Ethics and Crisis Management

Edited by

Lina Svedin, PhD
University of Utah

INFORMATION AGE PUBLISHING, INC.
Charlotte, NC • www.infoagepub.com

Library of Congress Cataloging-in-Publication Data

Ethics and crisis management / edited by Lina Svedin.
    p. cm. – (Ethics in practice)
  Includes bibliographical references.
  ISBN 978-1-61735-496-0 (pbk.) – ISBN 978-1-61735-497-7 (hardcover) –
ISBN 978-1-61735-498-4 (e-book)
  1. Emergency management. 2. Crisis management–Case studies. 3.
Management–Moral and ethical aspects. I. Svedin, Lina, 1974-
  HV551.2.E84 2011
  174'.936334–dc23

                                 2011020339

Printed in the United States of America

Ethics and Crisis Management

A volume in
Ethics in Practice
Robert A. Giacalone and Carole L. Jurkiewicz, *Series Editors*

CONTENTS

Foreword vii
Mary C. Gentile

Preface ix

Acknowledgements xi

1   Introduction 1
Lina Svedin

2   Inherent Ethical Challenges in Bureaucratic Crisis
Management: The Swedish Experience with the
2004 Tsunami Disaster 21
Pär Daléus and Dan Hansén

3   Value Conflicts in Foreign Policy Crises: How the United States
and the U.K. Wrestled with the Ethical Dilemma of Going to
War in Iraq 37
Fredrik Bynander

4   International Humanitarian Assistance: Legitimate
Intervention or Illegitimate Interference? 57
Lieuwe Zijlstra, Andrej Zwitter, and Liesbet Heyse

5   Drowning in Discretion: Crisis Management Ethics and the
Problem of Aporia 75
Arjen Boin and Paul Nieuwenburg

6   The Ethical Dilemmas of Straddling the Public–Private Divide
in Economic Crises 97
Lina Svedin

v

7 Chasing Evil, Defending Atrocities: Blame Avoidance and
   Prisoner Abuse During the War in Iraq 119
   Sanneke Kuipers, Kasia Kochańska, and Annika Brändström

8 Communication in Crises of Public Diplomacy: The Quest
   for Ethical Capital 141
   Eva-Karin Olsson

9 The Politics-Administration Dichotomy and the Failure
   of Symmetrical Responsibility Doctrines......................... 163
   Helena Wockelberg

10 The Purpose, Functions, and Ethical Dimensions of Postcrisis
   Investigations: The Case of the 9/11 Commission 183
   Charles F. Parker

11 Uncertainty, Accountability, and the Conduct of Postcrisis
   Inquiries.. 199
   Daniel Nohrstedt

12 Conclusions... 217
   Lina Svedin

   About the Editor... 247

   Contributors List 249

   Index 253

FOREWORD

Mary C. Gentile

Lina Svedin, along with an impressive group of international co-authors, have accomplished the seemingly impossible. They have managed, in one readable volume, to assemble a comprehensive overview of the core questions and the analytic frameworks at the intersection of ethics and public crisis management—from both a descriptive and a normative perspective; to share a wide-ranging set of relevant and current illustrative cases, ranging across the domains of financial markets, international relations, domestic security, and military operations; and finally to frame all this across the three levels of relevant analysis: systemic, organizational, and individual.

By so doing, they have begun to address and resolve one of the key lessons in their own work: that seemingly paradoxically, crises can and must be anticipated in order to enhance our ability to manage them ethically as well as effectively.

In my own work with values-driven leadership development, particularly in the business world, I have recognized the need for three types of preparation: *raising awareness, mastering analysis,* and *practicing action.* That is, we *raise awareness* by reviewing and categorizing the types of ethical challenges that are common to public crises, and we thereby begin to "normalize" them. The many examples in Svedin's volume attest to the predictability of the kinds of values conflicts we might confront, if not the precise timing and domain in which they will occur. This "normalization" means we anticipate and even practice our analysis and responses in advance.

Ethics and Crisis Management, pages vii–viii
Copyright © 2011 by Information Age Publishing

We *master analysis* by examining the lessons of history, recognizing patterns that help counter the tendency toward the ethical rationalization or excuse of assumed "exceptionalism." Very few of the thorny and complex ethical contradictions described in this text—such as the conflict between the accountability enforced through public transparency, on the one hand, and the protection of both individual rights and public safety pursued through confidentiality, on the other—are new. By reviewing the lessons of history, we not only recognize these conflicts when they occur, we are better prepared to both make informed decisions and, importantly, to communicate and justify those decisions to the affected stakeholders.

Finally and importantly, this volume invites us to *practice action* by going beyond the realm of ethical analysis and the development of taxonomies of ethical challenge, to actually invite a consideration of the kind of choices that individuals can and do make when facing the management and response—especially a "first response"—to public crises. The individual choices made, their consequences, as well as suggested and potentially better alternatives are all shared here, enabling the reader and student to engage with this material at the personal level and begin to "pre-script" him or herself to act responsibly and effectively.

In the end, it is this last emphasis—upon preparing for and practicing *action*—that takes this book beyond the realm of academic debate and theoretical questioning to the gritty and necessary task of preparing future public leaders to respond to the kinds of crises that impact and sometimes determine the course of all our lives. This book is an impressive example of knowledge in the service of responsible and effective action, and in that way, it models the very journey its readers are invited to pursue.

Mary C. Gentile, PhD is Director of *Giving Voice To Values*, Babson College, http://www.givingvoicetovalues.org/

PREFACE

To many, effective crisis management is viewed as a "mission impossible," an onerous task best done behind closed doors and far away from public scrutiny. Whether by gut instinct, common sense, or by detailed operational plans, preparing for crises is viewed by policy practitioners with a mix of fear and disdain.

Yet decades of social science research and training have conclusively demonstrated that crisis management is *not* a mission impossible. Individual decision makers and organizations can and do improve at preparing for and managing crises through training and analytical work between crises. Crises force policymakers to make quick decisions, decisions that can send a response down a policy path that is hard to redirect. Practitioners must be able to discern signals from noise, as well as effectively prioritize in situations where conflicting societal values present a policy minefield. Likewise, clarifying the consequences of alternative policy options in the heat of crisis is a formidable challenge for even the most seasoned practitioner. Unfortunately the last few decades have also shown us just how devastating the impact of crises handled poorly can be.

Some would argue that managing these skills with a critical eye to the value judgments and the moral reasoning that go into decision making and strategizing is too much to ask of our public servants and political representatives. I would respectfully disagree. The power vested in pubic offices, the design of representative democracy, and the collective experiences that hold our social fabric together demand it. By examining what inherent ethical challenges crises present, how public actors have tried to meet these challenges, and how their efforts have been judged in the aftermath of events, this volume takes important first steps toward meeting this demand.

Ethics and Crisis Management, pages ix–x
Copyright © 2011 by Information Age Publishing
All rights of reproduction in any form reserved.

The ground we are trying to break with regard to ethics and crisis management is uneven and full of rabbit holes. Strong psychological and political dynamics contribute to both an inability and unwillingness to state or examine the rationales behind decisions made and strategies adopted in the heat of the crisis. Not surprisingly, postcrisis evaluations often turn out to be grounds for blame games rather than the truth-seeking and performance-improving tools they aspire to be. As a consequence, policymakers, bureaucrats, and the general public still find themselves ill-equipped to take on the challenges that ethics in crises and crisis management entail.

This book is designed to start filling this gap by initiating a discussion on ethics and crisis management that will hopefully help practitioners better deal with this vital aspect of crises and crisis management. The effort to support and enhance public performance in regard to ethics has two primary bases. First, we will show that an ethical management of crisis is central to upholding the legitimacy of governing institutions. Likewise, ethical management is key to sustaining public trust in these institutions. Second, we will illustrate that ethics matter, particularly in crises, because of the consequential nature of decisions in crises and the vulnerability that the public feels in the face of threat, urgency, and uncertainty.

The public sector is not widely recognized for its ability to learn, adapt, and overcome challenges presented by the ever-shifting nature of public needs. One of the advantages of the public sector is its reliance on what is designed to be predictable and just procedures and rules. With this as its base, public crisis management has in place many of the mechanisms needed for ethical policymaking and scrutiny of reasoning. Furthermore, there has been a growing professionalization of the cadre of policymakers and street-level bureaucrats who respond to crises in the public realm. There is also a growing recognition of the importance of ethics in public affairs, as most MPA programs now include a course specifically on ethics for public administrators. My hope is that this volume will capitalize on these favorable conditions and provide a means by which we can improve and institutionalize more ethical conduct in crisis situations.

—**Lina Svedin**
Salt Lake City, Utah

ACKNOWLEDGEMENTS

While I am responsible for any shortcomings this volume might exhibit, many people share with me the credit for its merits. First and foremost, I would like to extend a great thank you to Carole Jurkiewicz for encouraging me to put this volume together. As editor and instigator of this project, I would also like to thank all of the chapter contributors for taking a leap of faith with me and for being willing to engage in new research, wearing a new pair of glasses in many cases.

I would also like to sincerely thank Mary Gentile for her inspirational work, her encouragement, and for taking the time to share some of her thoughts in the Foreword to this volume. Richard Green, Christopher Simon, and David Rudd at the College of Social and Behavioral Science at the University of Utah have provided encouragement and institutional support during this process, for which I am very grateful.

A heartfelt thanks also to Nicolas Swisher and Emily Mader for copy editing support on chapters 1 and 10, and to Daniel Patterson for copy editing support on chapter 6. Special thanks also go to Robert Stevens for substantive comments and subject matter feedback on chapter 6, and to my hardworking students in *Policy Analysis* and *Governance and the Economy* 2010 for thought-provoking discussions and perspectives. And finally, a great big thank you to my mom, Harriet Svedin, who provided excellent childcare support during the time much of this book was written.

Lina Svedin
Salt Lake City, Utah

CHAPTER 1

INTRODUCTION

Lina Svedin

INTRODUCTION

Scholars of crisis management have thus far done little to help decision makers and crisis practitioners deal with the many ethical dilemmas of crisis management. Despite a growing recognition among practitioners of public administration of the centrality of ethics in crises, very little research has focused on this dimension in crisis management. This volume addresses the empirical gap in crisis research and sets up a framework for analyzing the ethical dilemmas that face crisis managers. Our hope is to generate a focused discussion on this important topic among both scholars and practitioners.

The daily process of service provision and public administration is filled with value judgments and trade-offs. Public sector management and policy analysis are particularly challenging as decision makers and administrators must answer to multiple principals in addition to considering multiple stakeholder groups, many of whom do not agree on what values should be given preference in any one situation. The management of value conflicts, the safeguarding of just and fair processes in the development and implementation of public policy, and openness in government are all key elements supporting public trust in state institutions.

Ethics and Crisis Management, pages 1–20

In crises, the functioning of these governing institutions, particularly the decision makers who operate within them, are tested. Amplified media attention paid to the management of a crisis, combined with the very characteristics that make up a crisis, that is, a perceived threat to core values, urgency, and uncertainty, place public decision makers in the quandary of having to make complex ethical judgments under great uncertainty, time pressure, and heightened scrutiny. When insufficient attention is paid to the ethical dimensions of a crisis, a lack of closure might be the result; tensions surrounding the issue are likely to crop up time and again (see Page & Wessely, 2006).

The public's perception of how crisis managers deal with value conflicts and whether or not they perceive the process by which decision makers make hard and controversial decisions as legitimate and fair are key to the overall public assessment of whether the crisis was managed well or not. The consequences can be steep in cases where the management of a crisis is viewed as having been mishandled. The careers of decision makers can end and governments can be thrown out of office. The allocation of resources to individual agencies and the degree of independence an agency is granted are also influenced by their performance in crises. Agencies and departments viewed as having handled a crisis poorly sometimes see their budgets and responsibilities curtailed in favor of another agency or entity in the next round of budget negotiations. Overall trust in government is also affected by how the public views the efforts of institutions to manage risk and how they handle public threats that materialize. The perceived failures of the state in not carrying out its most basic functions, not protecting its citizens, and not exercising its power with discretion and good judgment undermine the willingness of people to entrust their lives and money in and to that state.

While ethics is a core part of most MPA and MBA curriculums today, there has been little scholarly discussion of how ethics play into and are dealt with in situations when it matters most: in crises. This introduction to the volume on ethics and crisis management provides a survey of what ethics in crisis management is (how we view it). It looks at different types of rationales that inform policy options, including crisis management options, and criteria that policymakers can use to base their decision on in these situations. The chapter also outlines necessary components for the evaluation of ethics of crisis decision making and makes the argument that crises test governing institutions, not only in their capacity to manage but also in terms of the relationship between the government and the governed. Finally, this Introduction provides a sketch of three key themes in ethics and crisis management and places the focus and content of the empirical chapters of the book within these themes.

ETHICS IN CRISIS MANAGEMENT

Ethics, in this book, refers to the reflective study of moral choice and behavior. As such, this book takes an unusual *metaethical*[1] approach to thinking about the ethical underpinnings, arguments, and criteria that drive decision making, actions, and perceptions in crises. The cases and arguments presented in this volume are designed to cast light on the nature and meaning of normative claims as well as the kinds of reasoning decision makers have employed within the specific context of crises, situations they perceive as characterized by threats to values and filled with urgency and uncertainty.

We can distinguish between *descriptive ethics*, which "involves the analysis of descriptions of customary morality," and *normative ethics* which is "concerned with the analysis, evaluation, and development of normative statements that provide guidance to those trying to solve practical problems" (Dunn, 2008, p. 345). Crisis management involves ethical reasoning. Managing crises involves determining what the desired ends of a crisis situation are and how we prefer or feel we ought to get there (the means by which we achieve these ends). When sitting in the "hot seat" (Flin, 1996), some would argue, there is not enough time for crisis managers to go through this kind of calculated process of ethical reasoning.

There are, however, plenty of ways in which crisis decision makers are given decision-making support. Often, a number of actions (means by which to secure an already established desired end) have been institutionalized through standard operating procedures (SOPs), protocols, trainings, action checklists, and emergency phone numbers, all specifically designed to ensure that decision makers take the *right actions* and make the *right decisions* in the heat of things. There is also decision-making support in terms of gathering and analyzing the sometimes problematic flow of information in crises. Often, the information that decision makers need to make analytically solid decisions is lacking. The available information covers only a very small part of the situation; sometimes it's contradictory, sometimes it's vague or ambiguous, sometimes it's primarily in the form of questions from the media and public, or sometimes it's technically challenging, requiring substantial professional knowledge to be deciphered into actionable information.

On Rationales

Ethical decision and action dilemmas in crises can be characterized by what President Lyndon Johnson and his undersecretary Robert Wood said: "Our problem is not to do what is right. Our problem is to know what is right" (Dunn, 2008, p. 3).

We can distinguish between six different types of rationality that inform recommendations and policy options: technical rationality, economic rationality, legal rationality, social rationality, and substantive rationality (comparing multiple forms of rationality) (Dunn, 2008, p. 221). Technical rationality evaluates options based on their ability to promote effective solutions to problems. Economic rationality is based on the degree to which an alternative provides an efficient solution.[2] Legal rationality looks to whether policy options abide by established rules and precedents. Social rationality judges options based on their ability to promote and improve valued social institutions.[3] Finally, the discussion and comparison of rationales in relation to a problem is what characterizes substantive rationality. This form of rationality advocates a comparison of rationales in order to find the most appropriate choice, given the circumstances of the situation (Dunn, 2008, p. 221). In many cases, several of these rationales are combined and used as the basis for decisions as good policy tries to meet many needs simultaneously.

However, just as often, two or more of these rationales compete or conflict with each other in any one course of action. For example, during a 10-week power outage that hit downtown Auckland in 1997, the mayor of Auckland decided to make a portable freezer truck available to affected small restaurants and businesses. The goal was to make it possible for these small businesses to operate on a limited scale during the outage so they would survive and provide some essential services to the area. The rationale of the mayor can be characterized as social, in that he was upholding the value of providing some kind of aid to the victims of the crisis who were least able to care for themselves and keeping a symbolic blood vessel pumping in the heart of the city. This rationale—however legitimate in its own right and well intended in its execution—conflicted with the technical rationality of the city's health department, which had been trying to keep people safe from food poisoning by preventing businesses from serving potentially unsafe food. On a number of occasions, health officials had even gone so far as to pour bleach on the improperly stored and unsafe food small restaurants were serving. From the health department's technical point of view, the portable freezer was a nightmare, as it would it be difficult to keep track of which businesses used the freezer and if the food in the freezer was handled properly. The health department shut it down immediately as a health precaution (Newlove, Stern, & Svedin, 2003).

Another recurring ethical challenge in crises is posed by evacuations. Evacuations present legal and economic challenges and are often rife with social tensions. Many countries have laws that allow authorities to mandate evacuations. If an evacuation is ordered, the cost of that evacuation typically falls on the public sector. For example, public servants, often police, must help evacuate those who need help and then must protect the evacuated homes and businesses, all actions that are quite costly. Consequently, technical questions of when and how many people to evacuate become paramount, although the information to make good decisions about these things is never straightforward. Frequently, people who are ordered to evacuate resist, which leaves the public sector in the legal, technical, and social gray area of what to do with citizens who refuse to leave their properties. Should they be arrested? Should they be forced from their homes? Or should they be left to fend for themselves, thus risking the possibility of having to later send out rescue teams after those who remained behind when conditions worsen?

The Red River flood of 1997 in North Dakota illustrates these challenges. Because spring floods were nothing new to the Red River area, many residents felt they had adequate protection, believed the flood would not be as severe as forecasted, or simply did not want to leave their homes. Government crisis managers sent out teams of psychologists to change the minds of residents who were clinging to their right to stay and defend their property. While this approach was effective, it was also time-consuming. It required valuable resources and resulted in a vast need for police patrols to secure the evacuated properties (Svedin, 2001). From an ethical standpoint, a public institution targeting citizens in crises with teams of psychologists to surreptitiously get them to do what you want them to do, rather than face the music of a more straightforward approach, might be considered questionable.

On Decision Criteria

How then do decision makers in crises go about making decisions in situations where the rationales for actions conflict? What are the criteria against which we can judge the legitimacy of any one decision?

We can consider decision criteria as "explicitly stated values that underlie recommendations for actions" (Dunn, 2008, p. 221). In policy analysis, these decision criteria are sometimes divided into six main types: effectiveness, efficiency, adequacy, equity, responsiveness, and appropriateness (Dunn, 2008, p. 221). *Effectiveness* refers to whether a certain action will lead to a specified result. *Efficiency* refers to how much it will take, or cost, to achieve a specific level of effectiveness. *Adequacy* is a measure of the degree to which a specific "level of effectiveness satisfies the needs, values, or opportunities that gave rise to the problem" (Dunn, 2008, p. 222) that decision makers are trying to solve. *Equity* refers to the distribution of cost and effects generated by actions among groups of citizens. *Responsiveness* measures the degree to which any one group's needs, values, or preferences, are being satisfied by the action. Finally, *appropriateness*, like the substantive rationale, compares several different criteria and evaluates whether or not the objectives of the action are the right ones for society, based on their value and how realistic the assumptions that underline the objectives are (Dunn, 2008, pp. 222–227).

In making decisions about policy alternatives or actions, decision makers can base their selection on any one of these values. While it might seem unreasonable that decision makers should consider this level of specificity when they choose their courses of action in crises, these choices are in fact made even when they are not explicitly stated. Sometimes, after the fact, they are obfuscated in language and justifications like, "it was the only thing to do," "it was a gut decision," or "it was common sense." Common sense, as the intense debate in the aftermath of many crises shows, often turns out not to be so common after all. Because of this lack of a shared sense, and the fact that the values promoted demote other competing values, it is critical to recognize the underlying choice. Furthermore, it is important to recognize decision criteria, because choices in crises matter so much. They matter in consequence at a very practical level to those directly subject to the decisions made, and they matter at a moral level to society at-large. However, the psychological and political desire to avoid moral conflicts[4] often leaves decision criteria in *the fog of war* (von Clausewitz, Maude, & Graham, 2008; Morris, 2004); that is, despite the need for a collective situational awareness and data assessment in order to plan military strategy and actions, this awareness and assessment become distorted and unattached from reality because of the participants' wishes and perceptions.

Evaluating the Ethics of Crisis Decisions

If decisions made in crises are to be evaluated and decision makers held accountable for their actions and behaviors, it has to be possible to identify what rationale(s) and decision criteria were used and what underlying value(s) the decision(s) were meant to uphold. Evaluation of ethical decisions and actions in crises is the analysis of whether the process that produced the alternatives (the process by which the group came to a decision or a consensus) and the choice of which value(s) to uphold were justified.

This evaluation can be *individual* when each voter makes a judgment of whether or not the process was good and whether the right values were protected. The evaluation may also be *institutional* in that it might be reviewed and judged in a court system where professionals or appointees serve a well-defined institutional function. And it might be *group* based, in the sense that a commission or an inquiry group, temporarily assigned to represent groups of stakeholders, review and evaluate the process and the values upheld. The conclusions and/or recommendations of the commission or inquiry are then a collective judgment on the ethics of process and actions.

Is there a way to sanction unethical decisions or actions that take place in crises? In a word, yes. There are formal legal sanctions of certain defined types of unethical behavior. There are also formal legal sanctions in many countries for unethical decisions, for instance when decisions made in crises have been reversed or voided in the aftermath by a constitutional court or institution imbued with a constitutional protection mandate. There are also sanctions of larger quasi-legal norms, such as with international human rights, where decisions made in wars and civil unrest have been judged as war crimes or crimes against humanity by the International Court of Justice.

Secondly, there is also the sanction of public scrutiny and judgment in the media. Many decision makers have had to leave their posts, governments have fallen, and major government policies have had to be changed or reversed when certain questionable actions were exposed and subsequently scrutinized in the public eye of the media. Countries that do not sanction behaviors and decisions in crises that were perceived by the public and the media as unethical might face a long shadow of discontent and lack of closure. These long-shadow crises are the ones that never seem to end. They change form over time, and the focus of the crisis might change, even creating a secondary credibility crisis or rift in the social fabric of a society (see Hagström & Sundelius, 2001), but they live on like an untreated wound that has become infected, bursting open from time to time to let out an oozing gush of bad feelings, mistrust, and grievances (see Haspers, 1998; Huizink, Slotti, & Witteveen, 2006; Slottje et al., 2007).

But there are also values that cannot be effectively protected or upheld if it is known that these values are the basis of an action or a decision, such as in situations where transparency undermines the legitimate effect sought. Examples would include policies aimed at restoring confidence in economic markets in times of crisis (Stern & Sundelius, 1997), symbolic actions aimed at quelling civil unrest or bringing closure to national mourning ('t Hart, 1993), and many decisions aimed at strengthening national security (Allison, 1971; Bynander, 2003; Piskalyuk, 2004). Is there a way that society can evaluate and judge the ethical components of these actions and decisions? There are special venues and mechanisms for ensuring ethical behavior in policy areas where information sharing is legitimately restricted. The track record of these accountability and sanctioning mechanisms is somewhat varied. Sometimes proper judgment and sanctioning can take place only after the seal of classification has been lifted (sometimes it never is) and investigative journalists and researchers start digging through archives.

The functions of *evaluation, judgment,* and *sanctioning* of public performance in crises, and their political costs and benefits, cause decision makers to respond in a number of different ways to the ethical challenges that crises inherently bring. For example, decision makers avoid, rationalize, justify, politicize and mask, label and define, communicate through symbolism, and they lie, cheat and steal; all in order to manage the perceptions of those who have the ability to evaluate, judge, and sanction. Conversely, decision makers also reason, debate, disagree, protest, quit, and repent in the name of what they think is right. Managing perceptions in crises is a vital part of crisis leadership, but it is also an ethical tightrope that decision makers walk as they navigate between tragic choices and the potential of devastating consequences.

ETHICS, ACCOUNTABILITY, AND TRUST IN GOVERNMENT: THE CRISIS TEST

Crises test the very fabric of our governing institutions. They threaten core societal values and require decision makers to make key decisions under conditions of sometimes great uncertainty and intense time pressure. While there is a great degree of public acceptance of decision making becoming centralized and information being confined to a select few in crises, trust in government is intrinsically linked to the ability to hold decision makers accountable for the crucial decisions they make in crises. The mechanisms set in place for exerting accountability under *normal* administrative conditions are often suspended in crises for reasons of expediency and effectiveness; but who is held responsible by whom in the aftermath of a crisis? The ability to hold top-level decision makers and public servants responsible for their actions, or lack of action, in situations that matter most is a crucial part of the ongoing relationship of trust between governing institutions and those they govern. This relationship is affected by the perception of public decision makers' reasonable risk taking, competent analysis, and timely action. If the public cannot make judgments about these things in relation to a crisis, the confidence in those very decision makers is going to be cast in shadows and mistrust. This book takes a closer look at inherent ethical challenges in crises and how policymakers and bureaucrats respond to them in an effort to identify ways to encourage ethical conduct in the management of crises and improve public performance in these situations.

Trust and confidence play significant roles in successful crisis management. Ludvig Beckman (2004) states that governments and agencies across the world are working on improving what is often termed society's crisis management ability. The core task that decision makers are taking on in this work, Beckman states, seems to be to secure the publics' *confidence* in society's ability to manage crises:

> If government actions in crises are successful, society is perceived as "robust" and faith in government increases. If these actions fail—if the wrong decisions are made, organization is poor and resources insufficient—the government

instead appears ineffective, which decreases public confidence. (Beckman, 2004, p. 15, my translation)

In line with this mode of thinking, the Swedish government stated in the early 2000s that, "'it is crucial for the public to have confidence in the democratic system's ability to manage situations that arise'" (Beckman, 2004, p. 15, my translation)

Even though fostering public confidence in governing institutions is critical, strengthening society's ability to manage crises cannot, as Beckman points out, solely serve this purpose. In order for a state governed by law to function well, citizens need to put pressure on their governing institutions and public servants in order to operate in a way that is *just* and *ethical*. The evaluation of crisis management should therefore be based not only on *effectiveness* criteria but also on *legitimacy* criteria (Beckman, 2004, p. 16). In accordance with Beckman's assertions, we argue that good or successful crisis management needs to be both *effective* and *legitimate* in its analyses, actions, and decisions. In situations characterized by great uncertainty and urgency, *effective*, *just*, and *ethical* analysis and action might be particularly challenging, something we need be mindful of when evaluating public performance. However, because of the consequential nature of decisions in crises, it is critical that these decisions are accounted for. Spin can make any action seem to stem from good leadership, but only critical review can tell us whether or not government actions are *reasonable* and *just*. Without well-functioning accountability mechanisms and the pursuit of accountability in crises, the public is unable to make this kind of critical judgment and will not be able to exert the kind of pressure that promotes *just* and *ethical* behavior in crises.

There is also the possibility of using accountability processes in crises for truly positive ends, such as strengthening the public's trust in government and improving the relationship between those governing and those governed. In this sense, accountability in crises becomes more than a receipt for good or bad public performance in crises. This utilitarian approach to administrative tools suggests that if we can design or improve existing accountability mechanisms in a way that allows the public to *evaluate* and *judge* the analyses and actions of their leaders and in the case of poor performance to *sanction* this performance, then trust in governing institutions will increase.[5]

A discussion about the nature and impact of ethics in crises and crisis management is long overdue, from both a theoretical standpoint, but more importantly, from a practical, societal impact standpoint.

OUTLINE OF THIS BOOK

This book will address and explore ethics in crisis management within three key themes. The first theme centers on what seems to be inherent ethical challenges in crisis situations. These challenges appear as fundamental and inescapable juxtapositions and conflicts that crisis managers face once great urgency and uncertainty start surrounding core values at stake. The second theme focuses on individual and organizational actors, more specifically, the ethical dimensions of decision making and the implications of ethics in relation to specific behaviors that crisis managers engage in when faced with adverse circumstances. The third theme is concerned with ethical dimensions of the institutional processes and mechanisms engaged in crises, specifically post hoc processes designed to investigate, evaluate, and account for what happened in the crisis and how it was managed.

Theme I: Inherent Ethical Challenges in Crises

The state is supposed to protect its citizens from harm, but can it do this with any real administrative capacity? In the classical conception of the social contract between citizens and their governments, the public gives up part of its freedom and resources, and grants the governing body a monopoly on violence in exchange for collective protection and basic services. As an extension of this basic agreement, people expect the government to plan for and respond to harms that threaten their welfare. This seemingly basic understanding and expectation quickly becomes complicated in contemporary crises. Many crises threaten people's fundamental values, rights, and freedoms, and they do so with synchronicity and simultaneity. In other words, several fundamental (and thus important) values and freedoms are at stake simultaneously and compete with each other for priority and protection. Consider for instance, the right of outlaw bikers to organize and assemble versus other citizens' rights to safety in situations when rival gangs are waging urban war on each other (Svedin, 1998). Or consider freedom of enterprise and citizens' right to affordable energy and the threat that a potential nuclear accident poses to the rights and freedoms of future generations and the irreparable damages it may cause to the environment (Stern, 1999). Finally, think of individuals' right to *habeas corpus* and the need to isolate and render impotent those who plan to create crises in the form of violent terrorist attacks.

Many of these value conflicts are inherent in the social activities of a society in normal times, yet through debate and drawn-out negotiations, we seem to muddle through the decision-making process of which value to prioritize. In crises, however, these conflicts are pushed to the surface and demand quick and authoritative decisions in ways that put crisis managers in a highly visible, contentious, and often uncomfortable place of having to make *tragic choices*. These choices create a sense of tragedy within the individual because they contain a conflict of fundamental ethical principles. For example,

> compassion requires us to regard all human lives as priceless and to preserve them at all cost. But utilitarianism dictates that scarce resources be allocated to achieve the greatest good. Hence, life-and-death human needs must be prioritized. When some lives must be given up in favor of others, such choices are regarded as tragic. This sense of tragedy, however, can vary depending on how tragic choices are made. (Fung, 1998, p. 71)

How value conflicts were handled by those in charge is a common point of public evaluation in the aftermath of a crisis, and it is one that leads to judgments being made about the overall management of that crisis which, in turn, might lead to the sanctioning of individual decision makers.

In light of the many tasks and challenges decision makers face in crises, some scholars have argued that crisis management is a mission impossible (Boin & 't Hart, 2003; McConnell & Drennan, 2006). Mitroff (2004, p. 5) describes the fundamental functions of crisis leadership as (a) performing a crisis audit of the strengths and vulnerabilities of the organization before a crisis materializes and developing skills and capabilities that can be used to manage a crisis; (b) putting the identified precrisis capabilities and skills to work during a crisis; (c) reassessing the leaders' and the organizations' performance in the aftermath of a crisis and; (d) implementing needed changes to make a more effective response possible in the future. One of Mitroff's key points is that crisis leadership should be anticipatory and preventative rather than reactive.[6] Actual crisis management ability is, I would argue, inherent in good crisis leadership, not in the ability to create a *perception* that such leadership exists (see for instance Beckman, 2004). The ideal assessment of public performance in crisis accountability processes is one that measures the extent to which public servants and elected officials fulfilled these four functions that Mitroff highlights.[7]

Crisis leaders also need to be able to take a *big-picture* approach to crises, assessing how discrete events and vulnerabilities might interact and thereby create major crises (Mitroff, 2004, pp. 11–14). Triggering events in crises are often easier to identify than the underlying causes and factors that produced the conditions for a crisis to form. Crisis leaders taking a big-picture approach also try to discern what kind of subsequent crises might follow if the current crisis is not handled well. The type of critical thinking that leaders need to do to successfully engage in crisis management in a highly integrated and massively complex world, Mitroff (2004) argues, is "the ability to be aware of, to examine, and to challenge one's fundamental assumptions of the world; the ability to 'connect the dots,' i.e., to see the 'big picture'; and the ability to think 'way outside the box' of conventional thinking" (Mitroff, 2004, p. 11). In many crises,

> It is not known how other critical factors, such as all of the stakeholders or key players, will "rise to the surface" in response to how the initial crisis is handled. As a result there is tremendous technical and ethical uncertainty regarding what one should do, especially with respect to how much responsibility one should assume from the beginning. (Mitroff, 2004, p. 25)

Good crisis leadership, therefore, also involves *leading*, as opposed to *managing*, in the ethical and technical uncertainty that is present in all crises (Mitroff, 2004, p. 25, my emphasis).[8]

Assuming that crisis management is not mission impossible, and that public office holders and public servants can learn to become crisis leaders, there are still plenty of inherent challenges to ethics in crisis management. One primary challenge is that citizens still make bad choices despite the state's best efforts to protect them. Research on risk tells us that what people are afraid of and the actual dangers they face do not always overlap. Flood management efforts have, for example, seen plenty of citizens refuse to heed public advice on evacuations and relocation of housing (Svedin, Luedtke, & Hall, 2010). Another challenge is that of perceptions. Whether a crisis is viewed as well or poorly managed is very much in the eye of the beholder, and the very conception of whether or not a situation presents a crisis is largely based on individual perceptions of threat, urgency, and uncertainty (cf. Rosenthal, Charles, & 't Hart, 1989b; Stern, 1999; Sundelius, Stern, & Bynander, 1997).[9] Crisis scholars setting out to examine a case often have to start by asking the question: a crisis for *whom?* Ethics is a highly subjective endeavor, but this does not mean that it is unprincipled or that it should be considered a private matter. On the contrary, since public crisis management uses public power vested in governing institutions by its citizens, it is a very public matter. In this regard, crises that call into question the very relationship between the government and the governed pose a particularly challenging situation for crisis decision makers.

Another type of highly relevant ethical dilemma in crisis management is a crisis created by a government for the purpose of drawing public attention away from government performance in other areas. An example would be starting a foreign policy incident or crisis in order to draw attention away from a domestic crisis or scandal, or to rally support for the state's leader.[10]

A number of chapters in this book explore these and additional inherent ethical challenges in crises. The chapter by Pär Daléus and Dan Hansén examines the contradictory impulses of the Swedish bureaucracy in its response to the 2004 Indian Ocean tsunami: to follow rules and safeguard organizational values, and yet act in the ambiguity and immediacy of this extraordinary situation. Fredrik Bynander, in his chapter, investigates the ethical ambiguity of upholding or defending core values in foreign policy crises by going to war. In a similar vein, Lieuwe Zijlstra, Andrej Zwitter, and Liesbet Heyse look at the ethical dilemmas and issues of legitimacy facing decision makers intervening in response to humanitarian crises.

Theme II: Actor-Centered Ethics

There are a number of ways in which ethical judgments can be made about actors' decisions and behaviors in crisis. Regarding the process of decision-making researchers and citizens affected by the crises can make judgments about the quality of the decision process. Were all the actors with a stake in the crisis involved? Were they given sufficient and accurate information, or were they misled by the information provided during the process of making specific decisions? How were issues decided? By majority vote (which would involve more contention and alliance building than a decision that was based on unanimity)? Were there rules established when the group came to make a decision, or was the process of getting a decision up for grabs, thus allowing stronger actors to bully weaker ones? It is also possible to make judgments about the ethics of reasoning and decision criteria employed during crises. Was the rationale used good or appropriate given the knowledge of the circumstances, and was the projected distribution of costs and benefits for groups affected fair/justified? Were the assumptions that the objectives set out reasonable and tenable? Were the criteria for choosing one course of action over another appropriately selected? Did decision makers reason about why they chose one course of action over another and thereby make the choice visible and who made the choice clear?

Considering the behavior of decision makers, citizens and researchers can judge whether or not those leaders acted in accordance with the values that they had previously espoused or that they had been charged with upholding. Furthermore, we can judge the extent to which decision makers in crises acted clandestinely (limiting the ability of others around them to judge their actions), and the extent to which those secret actions and behaviors were kept secret for a good cause (in the interest of public values that could not otherwise be protected, such as national security) or for personal gain (protecting personal gains, avoiding losing personal gains, or avoiding public judgment of actions).

Finally, there is the judgment question of whether or not decision makers should have acted or even become involved in the first place. The nature of crises presents decision makers with competing pressures and opportunities. Crises, in essence, present competing logics from which elected officials and professional administrators must choose, such as the logic of *avoiding responsibility* (for that which is perceived as having gone badly) in contrast to the logic of *assuming responsibility* (for all that is perceived as successful in the management of a crisis). Prior research has indicated that this balancing act takes considerable skill and might have disastrous effects when managed poorly. To skillfully navigate the mandates of formal rules and to apply these in a way that best suits the crisis, or the decision maker who finds him or herself in that crisis, can be seen as an essential leadership skill. To assume and avoid responsibility in crises is an inherent part of the political game of gaining favor and avoiding losing power. But what about the professional public servants; do they engage in the kind of strategic assumption and avoidance of responsibility in crises that elected officials have been known to do? Do elected officials blame the bureaucracy, or even specific civil servants for decisions and actions, or inaction, in crises? To what extent can public servants defer ultimate responsibility to elected officials by dint of those leaders' mandate to *steer* the bureaucracy?

The chapters by Arjen Boin and Paul Nieuwenburg; Lina Svedin; Sanneke Kuipers, Kasia Kochanska, and Annika Brändström; and the chapter by Eva-Karin Olsson in this volume look specifically at the ethical dimensions of actors' decision making and behavior in crises. Boin and Nieuwenburg's chapter examines the decisions made by first responders in a New Orleans hospital in the aftermath of hurricane Katrina when faced with several tragic choices. Svedin explores how the U.S. government has tried to navigate the public-private division of responsibility in relation to recent economic and financial crises. Kuipers, Kochanska, and Brändström offer insights into the ethical debates and blame games surrounding American and British prisoner abuse during the war in Iraq. Finally, Olsson's chapter explores leaders' crisis communication strategies in moral crises that take place in highly complex, religiously and cultural diverse, transnational environments.

Theme III: Ethical Aspects of Crisis Processes

In addition to good leadership and sound decision making, crisis management relies on institutional processes and the mechanisms embedded in institutional arrangements. Institutional processes are established to safeguard due process and transparency under *normal* administrative circumstances. However, in crises there are strong incentives to ignore or set aside these processes for the sake of *expedience* or management *effectiveness*. The push to ignore institutional *due process* in the heat of a crisis has ethical implications and puts at risk both the crisis managers and the public that they are expected to protect. Institutional processes and mechanisms often assign responsibility and authority to actors and, as such, protect them from undue influence and set limits on what others can and cannot expect them to do. Once regulatory mechanisms and institutional processes are set aside in a crisis, actors enter a no-man's-land in which responsibility may be shifted or forced upon them in a way not previously anticipated. Looking at this kind of situation after the fact, the spotlight on individual decision makers becomes much sharper as decisions and actions have been based solely on personal judgments and discretion rather than on routines and rules. The public also risks harm when decision makers' poor personal judgments cause institutional processes to be disregarded and when the suspension of mechanisms of *accountability* and *due process* lead to a lack of *transparency*.

In order to piece together the details of fast moving, ambiguous, and complex crises, there are specific institutional processes and record keeping methods that depend on transparency being in place. Frequently, these processes take place after the acute phase of the crisis has passed. These post hoc operations help create meaning for ordinary citizens out of the extraordinary events that shook their society and the core values it is built on. These processes (investigations, commissions, hearings, and reports), through their organizing and classifying effects, assign responsibility to individuals and groups based on the actions they took (or did not take) during the crisis and provide vital information for sustaining democracy. Ultimately, well-functioning accountability mechanisms and post hoc processes should provide information that allows the public to locate responsibility and evaluate the ethics of decision makers.

Exerting accountability in crises, or in relation to crises in cases in which accountability can only be established after the fact, involves a balancing of the two logics of responsibility. For decision makers, it means taking responsibility for those things that would appropriately fall within their office's area of responsibility, but also to avoid taking responsibility for those things that would not. This may seem like a straightforward proposition, but the imperatives of crises sometimes push decision makers to assume responsibility for things and in situations where they have no authority. In such cases, decision makers either fail to appreciate the potential consequences of a decision or action they might take or tread on the responsibility of another actor, or both. Furthermore, it is tempting to assume responsibility for actions and decisions made that were actually the result of happenstance. When this happens, identifying real holes in the response and planning on the part of managers in the involved institutions is regrettably circumvented. Claiming responsibility for outcomes in crises that actually turned out opposite of or contrary to the measures put in place to manage the crisis can similarly present a false understanding of cause and effect and thus hinder learning in the aftermath of crises.

In cases where post hoc processes reveal abuses of power in crises, postevent proceedings may attract a great deal of public attention, which might subsequently spawn additional crises. As history has shown, such public sector scandals can have a very damaging effect on the public's trust in governing institutions (Johansson, 2004), including spurring cynicism about politics and public performance.

Ethics remains a rather murky and subjective area of politics, something which sometimes spills over and leaves the ethics of public administration unclear (Wockelberg, 2005). Accounting for the ethical dimensions of crises and crisis management is important, not only for its symbolic effects on the possibility of crisis termination and a return to *normalcy* ('t Hart, 1993), but also for its long-lasting effects on public trust in governing institutions. Abuse of power and poor judgment in situations in which the public perceives itself as most vulnerable and in need of leadership seem to have stronger effects on people's trust in the system than abuses of power under normal administrative circumstances.

The last section of chapters in this book looks more closely at these institutional processes that place ethics at the very heart of crisis management. Helena Wockelberg takes on the institutionalization of the politics-administration dichotomy and examines the ethical implications of contemporary failures to match delegated powers with responsibility, particularly in relation to the 2004 Indian Ocean tsunami disaster. Charles Parker's chapter on the 9/11 Commission highlights how ethical considerations can impact the role, functioning, and consequences of postcrisis inquiries and impact the management of future crises. Exemplified by the Pitt review of the 2007 floods in the United Kingdom, the last empirical chapter in this volume, written by Daniel Nohrstedt, examines how postcrisis investigations appraise moral judgments made by decision makers in crises.

In the final chapter of the book, our concluding discussion brings together the various points of view and cases found in this volume and centers on the fundamental challenges of crisis management. This discussion touches on the tragic choices decision makers often face in crises, whether crisis management really is a mission impossible from an ethical point of view, how decision makers should deal with the bad choices and behaviors of others, and how ethics is linked to accountability and public trust in governing institutions. This concluding chapter also pulls together lessons learned (often the hard way) about whether or not to intervene, criteria for making critical decisions and evaluating policy, about assuming and avoiding responsibility, and about communicating ethically in crises. The implications of our discussion of ethics in crisis management are also reviewed with an eye to practitioners and how we may structure the response to crises in a way that promotes ethics and improves organizations' performance in these situations.

NOTES

1. "Metaethics is the attempt to understand the metaphysical, epistemological, semantic, and psychological, presuppositions and commitments of moral thought, talk, and practice. As such, it counts within its domain a broad range of questions and puzzles" and it "explores . . . the connection between values, reasons for action, and human motivation, asking how it is that moral standards might provide us with reasons to do or refrain from doing as it demands, and it addresses many of the issues commonly bound up with the nature of freedom and its significance (or not) for moral responsibility." (Stanford Encyclopedia of Philosophy, 2007)

2. This refers to economic efficiency, i.e., the lowest cost per unit of social goods produced.

3. This rationale supports the institutionalization and extension of social institutions such as the right to democratic participation.

4. There are powerful psychological mechanisms that help people avoid, forget, skew, or otherwise rationalize away moral conflict, which in the moment, enables them to commit horrible acts that go against some part of their conscience, and if asked about it afterward, simply cannot remember, or they are able to justify, minimize, rationalize, or deny any wrongdoing with their mental worldview intact. Political desires have spawned cover-ups, perjury, shredding of paper trails, failures to document decisions, and who the present decision makers were, as well as intense and conscious efforts at spin and damage control.

5. The public's role in holding actors accountable and what it means to hold someone accountable is outlined in more detail in Chapter 2.

6. This proactive stance is different from the predominantly reactive nature of crisis management. Mitroff argues that states often have excellent emergency response systems but terrible crisis anticipation systems (2004, p. 14)

7. The assessment would evaluate to what extent leaders had led well by seeking information, analyzing needs, developing capabilities, and applying these skills and resources in the crisis; and in the aftermath of the acute crisis, assessing their own performance and initiating changes to improve performance.

8. An aggravating and challenging aspect of leading these kind of assessments and actions is that decision makers often cannot "delay action for too long because such delays will not only add to the crisis, but set off new ones as well" (Mitroff, 2004, p. 25)

9. Three of the most frequently cited crisis definitions in research on crisis management include this perceptual component. For instance; A crisis poses (a) a threat to basic values, with a simultaneous or subsequent awareness of (b) a finite time for response, and of the (c) high probability of involvement in military hostilities (Rosenthal, Charles, & 't Hart, 1989a); A crisis poses (a) a serious threat to the basic structures or the fundamental values and norms of a social system which, (b) under time pressure and (c) highly uncertain circumstances, necessitates making critical decisions (Sundelius et al., 1997, my translation); A decision-making crisis is a situation, deriving from a change in the external or internal environment of a collectivity, characterized by three

necessary and sufficient perceptions on the part of the responsible decision makers: (a) a threat to core values, (b) urgency, (c) uncertainty (Stern, 1999; Stern & Sundelius, 2002).

10. For a discussion on the rallying-around-the-flag effect of foreign policy crises, see for instance Baker and Oneal (2001), Gowa (1998), and Hetherington and Nelson (2003).

REFERENCES

Allison, G. (1971). *Essence of decision: Explaining the Cuban missile crisis.* Boston: Little, Brown.

Baker, W. D., & Oneal, J. R. (2001). Patriotism or opinion leadership?: The nature and origins of the "rally 'round the flag" effect. *Journal of Conflict Resolution, 45*(5), 661–687.

Beckman, L. (2004, Spring). Krishantering och legitimitet: Den legitima krishanteringen—inte enbart effektiv och förtroendeskapande. *Politologen,* 15–24.

Boin, A., & 't Hart, P. (2003). Public leadership in times of crisis: Mission impossible? *Public Administration Review, 63*(5), 544–553.

Bynander, F. (2003). *The rise and fall of the submarine threat: Securitization of underwater intrusions in Sweden 1980–2002.* Uppsala, Sweden: Uppsala Universitet.

Dunn, W. N. (2008). *Public policy analysis: An introduction* (4th ed.). Upper Saddle River, NJ: Pearson-Prentice Hall.

Flin, R. (1996). *Sitting in the hot seat: Leaders for teams for critical incident management.* Chichester, UK: Wiley.

Fung, K. K. (1998). Decentralizing tragic choices: Pooling health risks with health unions. *The American Journal of Economics and Sociology, 57*(1), 71–94.

Gowa, J. (1998). Politics at the water's edge: Parties, voters, and the use of force abroad. *International Organization, 52*(2), 307–324.

Hagström, A.-Z., & Sundelius, B. (2001). *Krishantering på göteborska: En studie av brandkatastrofen den 29–30 oktober 1998* (Vol. 15). Stockholm: Ateljé/Faktor AB.

't Hart, P. (1993). Symbols, rituals and power: The lost dimensions of crisis management. *Journal of Contingencies and Crisis Management, 1*(2), 36–50.

Haspers, A. (1998). The MV Estonia catastrophe. In E. Stern & F. Bynander (Eds.), *Crisis and internationalization: Eight crisis studies from a cognitive-institional perspective* (Vol. 2, pp. 286–315). Stockholm: Swedish Agency for Civil Emergency Planning.

Hetherington, M. J., & Nelson, M. (2003). Anatomy of a rally effect: George W. Bush and the war on terrorism. *PS: Political Science & Politics, 36*(1), 37–42.

Huizink, A. C., Slotti, P., & Witteveen, A. B. (2006). Long term health complaints following the Amsterdam air disaster in police officers and fire-fighters. *Occupational and Environmental Medicine, 63*(10), 657–662.

Johansson, P. (2004). *I skandalers spår: Minskad legitimitet i Svensk offentlig sektor.* Unpublished dissertation, Gothenburg University, Gothenburg, Sweden.

McConnell, A., & Drennan, L. (2006). Mission impossible? Planning and preparing for crisis. *Journal of Contingencies and Crisis Management, 14*(2), 59–70.

Mitroff, I. I. (2004). *Crisis leadership: Planning for the unthinkable.* Hoboken, NJ: John Wiley and Sons.

Morris, E. (Writer) (2004). *The fog of war: Eleven lessons from the life of Robert S. McNamara.* In M. Williams, J. Ahlberg (Producers), & E. Morris (Producer, Director). Culver City, CA: Columbia TriStar Home Entertainment.

Newlove, L., Stern, E., & Svedin, L. (2003). *Auckland unplugged: Coping with critical infrastructure failure.* Lanham, MD; Boulder, CO; New York; Oxford, UK: Lexington Books.

Page, L. A., & Wessely, S. C. (2006). Group health complaints following an air disaster: A "second disaster." *Occupational and Environmental Medicine, 63*(10), 647–648.

Piskalyuk, Y. (2004). *Construction of the dam by the Russian Federation towards the Ukrainian island of Tuzla.* Syracuse, NY: Syracuse University.

Rosenthal, U., Charles, M. T., & 't Hart, P. (1989a). *Coping with crises: The management of disasters, riots, and terrorism.* Springfield, IL: C. C. Thomas.

Rosenthal, U., Charles, M. T., & 't Hart, P. (1989b). The world of crises and crisis management. In U. Rosenthal, M. T. Charles, & P. 't Hart (Eds.), *Coping with crises: The management of disasters, riots, and terrorism.* Springfield, IL: Charles C. Thomas.

Slottje, P., Twisk, J. W. R., Smidt, N., Huizink, A. C., Witteveen, A. B., van Mechelen, W., et al. (2007). Health-related quality of life of firefighters and police officers 8.5 years after the air disaster in Amsterdam. *Quality of Life Research, 16*(2), 239–252.

Stanford Encyclopedia of Philosophy. (2007). *Metaethics.* Retrieved March 31, 2010, from http://plato.stanford.edu/entries/metaethics

Stern, E. (1999). *Crisis decisionmaking: A cognitive institutional approach* (Vol. 6). Stockholm: Swedish National Defense College.

Stern, E., & Sundelius, B. (1997). Sweden's twin monetary crises of 1992: Rigidity and learning in crisis decision making. *Journal of Contingencies and Crisis Management, 5*(1), 32–48.

Stern, E., & Sundelius, B. (2002). Crisis management Europe: An integrated regional research and training program. *International Studies Perspectives, 3*(1), 71–88.

Sundelius, B., Stern, E., & Bynander, F. (1997). *Krishantering på Svenska: Teori och praktik* (Vol. 1). Stockholm: Nerenius Santérus Förlag.

Svedin, L. (1998). Mc-krig i Sverige och Skandinavien 1994–97 [Biker-wars in Sweden and the Nordic countries 1994–97]. In F. Bynander & E. Stern (Eds.), *Crisis and internationalization: Eight case studies from a cognitive-institutional perspective* (pp. 128–143). Stockholm: Swedish Agency for Civil Emergency Preparedness.

Svedin, L. (2001). *Perception as a stepping-stone to cooperation.* Unpublished master's thesis, Stockholm University.

Svedin, L., Luedtke, A., & Hall, T. (2010). *Risk regulation in the United States and the European Union: Controlling chaos.* New York, NY: Palgrave Macmillan.

von Clausewitz, C., Maude, F. N., & Graham, J. J. (2008). *On war.* Radford, VA: Wilder Publications.

Wockelberg, H. (2005). Etik som politik, fler frågor än svar? [Ethics as politics, more questions than answers?]. In L. Köling Abjörner (Ed.), *Etik i medborgarens tjän-st—en antologi om förvaltningsetik* [Ethics in public service—An anthology on ethics in public administration] (pp. 98–109). Stockholm: Statens kvalitets- och kompetensråd.

CHAPTER 2

INHERENT ETHICAL CHALLENGES IN BUREAUCRATIC CRISIS MANAGEMENT

The Swedish Experience with the 2004 Tsunami Disaster

Pär Daléus and Dan Hansén

INTRODUCTION

Over the last decades, the concern with ethics within public bureaucracy has increased as political and administrative wrongs and scandals have been brought to light. There is reportedly "a perceived dramatic increase in government corruption" (Cohen & Eimicke, 1995, p. 97). Impairment of integrity, virtue, or moral principle on behalf of government is dramaturgically profitable for media (cf. Frederickson, 1993), which might have amplified the concern. As a consequence, governments have more harshly enforced administrative ethics (Huddleston & Sands, 1995). Typically, the growing concern has resulted in a widespread production of codes of conduct and

Ethics and Crisis Management, pages 21–36
Copyright © 2011 by Information Age Publishing
All rights of reproduction in any form reserved.

rules, which most often do not "[say] more than to obey law and, if the law is not clear, to do the right thing" (Cohen & Eimicke, 1995, p. 102). Related to the discussion on ethics is an apprehension with government transparency. In Westminster systems, the public servants have been able to provide frank advice to political powers, on the implicit agreement that they are themselves shielded from the verdict of posterity. This notion is now being challenged by *transparency lobbyists* who press for more openness in government (see Mulgan, 2009). The right thing to do, in situations where laws and regulations provide poor guidelines, arguably looks very different depending on where in the administrative complex one sits, to whom one is primarily accountable, and if the task environment is stable or not.

Crisis management is often depicted as a *mission impossible* (Boin & 't Hart, 2003) that calls for extraordinary and creative flexibility (cf. Stern, 2009). Doing the right thing (from a legal or rule-abiding point of view) is sometimes the wrong or corrupt thing to do, and occasionally, the wrong thing to do is the only legitimate course of action. The impossibility of crisis management, in this sense, is that the verdict of posterity is uncertain in the heat of events.

In this chapter, we explore how bureaucratic actors (including the political leadership), in pursuit of legitimacy in crisis situations, face ethical dilemmas as they either abide by or breach legal frameworks and often find themselves in legal grey zones. In so doing, we find it pertinent to develop ideal typical expectations regarding (a) the requirements for ethical accountability, and (b) postcrisis appraisals. Combined, the ideal types outline an analytical instrument for unearthing how criteria for ethical evaluation match actual postcrisis scrutiny. We will probe the case of how Sweden handled the 2004 Tsunami disaster. The Swedish bureaucracy and the case studied hold idiosyncratic elements; however, the case illustrates the problems of ethical dimensions, common to crises and bureaucracies in Western democracies, and is therefore useful as a case in point.

ETHICAL EXPECTATIONS ON BUREAUCRATIC BEHAVIOR

The great virtue of an ideal Weberian bureaucracy is that it is "an institutional method for applying general rules to specific cases, thereby making the actions of government fair and predictable" (Wilson, 1989, p. 334–335). The (Weberian) bureaucratic construction, including "hierarchical organization, extensive use of rules, impersonality of procedure, and the employment of specialists on a career basis" (Downs, 1964, p. 6), would seem to avert many ethically awkward situations that might befall the individual bureaucrat. His or her personal views or other individual qualities should not matter, nor be requested. The way in which bureaucracy in general is construed can hence be seen as an answer to some of the inherent ethical challenges implied in public decision making over resource allocation and issue priority. Bureaucracy, in its pursuit of *consistency* and *predictability*, promotes the value of *abidance by law and regulations*. For hierarchies to be purposeful, *obedience to authority* is vital.

One rationale behind hierarchical layers is the power superiors have in settling conflicts between units or individuals who have different perceptions of the basic goals of the bureau. A second rationale is that hierarchies can render communication within the bureau more efficient in terms of relaying information appropriately, instead of having all sharing all information with everybody else (Downs, 1964). Both rationales push accountability upward. The lower hierarchical levels cannot be expected to determine the agency's goals and values, and their control over information flows is limited. It is plausible therefore that different hierarchical levels in a public bureaucracy experience different ethical rationales. *Abiding by the law* and *obeying superiors* pertain to the ethical rationality of the bureaucratic floor. At the top, there is a *political rationality* that guides action in ethically tricky situations, which does not necessarily heed Weberian ideals of *fairness* and *predictability*. As long as the politics-administration dichotomy is preserved, ethical challenges inherent in the nature of bureaucracy are unlikely to manifest, even in times of crises.

Beyond the ideal typical bureaucracy, it is, however, quite likely that tension arises between *political morality* and *administrative expediency* (Skidmore, 1995, p. 35). Christopher Hood points out that delegation of formal responsibility can be seen as an *agency strategy* to avoid blame. Avoiding direct control limits the reward in situations where things go well but also limits the blame if something goes wrong (Hood, 2007). The political elite are in some sense responsible overall for what's going on in the machinery but have little choice but to delegate authority to the civil servants. Who then is responsible if things go wrong? The discussion above indicates an ethical dilemma inherent in bureaucracy; its construct paves the way for blame games between different levels of government. Hood's observations add to a general demise of Weberian ideals. Kathryn Denhardt made the point a few decades ago that the politics-administration dichotomy was helplessly outdated as theoretical guidance to unearthing bureaucratic mysteries. She argued instead that we should acknowledge the administrator as policymaker in order to develop ethical guidance for the value judgments he or she will inevitably encounter. The public has increasingly come to perceive that they have easier access to administrators than to legislators, and they consequently expect more *responsiveness* from administrators (Denhardt, 1988, pp. 61–65). Being *responsive* to the needs of the public of course requires occasional breaches of rules and regulations. Responsible action might therefore imply avoiding precedents by discarding responsiveness.

In sum, the bureaucratic scene for ethical choice is marked by a combination of sometimes contradictory ideals and realities. Weberian principles are present in the way bureaucracies are hierarchically organized and in the division of labor and responsibility that are chimerically endorsed. At the same time, there are demands on the whole width of bureaucracy to make value judgments that go beyond simple rule abidance.

Insight and Autonomy

Lennart Lundquist (1988, p. 143) suggested three criteria for assessing ethical behavior. The actor (a) has taken an *action* with effects that can be evaluated; (b) has *insight* into what is right and wrong, good and bad; and (c) has the *autonomy* to do what is good and what is right. The action criterion refers here both to the content of a decision and the process by which the decision is taken, such as its democratic status. Lundquist relates the second criterion to individuals' fundamental moral consciousness and ability to discern between right and wrong. When analyzing an established bureaucratic institution, it is more purposeful to use the criterion of *insight,* referring to whether the actor understands the situation and the potential consequences of his/her actions or inactions. Classical experiments, such as Milgram's experiment on obedience to authority, show that people might disregard basic ideas of right and wrong and subject themselves to authorities. Lundquist, however, argues that since the internal control of bureaucracies is imprecise, a bureaucrat can never blame actions on the control (or lack thereof) of superiors (Lundquist, 1988, p. 148). *Autonomy,* the third criterion, implies that the actor has the freedom (according to laws and social norms) to act and the ability (actual possibility to use the freedom, resources, competence, etc.) to do so (Lundquist, 1988, pp. 111, 143).

TABLE 2.1 A Typology for Assessing Ethical Behavior

		Autonomy	
		High	Low
Insight	High	A	B
	Low	C	D

Consequently, actors can have towering insight combined with a high degree of *autonomy* (A), *insight* of the need to take action, but lack the *autonomy* to act on that understanding (B) and vice versa (C). They may also lack both *insight* and *autonomy* (D). The cases of B and C may be questioned ethically, as there are rarely clear-cut lines defining where your responsibility to gain *insight* and to act on this *insight* starts and where it ends. In situation A, actors can and should be evaluated unapologetically on the ethics of their behavior and decisions.

In an ideal administrative setting, only actors in position A would be held ethically accountable. In line with Hood (2007), Wockelberg (see Chapter 9, this volume), and other students of politics, we have good reason to assume that also actors in positions B and C will be evaluated, held accountable, and judged based on their ethical stands.

LEGALITY, LEGITIMACY, AND POSTCRISIS SCRUTINY

Having both the *insight* into a problem and the *autonomy* to act on it, in what seems to be the right way, might not always mean that it will be valued as the ethical thing to do come postcrisis scrutiny. An analysis of how actions are judged in the postcrisis phase can be based on the notions of *legitimacy* and *legality* (cf. Beckman, 2004).

TABLE 2.2   A Typology of Postcrisis Evaluation of Crisis Action

		Legitimacy	
		Low	High
Legality	Legal	1	4
	Grey zone	2	5
	Illegal	3	6

With the benefit of hindsight, investigative commissions, the public, or the media might deem an action *illegitimate*, that is, breaching with social rules and norms even though it is *legal* (1), *legitimate* and *illegal* (6), *legal* and *legitimate* (4), and *illegitimate* and *illegal* (3). Positions 2 and 5 represent legal grey zones that tend to become apparent in crises (see Table 2.3).

TABLE 2.3   Empirical Observations of Insight, Autonomy and Postcrisis Evaluation

	Low legitimacy			High legitimacy		
Insight/Autonomy	Legal	Grey zone	Illegal	Legal	Grey zone	Illegal
	1	2	3	4	5	6
A	O: 5	O: 4	O: 2			
B		O: 7		O: 1		O: 6
C	O: 3					
D						

Table 2.3 aims to combine the situational basis for assessing ethical behavior (see Table 2.1) with the verdict of the posterity (outlined in Table 2.2). Combinations A1 and A6 (Table 2.3) represent situations where actors had a high degree of *autonomy* and *insight*, and they managed to do the right thing but did not abide by the law or alternatively, abided by the law and, as a consequence, were not able to do the right thing. Position B, situations where actors have a low degree of *autonomy* but a high degree of *insight*, is interesting, especially if found in combination with 1 (Table 2.3). It would indicate that the posterity had unrealistic expectations on the *autonomy* of the bureaucrat. Position C1 (Table 2.3) is equally interesting since it says that the expectations on people in the machinery with a high degree of *autonomy* are that they should be informed enough to have a good *insight* into the problem at hand. Positions B and C, most pointedly in combination with 1 and 6 (Table 2.3), represent inherent ethical dilemmas where hierarchical rules must be breached and/or professional responsibilities disrespected in order to come out with some decency in postcrisis evaluations.

The sections below outline a case study of the Swedish experience with the 2004 tsunami. The ambition in this chapter is not to provide an exhaustive account of how the events unfolded, but rather to recount episodes selectively. We will choose observations that represent a variation, in terms of the verdict of posterity, that illustrates the typology above. The selected observations are plotted in Table 2.3.

THE SWEDISH BUREAUCRACY DURING THE 2004 TSUNAMI DISASTER

When the tsunamis hit the shores of the Bay of Bengal on December 26, 2004, approximately 30,000 Swedes were escaping the Scandinavian winter on the beaches of Thailand. With over 500 Swedes dead and many thousands injured, the 2004 tsunami disaster constitutes one of the most tragic peacetime incidents in Swedish history. The Social Democratic government was criticized early on for reacting slowly to the crisis. Evacuation operations were delayed, information to the public was lacking or incomplete, and many people perceived the attitude displayed by politicians and civil servants as arrogant. Needless to say, the disaster triggered an intense blame game between the government, the political opposition, and the media (Brändström, Kuipers, & Daléus, 2008). The government's management of the disaster was subsequently scrutinized by a government inquiry commission (the Commission). The Commission was unique in explicitly placing responsibility for the failures in government first and foremost on the prime minister (PM), Göran Persson (SOU, 2005, pp. 104, 268), but also placing some of the responsibility with other ministers and key civil servants. "The staff of the Government Offices works with long term analysis and is not used to put everything aside to engage in major operative issues. They are not 'doers' in the same way as people from the economic life are" (Dagens Nyheter, 2005, authors' translation),[1] commented one of the members of the Commission. The postcrisis scrutiny continued in the parliamentary Standing Committee on the Constitution (the CoC), which held hearings with civil servants and ministers. The flawed crisis response led to a major restructuring of the government's crisis management system and was, according to high-ranking social democrats, a direct cause in the party being ousted from power in the 2006 general elections (Nuder, 2008, p. 272).

Initial Reactions

The tsunami certainly caught Swedish public administration snoozing at the wheel. The bulk of the staff was on Christmas leave, rendering the central bureaucracy close to empty. The ability to gain insight into the crisis, in terms of its scope and magnitude, was severely hampered by a reluctance to bother top-level officials. Like Chinese Whispers,[2] the alarming messages from the bottom of the administrative hierarchy transformed beyond recognition, to look quite harmless, before they reached upper echelons. The reasons for this transformation can be found in the pressure to respect hierarchy and in a fear on behalf of the middle management of overreacting in the eyes of political officeholders; that is, interrupting their vacations without a true cause.

The first report that came to the on-duty consular officer at the Foreign Ministry from the embassy in Bangkok said that an earthquake had taken place followed by tidal waves; cars were floating around, and up to 30,000 Swedes were in the area. The consular officer realized the catastrophic dimensions of the situation based on her own prior experience. She alerted her two closest superiors, the group leader and the head of the consular affairs unit, to the severity of the situation (Hansén, 2005, pp. 25–26). Based on this information, the latter called the highest ranking civil servant at the Foreign Ministry, the permanent undersecretary. The undersecretary did not find the news alarming; his understanding was that the relevant functions at the ministry were up and running, and that there was no coherent situational awareness to act on yet. He was, in fact, surprised to be awakened by such nonalarming news (Hansén, 2005, p. 33). The head of the consular affairs unit nevertheless felt that he had alerted his superior and saw no need to also call the political appointees at the ministry, especially not the Minister of Foreign Affairs. He would not take such action "unless war broke out" (SOU, 2005, pp. 104, 189). The on-duty officer was persistent, however, and called the head of the unit again to say that the situation was untenable. She was soon reprimanded by the group leader for bypassing her in the hierarchy. The group leader told her she was *hysterical* and instructed her to remain at her home (Hansén, 2005, pp. 33–34).

The on-duty officer was later commended (SOU, 2005, pp. 104, 184–185, 269) on her early and correct reaction to the crisis. She had insight but lacked autonomy to initiate further actions (observation 1: B4, in Table 2.3). The head of the consular unit and the group leader were criticized for not discontinuing their vacations to lead the crisis management efforts at the ministry. Further, the head was criticized for not informing the ministry political appointees of the event, as he was the responsible authority at the Foreign Ministry (SOU 2005, pp. 104, 273). They both, but the unit head in particular, had autonomy to act and insight into the unfolding events (observation 2: A3, in Table 2.3). The actions were thus judged as illegal.

One argument for upholding bureaucratic hierarchies is to render communication more efficient. It is obvious, however, that various distortions of the vertical mediation of information had a counterproductive effect on the initial reaction of the Swedish government. Information came to the PM and the Minister for Foreign Affairs in the morning of December 26. The PM saw the international news that reported on an earthquake in the Indian Ocean. He had routine contacts with his undersecretary, but their contacts were not directly related to the disaster. The Minister for Foreign Affairs got similar information from the civil servants at the Foreign Ministry. She was informed that many Swedes were in the area, but that there was no information reporting on dead or injured Swedes. She assumed, because no one in the line organization contacted her, that everything was working smoothly. Both the PM and the foreign minister understood from their co-workers that the Minister for International Development Cooperation, Carin Jämtin, was handling the situation and commenting on it in the media (KU8, 2005/06, pp. 115–118).

The CoC recognized that the information that the PM and the Minister of Foreign Affairs received was not that alarming, nevertheless the CoC criticized the ministers for not actively following the media reporting on the event on the morning of December 26 (KU8, 2005/06, pp. 197–198, 207–208). That is, in terms of legality, the civil servants failed to deliver information to the ministers, but in their position, it was not legitimate for the ministers to be unaware of a disaster of such magnitude. They were judged as having acting illegitimately even though they clearly lacked insight (observation 3: C1, in Table 2.3).

Organizational Responsibility

A prominent argument for upholding hierarchies is the need for settling conflicts between units or individuals who might interpret goals differently.

In this situation, an ethical dilemma appears related to the concept of *significant choice.* That is, giving the relevant bodies information to be able to make rational choices on significant issues (such as the hazards associated with smoking). This is what Seeger, Sellnow, and Ulmer (2003) call "information based ethics" (pp. 235–236). It applies here in both hierarchical directions. The superior level needs to know that there is a conflict to solve, including the various components and stakes that make up the dispute. The lower hierarchical levels need clear and unambiguous outcomes from the deliberation of their superiors' positions. In this case, bottlenecks were created because higher administrative levels were not informed of an ongoing dispute, and later on, the highest levels conveyed turbid messages down the hierarchical chain to operational staff.

Indeed, the initial reactions to the disaster came to plague the subsequent response. What should the government respond to? An initial plan to send relief to traumatized Swedes in Thailand was initiated by the Swedish Rescue Services Agency (SRSA) on Sunday, December 26. However, funding was needed, so they needed approval by the Cabinet. Organizational disputes and miscommunication began between the SRSA, the Ministry of Defense, and the Foreign Ministry. Initially, it was decided that the Foreign Ministry was in charge and was to decide on financial issues. When the issue was raised at the Foreign Ministry, civil servants declined aid from SRSA to Thailand as there was no formal request from the Swedish embassy. Similar problems occurred at the Ministry of Defense (Hansén, 2005, pp. 44–45). Again, ministry middle management abided by formal rules, and the machinery came to a halt. Civil servants confirmed in the Commission inquiry that there is an instinctual reaction within the two ministries stating that "if you make a decision then you have to finance it" (Hansén, 2005, p. 49). Trying to keep the ministries' finances intact, it was easier for both ministries to pass the buck. Miscommunication remained a problem until a final decision was made at noon on December 28 to send a team from SRSA to Thailand (Hansén, 2005, p. 49).

The actions of the Minister of Defense and Minister for International Cooperation were not deemed legitimate, as their respective ministries were the most affected, they had some insight into what was going on, had the autonomy to act and put an end to the disputes (KU8, 2005/06, pp. 208–209). Their actions, while admittedly in a legal grey zone, were not seen as legitimate by the postcrisis inquiry (observation 4: A2, in Table 2.3). Their culpability in this case can be seen as a consequence of the *problem of many hands.*

Financing Actions in Thailand

When scrutinizing the actions of the Swedish civil servants in the 2004 tsunami disaster, it becomes clear that fuzzy mandates dominated their work processes, making it hard for these civil servants to determine their own responsibility for actions taken and actions shunned. The nebulous work processes and the vague status of decisions/signals of the political leadership can be understood in terms of planning for a foreseen accountability process.

The PM's office was to play a limited part in the crisis, as the Foreign Ministry had taken the initial lead. At the first meeting held with the PM, a ministerial group was put together. The group headed by the PM was not to make any *formal* decisions but to inform, discuss, and if need be, make sure that a Cabinet quorum could convene quickly. The informal status warranted the Chief of Legal Affairs to decide that minutes did not need to be taken at these meetings (KU8, 2005/06, p.115). The discussions held by this very important group therefore remain unknown, but it is safe to say that the discussions affected the management of the crisis. The issue of how to finance the rescue operations in Thailand, including the SRSA mission, was discussed in the group on December 28. The group did not make any formal decisions, however, but rather decided to send *signals* to the Government Offices via another group (constituted by state secretaries from affected ministries) that it was better to double the efforts rather than to make no efforts (KU8, 2005/06, part 1, pp. 115, 196).

Both the Commission and the CoC later criticized this arrangement, asserting that a formal Cabinet decision would have emphasized the importance of putting aside the issue of who would finance the mission (KU8, 2005/06, pp. 207–208; SOU, 2005, pp. 104, 252, 267). The CoC argued that even though the ministers did not act illegally, a formal cabinet decision would have been better in the sense that it would have reduced ambiguity. The PM, the Minister for Foreign Affairs, and Minister of Finance were criticized, as they had been in a position to initiate such a decision (KU8, 2005/06, pp. 207–208). Furthermore, the CoC emphasized the importance of keeping records of decisions (KU8, 2005/06, p. 197). Thus, even though it was legally correct to make informal decisions, it had no legitimacy in the eyes of the postcrisis examiners (observation 5: A1, in Table 2.3).

Consular Issues and Repatriation

The discussion above portrays the process by which funding for action was provided. As the waves swept people and their belongings away, thousands of Swedes found themselves without shelter, money, or passport. The law on economic consular aid stipulates that an embassy can grant economic aid in form of *help to self-help* to a citizen in an emergency. Aid must be requested in writing, and the loan is to be repaid at an interest rate of 10% (SOU, 2005, pp. 104, 85–89). Victims who found their way to the embassy in Bangkok and the Consulate in Phuket were requested to identify themselves and sign an IOU notifying them of the interest rate. As more and more people turned up, the embassy civil servants lacked directives on how to act and felt that the rules were a problem. They needed a decision on whether the rules could be put aside or not. On Tuesday, December 28, 2004, they received the news that money should be paid against a receipt signed by the recipient. Uncertain about their ability to circumvent the rules, civil servants applied the rules differently in Bangkok and in Phuket. Those civil servants who were used to working with consular affairs applied rules strictly. Interestingly, those who had no experience working with consular affairs assumed a more liberal approach to the rules (SOU, 2005, pp. 104, 226). The head of the Consular Affairs Unit in Stockholm said that the austere personnel acted correctly, as they cannot make exceptions in relation to the law. At first, *political signals* were conveyed to the head of the consular unit from a formal crisis management group at the Foreign Ministry. The rules were to be put aside and no interest should be charged, a decision that was later formalized on Tuesday, December 28, (Daléus, 2005, pp. 105–106).

A similar chain of events took place when it became apparent that Sweden needed more air power to bring stranded Swedes home. The Cabinet announced early on, at a press conference, that travel agencies were primarily responsible for repatriating the Swedes they had flown to Thailand (Information Rosenbad, 2004). However, at a meeting with a crisis management group at the Foreign Ministry, it was apparent that the travel agencies would not be able to repatriate all Swedes; the Cabinet needed to take action (Hansén, 2005, p. 58). A meeting was held between Scandinavian Airlines (SAS) and the Foreign Ministry on Tuesday, December 28. SAS did not have the capacity for a large-scale evacuation until New Year's Eve. After the meeting, civil servants at the Foreign Ministry in Stockholm were given the instructions to procure air capacity. There was *political pressure* to get things done and not wait for SAS. The staff at the Foreign Ministry reasoned that there was not enough time to abide by the Public Procurement Act; the directives were that money was no problem, and the main thing was to get as many airplane seats as possible out of Thailand (Hansén, 2005, pp. 58–59).

The system of weak signals made the civil servants responsible for deciding what could be done and how. Had they done too much, it would have been up to them to defend their actions in the aftermath. The Commission expressed sympathy for the efforts to deviate from the strict regime on economic consular aid and bypass strict regulations set by the Public Procurement Act. The Commission suggested that the loose instructions given to the civil servants made them responsible for making the call whether to stick to traditional regulations or to engage in *acute crisis management*

(SOU 2005, pp. 104, 267). Thus, in the Commission's view, the actions were legitimate, but in a formal sense they were illegal (observation 6: B6, in Table 2.3). In this observation, legitimacy was not based on legal actions, but rather on its opposite: breaking the law and setting aside rules.

Truthful or Responsible Communication?

Public officials face truly severe ethical dilemmas in crises when it is time to communicate what is happening to the public. It might be ethically defensible, at certain times in crises, to lie to the public in order to avoid panic, or to withhold information in order to save lives, or to protect the privacy and psychological well-being of victims (Seeger et al., 2003, pp. 235–236).

For days, it was unclear how many Swedes had perished or were injured in the 2004 tsunami disaster. Public officials (politicians and civil servants alike) had to carefully balance the information they went public with. On the afternoon of December 26, the media relations manager at the Ministry for Foreign Affairs said on TV that there were unconfirmed reports that Swedish citizens had died in Thailand and that the number of dead was probably under 10 (Uppdrag Granskning, 2005). This was part of the formal communication strategy from the ministry to only speak of confirmed dead, and at the beginning of the crisis there were no confirmed deaths (SOU, 2005, pp. 104, 202). Later on, when she was asked if she thought at the time that more Swedish citizens had died, the media relations manager said, "Oh yes. But we are a government agency; we cannot speculate on whether there are 3,000 or 300" (Uppdrag Granskning, 2005). A civil servant at the embassy in Bangkok confirmed on radio that two Swedish citizens had died; he was then criticized by the Foreign Ministry back in Sweden. They argued that such information would only add to the pressure on the already strained Government Office switch board (SOU, 2005, pp. 104, 202). At press conferences, the PM and other politicians provided statements that indicated a more and more severe situation at hand. At the first government press conference, the PM said that "there's talk about ten dead" (Information Rosenbad, 2004), but he deemed it risky to commit to a specific number. On December 28, a media relations manager at the Ministry for Foreign Affairs said that the ministry did not have confirmed numbers but "we can only expect the worst" (Dagens Nyheter, 2004).

The CoC was critical of how the government reported on the number of deceased and missing Swedes. They argued that the restrictive attitude regarding when and how to disclose the number of dead stood in sharp contrast to what the media was reporting; the government's restrictiveness early on probably reinforced a nonalarming image of the disaster, the CoC argued. At the same time, the CoC suggested that it was right not to speak publicly of unconfirmed numbers of dead, but that the political leadership should have emphasized that they feared a large number of Swedes had died (KU8, 2005/06, p. 206). The Commission was also critical in this regard and proposed that the short-term damage, in terms of an overloaded switchboard, was outweighed by the potential long-term damage to the public's trust in government (SOU, 2005, pp. 104, 202). Hence, civil servants and politicians alike faced the ethical dilemma of not being able to assess the consequences of either saying too much or saying too little. The formal way that officials handled information regarding the number of dead and injured was not illegal because there are, in fact, no rules established for how to inform the public about such matters. Officials in charge of speaking to the media had insight into the matter of the potential number of missing and dead Swedes, but dared not go public with numbers they were not certain of. These actions were seen as illegitimate by the postcrisis inquiry, however, as other countries had better systems for approaching the problem, and the information the government provided caused more confusion than it helped the situation (SOU, 2005, pp. 104, 202) (observation 7: B2, in Table 2.3).

CONCLUSIONS

In this chapter, we set out to formulate a typological framework for analyzing ethical challenges in the assessment of crisis management efforts. Very simply, the typology matches expectations about who can be ethically held responsible, with observations of who actually was held accountable in postcrises processes. This match provides a first cut at how ethical dilemmas in bureaucracies affect crisis management at all levels of government, from civil servants, at the lowest level, all the way up to the prime minister, at the highest level.

Foremost, our analysis shows that a strict division between politics and administration (the politics-administration dichotomy) cannot be expected to be endorsed or supported by examiners in postcrisis evaluations. The Weberian ideal of delegating authority to civil servants does not correspond with the postcrisis analysis of legitimacy we saw in the 2004 tsunami disaster case. The observations show that high-ranking politicians who lacked insight were still held accountable for organizational failures. They were considered responsible overall for what happened and, to a significant degree, the shortcomings of individual civil servants, as illustrated by the unwillingness to assume responsibility at the Ministry for Foreign Affairs and the Ministry of Defense. This is also illustrated by the initial reactions that the postcrisis commissions expected the political leadership to display. Even though the prime minister and minister for foreign affairs did not get information, they were, in the postcrisis evaluation, expected to have been more active in attaining additional information from the media. This case, hence, suggests that in crises, *autonomy* outweighs the criterion of *insight* in the ethical evaluation of actions.

The analysis shows congruence with Skidmore's (1995) claim that tension between different levels in a bureaucratic hierarchy is likely. The study identifies the bureaucratic middle management as situated in an ethical crossfire. In this case, the lower levels were preoccupied with the consequences of their actions, whereas middle managers looked to concerns about the actions in and of themselves. The tension was illustrated in the relationship between the on-duty officer, her closest superior (the group leader), and the head of their unit. The on-duty officer worked persistently to make things happen, whereas her superiors were more reluctant to disturb their high-level superiors and political appointees without having confirmed deaths of Swedish citizens. The civil servant at the embassy who spoke out on the radio about the number of deceased Swedes is yet another illustration of the lower bureaucratic levels' concern with achieving results; again, this action was reprimanded by superiors at the ministry in Sweden. Tensions between a political rationality and administrative expediency were expected, but the findings of great anxiety inside the bureaucracy due to diverging rationalities deserve further theoretical elaboration.

The typology presented in this chapter (see Table 2.3) helps illustrate that illegitimate processes may still provide legitimate outcomes. As illustrated by the handling of IOUs and the procurement of additional air capacity, there was a need to bend (or even break) standard operating procedures in order to handle the crisis. The government was not criticized for this, but rather was seen as having acted naturally in response to an unprecedented disaster.

Conversely, the process leading to the decisions on how to finance actions was criticized and deemed illegitimate, as it did not show sufficient amounts of political will. Furthermore, abiding strictly by the law, might on the contrary be viewed as rigid and unimaginative, as illustrated by the group leader's actions and the embassy civil servants' management of consular aid. This goes to show that the legal grey zones identified in this chapter that many bureaucrats find themselves in, give them room to maneuver but also make them vulnerable to criticism.

The observations in this study are representative of the 2004 tsunami disaster; however, it is unclear at this point if they also represent a larger phenomenon. Relevant questions for future research might be raised to determine this. Only two out of seven observations were deemed highly legitimate, and in both situations, the actions were carried out by lower-level civil servants. The other five situations involved actions carried out by higher ranking officials or top-level politicians and were seen as illegitimate. If generalizable, in what way would such results affect the public's trust in government? If this is an accurate picture of how postcrisis scrutiny tends to keep higher levels responsible for actions and inaction, then is the Weberian dichotomy of civil servants and politicians outdated? Furthermore, if the middle managers are more likely to be scrutinized and held publically accountable, will that make them more *ethically apt*? If civil servants can no longer hide behind political superiors, should we expect them to start behaving differently? The problem is inherent as their loyalty is split between the public, who demands *responsiveness* and the their own organization for which *responsibility* is key.

It is possible that bureaucrats, if given a free mandate to act, will be more responsive and behave proactively rather than reactively. However, such discretionary power in the hands of civil servants will undermine the Weberian notion of how ideal bureaucracies function, and the implementation of decisions might shift from being predictive to arbitrary. This underlines that the ethical dilemmas of bureaucracies in crises are truly inherent. Hierarchies, organizational loyalty, and a foreseen shadow of accountability are elements, present in this case, that affected how both civil servants and politicians acted. We invite scholars to further develop the framework used here through comparative analysis of crises in other contextual settings. Quantitative studies might yield answers as to what actions are viewed as legitimate/illegitimate in bureaucracies in a wider number of cases and might further the understanding of the role of middle managers in times of crisis.

NOTE

1. This and subsequent quotes by Swedish actors have been translated by the authors.
2. In the game variously known as Chinese whispers, Telephone and Pass the Message, the first player whispers a phrase or sentence to the next player. Each player successively whispers what that player believes he or she heard to the next. The last player announces the statement to the entire group. Errors typically accumulate in the retellings, so the statement announced by the last player differs significantly, and often amusingly, from the one uttered by the first. The game is often played by children as a party game or in the playground.

REFERENCES

Beckman, L. (2004). Krishantering och legitimitet: Den legitima krishanteringen— inte enbart effektiv och förtroendeskapande (särtryck ur *Politologen* våren 2004), Stockholm: Krisberedskapsmyndigheten.

Boin, A., & 't Hart, P. (2003). Public leadership in times of crisis: Mission impossible? *Public Administration Review, 63*(5), 544–553.

Brändström, A., Kuipers, S., & Daléus P. (2008). The politics of tsunami responses: Comparing patterns of blame management in Scandinavia. In A. Boin, A. Mc-Connell, & P. 't Hart (Eds.), *Governing after crisis: The politics of investigation, accountability and learning.* Cambridge, UK: Cambridge University Press.

Cohen, S., & Eimicke, W. (1995). Ethics and the public administrator. *The Annals of the American Academy of Political and Social Science, 537*(1), 97–108.

Dagens Nyheter. (2004). *UD lämnar inte ut dödssiffror.* Retrieved December 28, 2004, from http://www.dn.se/nyheter/sverige/ud-lamnar-inte-ut-dodssiff-ror-1.340711

Dagens Nyheter. (2005). *Marianne Nivert efterlyser ansvar.* Retrieved December 2, 2005, from http://www.dn.se/nyheter/sverige/marianne-nivert-efterlyser-ansvar-1.418507

Daléus, P. (2005). Flodvågskatastrofen: Massmedias och myndigheters framställningar av hanteringen. In *SOU 2005: 104 Sverige och tsunamin: Granskning och Förslag.* Stockholm: Fritzes.

Denhardt, K. (1988). *The ethics of public service: Resolving moral dilemmas in public organizations.* New York: Greenwood Press.

Downs, A. (1964). *Inside bureacracy.* Chicago: Real Estate Research Corporation.

Frederickson, H. G. (1993). *Ethics and public administration.* Armonk, NY: M.E. Sharpe.

Hansén, D. (2005). Den Svenska hanteringen av tsunamikatastrofen: Fokus på regeringskansliet. In *SOU 2005: 104 Sverige och tsunamin: Granskning och Förslag.* Stockholm: Fritzes.

Hood, C. (2007). What happens when transparency meets blame-avoidance? *Public Management Review, 9*(2), 191–210.

Huddleston, M., & Sands, J. (1995). Enforcing administrative ethics. *The Annals of the American Academy of Political and Social Science, 537*(1), 139–149.

Information Rosenbad. (2004). *Televised press-conference, the Government Offices of Sweden.* Retrieved December 27, 2004, from http://www.regeringen.se/sb/d/5046

KU8. (2005/06). *Konstitutionsutskottets betänkande: Granskning av regeringens krisberedskap och krishantering i samband med flodvågskatastrofen 2004,* Del 1, (parliamentary hearings) Utskottets text. Sveriges Riksdag.

Lundquist, L. (1988). *Byråkratisk etik.* Lund, Sverige: Studentlitteratur.

Mulgan, R. (2009, November 26–27). *Can public service advice be both frank and transparent.* Paper presented at the Public Leadership Workshop 2009, Canberra, Australia.

Nuder, P. (2008). *Stolt men inte nöjd.* Stockholm: Norstedts.

Seeger, M. W., Sellnow, T. L., & Ulmer, R. R. (2003). *Communication and organizational crisis.* Westport, CT; London: Praeger.

Skidmore, M. (1995). Ethics and public service. *The Annals of the American Academy of Political and Social Science, 537*(1) 25–36.

SOU. (2005). *Sverige och tsunamin–Granskning och förslag* (government report). Stockholm: Fritzes.

Stern, E. (2009). Crisis navigation: Lessons from history for the crisis manager in chief. *Governance, 22*(2), 189–202.

Uppdrag Granskning. (2005, March 1) (investigative TV show), SVT (Swedish television)

Wilson, J. Q. (1989) *Bureaucracy: What government agencies do and why they do it.* New York: Basic Books.

CHAPTER 3

VALUE CONFLICTS IN FOREIGN POLICY CRISES

How the United States and the U.K. Wrestled with the Ethical Dilemma of Going to War in Iraq

Fredrik Bynander

INTRODUCTION

Democratic leaders go to great lengths to demonstrate their discretionary powers in forming their state's foreign policies. They create bipartisan deals to preserve the preeminent role of government and to avoid parliamentary revolts in times of international conflict. They employ extraordinary legal rules for contingencies in the foreign policy arena. They make use of the state's security and intelligence communities to create partial information monopolies in international relations. Many of these practices are mandated in the constitutions and legal frameworks of states. Western democracies have further consolidated and more widely applied these practices since the advent of the War on Terror and its associated conflicts. However, as numerous Western governments have realized, they can backfire badly as the do-

Ethics and Crisis Management, pages 37–56

mestic logic of accountability and blaming kicks in. International relations operate in shades of grey; whereas domestic politics tend to concentrate on one story, and one societal value, at a time. This chapter examines how leaders and civil servants interact to manage the ethical challenge of conflicting values located in the international and domestic arenas respectively. It discusses in detail how complex value conflicts involved in international interventions affect the production, interpretation, and use of intelligence in two Western democracies: the United States and the U.K.

THE DYNAMICS OF ETHICAL FAILURE: FOUR HYPOTHESES

When George W. Bush ordered the commencement of the bombing campaign in Iraq on March 20, 2003, the timing was based on a flash report from the CIA that Saddam Hussein and his sons were gathered at a southern Baghdad compound, Doura Farms, which was targeted with cruise missiles and bunker-busting bombs. The tip was wrong. It was the latest in a long series of CIA mistakes, the most infamous of these being reports on Iraqi WMDs that had been served on a subscription basis to the White House in the President's Daily Briefs and the Senior Executive Intelligence Briefs (U.S. Senate, 2004). As Secretary of State Colin Powell prepared for his speech to the UN Security Council on the eve of war in February of that year, he spent hours upon hours with CIA Director George Tenet going over the intelligence on Baghdad's capabilities, questioning the CIA's reports and their sources. "Tenet looked him in the eye and told him it was rock solid" (Weiner, 2007, p. 568). In light of this, can the ethical failure[1] of legitimizing the invasion of Iraq thus be squarely placed with the CIA, or is the failure more complicated than that?

Was it the extreme pressure applied by the principals of the Bush team, rather, that threw the intelligence system out of orbit and produced the fiction and fables that the administration wanted to hear? I will try to shed light on these questions by exploring *value complexity* as an ethical dilemma when faced with a more or less acute security context, and relate the resulting dynamic to the intragovernmental relationships of *trust* and *professionalism*. I will not ignore the greater debate of ethics in international relations or the philosophical basis of ethics as such, but the working definition in this text is *instrumental* (or *descriptive*; see Chapter 1, this volume), that is, relating the realm of ethics to what a political *demos* can sustain as actions in their name (by their elected representatives) over time.

In an oft-quoted passage of his *Just and Unjust Wars*, Michael Waltzer (2000) argued that "the clearest evidence for the stability of our values over time is the unchanging character of the lies soldiers and statesmen tell" (p. 19) And he does present a convincing case displaying the cross-cultural delineations of the ethically acceptable in intrastate conflict. The issue of interest here, however, is not so much what would in essence constitute ethical behavior in any given circumstance, but rather how come so many of these *soldiers and statesmen* get caught presenting the same old lies in the face of public scrutiny.

One fundamental ethical challenge in the conduct of warfare is the divergent logics of justification[2] presented in the domestic and the international arena, respectively. States use violence against their citizens and other individuals within their territory. They generally do so with justifications based in domestic law and with reference to the integrity of the state. Using sovereignty as a defining concept, the state assumes the right to determine the national interest and to enforce its perceived essence in the relationship to its subject (Khong, 1992, pp. 102–104; Krasner, 1993; Putnam, 1988). The legal principles to dispute that privilege of the state are usually constitutional or founded in international frameworks such as the European Convention on Human Rights or international treaties with which states have no obligation to comply.

When organized violence is directed across national borders, a different legal and moral arena is entered. International law is no exact science, and domestic legitimization strategies are often more elaborate than international ones. Furthermore, international justification strategies tend to be directed toward the domestic political arena as much as they are toward the international arena (Tsebelis, 1991). The proceedings of the UN Security Council, before the Iraq invasion in 2003, showed a debate focused in equal measure on the transgressions of the Iraqi government, the legal foundations for sanctions against Iraq, and on the exposé of unwillingness that Russia, China, and France had displayed in regard to getting serious about the crimes committed by the Baghdad regime. Thus, the political posturing was taking place at the intersection of domestic and international politics, and it is seldom clear which argument is directed to which audience under such circumstances (see Putnam, 1988; Tsebelis, 1991). Obviously, states have their own agenda when faced with international conflict, and they invariably engage in strategies of furthering that agenda internally, and among friends and allies. The resulting debate, internally and internationally, will thus harbor varying degrees of value conflicts; conflicts that will need to be mitigated. The sections below develop four preliminary hypotheses that help describe and discriminate avenues for influence over value conflicts and governments' ethical performance in situations when they contemplate initiating intrastate war.

The first hypothesis, the *own hide hypothesis*, places value complexity at its core and highlights the tendency for internal ethical values to be consistently exaggerated at the expense of external ethical values in situations perceived as very consequential. In accordance with attribution theory, when the stakes are considered high or extremely high, the ethical values emphasizing the interests of the state are inflated, compared with those emphasizing, for example, international order. Correspondingly, organizational values (such as avoiding public embarrassment or heavy budget cuts) can trump the national demand for an organization to provide decision makers with unbiased information (Halversheid & Witte, 2008; Suedfeld, Tetlock, & Jhangiani, 2007). Very consequential situations compound generic value complexity by forcing an off-balance accountability structure (tilted toward institutions of strict accountability that are usually domestic). Since sanctions (legal, social, political) against individual decision makers are much more effective on the domestic and intragovernmental arena than the international arena, domestic values might take priority in the decision-making calculus.

The second hypothesis, the *shortcut hypothesis*, emphasizes that the drive to minimize uncertainty in high-consequence situations creates organizational pressures to ignore complexity, prioritize expediency over accuracy, and to distill evidence that supports the overall assessment held by the organization (March & Olsen, 1998). The latter behavior would entail the unintentional or intentional suppression of dissenting voices, the *doctoring* of anomalous information, and exaggerating the preferred policy's chances of success (Preston, 2001, pp. 9–11). Organizational schemata guide individual behavior by imposing compliance with preset rules, especially in situations characterized by uncertainty. This has been convincingly illustrated for risk acceptance (Heimer, 1998; Vertzberger, 1998) as well as the cognitive integration of value complexity (Renshon, 2008; Tetlock, 1985).

The third hypothesis, the *blind spot hypothesis*, points to organizational and professional deficiencies as instrumental in ethical failures. If decision makers are given a sufficiently erroneous image of their counterpart(s) and their own ability to influence the situation, then an ethically sound decision will be impossible and the decision outcome will be random (Vertzberger, 1998, pp. 52–56). The decision maker in this scenario will be acting on the basis of her own fears and convictions, rather than some (more or less) analytical ground for decision. Obviously, the sources of said deficiencies are under serious scholarly debate (Sagan, 1993, p. 11–7), but here, evidence of such deficiencies will be enough for the hypothesis to be viewed as a credible narrative.

In the fourth hypothesis, the *breaking eggs*[3] *hypothesis*, ethical deliberations can be decided by institutional metanarratives or ethical justification strategies that are implicit in the political or administrative system as such. In the case of foreign policymaking in Western democracies, at least two such institutional metanarratives can be found: a latent *cold war* narrative and a developing *War on Terror* narrative. These narratives work as justifications through the mechanisms of cognitive consistency. These situations

TABLE 3.1   Internal Logic of the Hypotheses

Hypothesis	Mechanism	Direction of influence	Outcome
"Own Hide"	Attribution error	Bottom-up	Domestic solution
"Shortcut"	Consensus seeking	Bottom-up	Groupthink
"Blind Spot"	Incompetence	Either way	Random
"Breaking Eggs"	Avoidance of complexity	Top-down	Predetermined

implore leaders to incorporate events into overriding metanarratives that order their reality (Rosati, 2000; Tetlock, 1982). On the one hand, a lingering *cold war* narrative views discrete events as significant primarily in terms of what they have in common rather than what distinguishes them. This has led to an ends-justifies-means mentality with regard to methods of warfare and intelligence gathering, an enemy-of-my-enemy mentality when it comes to alliance formation, and an emphasis on capabilities over intentions in the assessment of perceived enemies (Herrmann, Voss, Schooler, & Ciarrochi, 1997). On the other hand, the *War on Terror* narrative has undermined territorial integrity as a cornerstone in the previous balance-of-power mindset, and markers of religion, ideology, and ethnicity have now become crucial for security actors in order to discriminate between friend and foe.

It would be disingenuous to suggest that any of these hypothesized logics are mutually exclusive. On the contrary, in policy decisions that constitute ethical failures, it is highly likely to find more than one mechanism at work, and a quick glance at the example of the U.S. engagement in Iraq reveals the clear possibility that all four logics might have been applied. However, the predicted analytical advantage does not lie in the confirmation of one or another hypothesis; rather it lies in the development of a more detailed account of how the logics interact. It is, for example, possible to argue that the ubiquity of a systemic *breaking eggs* approach in the political system increases the likelihood of the other types of ethical reasoning and failure. By contrast, with regard to the justification of policy, does trying to win domestic arguments over the primary threat perception (e.g., War on Terror) conceivably force more prudent and diligent behavior in decision processes (e.g., avoiding shortcuts and blind spots to preserve legitimacy and primacy of interpretation)?

The link between these hypothesized decision processes and ethical failure is constituted by ignorance of long-term consequences that usually would conflict with decision makers' own ethical standards. The concern with a greater good forces a number of lesser evils into the policy process, which undermines the possibility of an outcome that abides by established ethical norms, and thus damages the primary actors as well as their institutional surroundings.

In order to draw reasonable conclusions about the administration of classified intelligence and discreet advice, we need to recognize both the limited (some would say inconclusive) empirical basis for such studies and the often self-serving account decision makers and advisors provide of actual deliberations and decisions.

The Cases

This chapter will examine early empirical accounts of the decisions by the Bush administration and the Blair government to invade Iraq in 2003. Obviously, the historical record is far from complete regarding the decision-making and intelligence processes that preceded the invasion, and facts that could potentially affect the validity of our findings might certainly surface as more classified material is made public. Nevertheless, the actions of these two governments have been more publicly scrutinized in closer proximity to the events in question than perhaps any other event of global political importance. Furthermore, the value complexity that drives the processes hypothesized here (see "Ethical Failures: Four Hypotheses" above), and that manifest themselves over the course of the decision-making process, are to a large degree in the public domain (such as the *evidence* presented by Secretary of State Colin Powell to the UN Security Council in February 2003).

Public hearings and investigative journalism have uncovered enough of the government processes related to the decision to invade Iraq for us to pursue a first test of our four hypotheses. It is also a fact that the justifications provided by the primary actors, as elaborated in speeches, testimonies, interviews, and autobiographies, are relevant to the assessment of our hypotheses and links we might see between them.

The United States

The primary, and extremely public, ethical failure of both of the studied governments in legitimizing their cause for war was their ultimately discredited claim that Saddam Hussein had the capacity to unleash weapons of mass destruction (WMDs) in 45 minutes. The more substantial argument presented to the United Nations Security Council was that Iraq was in material breach of UNSC resolution 1441,[4] in its refusal to cooperate with the UN weapons inspectors and provide evidence of the destruction of its known possession of WMDs, but the *pièce de résistance* was the repeated claim that Saddam indeed possessed and planned to deploy these weapons. In trying to trace the intelligence process that provided cover for the claim, we need to consider the end of the first Gulf War and the weapons inspection regime that was put in place under the auspices of the UN. The evasive tactics of the Iraqi military and political establishments rapidly eroded any remaining shred of credibility that the regime might have with the inspectors (or with the CIA, which was deeply involved in the search for elements of a weapons program). Faced with a culture of lies, the prevailing wisdom in the West was that whatever Saddam could get away with, he would (Blair, 2010, p. 413; Kay, 2004).

The head of the UNSCOM inspection team in 1995, Rolf Ekéus, liaisoned with compatriot telecom giant Ericsson and U.S. intelligence organizations to penetrate Iraqi military communications in order to find evidence of a weapons programs (Weiner, 2007, p. 565). Nothing was discovered, but the information obtained during this operation was used for target selection when the inspectors were pulled out in 1998 and the United States bombed Baghdad. The mutual distrust between Iraq and the United States greatly impacted not only the monitoring regime created in 1991 but also the United States' expectations and intelligence gathering regarding Iraqi weapons of mass destruction. UNSCOM had been first to interview Saddam Hussein's defected son-in-law, Hussein Kamal, in August 1995, but had not trusted his claim that he personally had overseen the destruction of all Iraqi WMDs after the Gulf War (UNSCOM, 1995).

The CIA was, throughout the end of the Cold War and with the depletion of resources that followed it, short on *human intelligence*—eyes and ears on the ground—in current and likely future hotspots of U.S. foreign policy (Berkowitz, 2003). This became painfully obvious as al-Qaeda ramped up the security agenda, and it turned out that their capabilities were largely unknown to the Western intelligence community (Woodward, 2006, pp. 49–52, 90). The CIA tried to make up for their poor intelligence capacity by offering large sums of money to defectors and regional experts with knowledge of the Iraqi military system. The result was a flow of low-quality intelligence that could not be verified or validated through other means (Kay, 2004).

The most (in)famous source regarding Iraq's WMD programs was *Curveball*: an Iraqi citizen who defected in 1999 and became a source for the German Bundesnachrichtendienst and who claimed he had been a chemical engineer working at a plant that manufactured mobile biological weapons laboratories. His information was always shrouded in doubt. The Germans would not allow direct access to Curveball, and his information was conveyed in English and Arabic, translated into German, and then translated back into English. He was known to be a heavy drinker who was wanted for theft in Iraq. He changed his story soon after his arrival in Germany and claimed that he had worked directly for Rihab Rashid Taha, a microbiologist who was known as Dr. Germ to Western intelligence agencies. Curveball was discredited by a number of sources, but his claims kept showing up in U.S. intelligence briefs and were used in Colin Powell's speech to the UN.

Curveball is only one of many highly doubtful sources that were used to build a case against Iraq on the issue of weapons of mass destruction. Reports of Iraqi purchases of *yellow cake uranium* from Niger, imports of aluminum tubes used to build uranium centrifuges, and conclusions on material found by UNSCOM to indicate production of nerve agent VX, were all found to be false by the Senate's select committee on intelligence in 2004 (Hersh, 2005, p. 204; U.S. Senate, 2004). What is more, the intelligence community could easily have disproved this before using the information in their briefs to the political leadership. Taken together, the reporting is solid evidence of what the intelligence community knows as *cherry picking*, the selective use of intelligence to make a case. The very nature of the intelligence world makes claims hard to falsify, and the political impact can obviously be substantial.

The relationship between the Bush administration and the intelligence community was, despite their common interest in finding *the goods* on Saddam Hussein, a tense one. The most visible sign of the distrust that existed between the levels of government was the politically motivated exposure of a covert CIA operative named Valerie Plame. Plame's husband, former Ambassador Joseph Wilson IV, had been sent by the CIA to investigate the rumor that Iraq tried to acquire yellow cake from Niger. He had quickly decided that the rumor was false, and when the allegation started to show up in government arguments for a war with Iraq, Wilson published an op-ed piece in the *New York Times*, entitled "What I didn't find in Africa." Plame's identity was revealed, allegedly as an act of retribution against Wilson, by Vice President Cheney's chief of staff Lewis "Scooter" Libby. Libby was convicted in federal court for his role in outing Plame (U.S. vs. Libby, 2005). Other senior figures of the Bush team were also implicated: Senior Adviser to the President Karl Rove, Deputy Secretary of State Richard Armitage, and the vice president himself. The affair exacerbated the conflict between the intelligence community and the administration.

That conflict had simmered ever since Donald Rumsfeld and Dick Cheney returned to posts in the federal government with the election of George W. Bush. They were both critics of the U.S. intelligence community in general and of the CIA in particular. Rumsfeld had, during his first stint as Secretary of Defense in 1975–1976, an infected fight with the CIA over budgets and had stated that the CIA was spying on him. Ironically, the director of central intelligence at that time was George H. W. Bush (Garthoff, 2005, pp. 113–116). Although Director Tenet became an insider in the Bush White House after 9/11, the CIA was effectively held at bay through budgeting by Rumsfeld, who allowed no representatives of the intelligence community at the Pentagon when the budget was negotiated (Garthoff, 2005, pp. 273–276). This distrust was well known in the intelligence community, and there was a sense of desperation in the CIA as the mission became more complex, and publically demanding, but the intelligence resources had already been eroded (Woodward, 2008, p. 137).

The result of these meandering efforts to substantiate the claims of Iraqi WMDs was eventually a full choir of top administration voices declaring,

> The Iraqi regime has in fact been very busy enhancing its capabilities in the field of chemical and biological agents. And they continue to pursue the nuclear program they began so many years ago. These are not weapons for the purpose of defending Iraq; these are offensive weapons for the purpose of inflicting death on a massive scale, developed so that Saddam can hold the threat over the head of anyone he chooses, in his own region or beyond. (Dick Cheney, speech to the Veterans of Foreign Wars (VFW) national convention in Nashville, Tennessee, August 27, 2002)[5]

> Year after year, Saddam Hussein has gone to elaborate lengths, spent enormous sums, taken great risks to build and keep weapons of mass destruction. But why? The only possible explanation, the only possible use he could have for those weapons, is to dominate, intimidate or attack. (George W. Bush, State of the Union Address, January 29, 2003)[6]

> The facts on Iraqis' behavior—Iraq's behavior demonstrates that Saddam Hussein and his regime have made no effort—no effort—to disarm as required by the international community. Indeed, the facts and Iraq's behavior show that Saddam Hussein and his regime are concealing their efforts to produce more weapons of mass destruction. (Colin Powell, Speech to the United Nations Security Council, February 5, 2003)[7]

If the administration had realized that the intelligence on Iraqi WMDs was phony, they would not have stressed this aspect of their causes for war as strongly. They would likely have prepared for a postinvasion debate and argued the poor human rights record of Saddam Hussein more strongly, for example. In a way, the leadership had duped themselves into believing information that was the product of doctored intelligence from suspicious sources. This manipulation, in turn, was a product of their own single-mindedness in dealing with the Iraq problem and the way they directed federal agencies to implement their view of that problem. All evidence suggests that Colin Powell walked into the UNSC firmly believing the story he was about to deliver to the world, or at least did not feel he had sufficient grounds to dispute the CIA material and thus resist his colleagues in their push for immediate war. Powell knew he risked his reputation and his legacy as a George Marshall-style soldier-turned-statesman, which gave him an unusual moral influence on U.S. foreign policy.

The U.S. Modus

The active communication of flawed intelligence came from several government units and was originally a product of poor sources on Iraq combined with rapidly growing political pressure after 9/11. The reliance on defectors in search of asylum, protection, and cash was never a solid basis for estimating the capabilities of Saddam's regime. Furthermore, the political urge to build a case for action crowded out concerns over the legitimacy of a war in the longer run. The intelligence community became increasingly aware that the Iraq policy was in relentless motion, and the constant worry of the intelligence leadership was of not being onboard, of not being useful to the administration when it was summoned. The results were errors of judgment in at least three stages of the intelligence cycle: the intelligence gathering was sloppy and did not meet professional requirements; the communication of the resulting analysis was overconfident and lopsided; and the reaction of the principals was not one of sound skepticism but of impatient calls for tougher conclusions, the return of lost nuggets from previous briefings, and erring on the side of recklessness (U.S. Senate, 2004; Weiner, 2007).

In terms of our hypothesized patterns of value biases, all four were present in the U.S. decision to go to war with Iraq. The U.S. administration overemphasized internal values domestically and internationally (how to sell the war, rather than establish a cause for war that would hold up across time). It clearly selected information that confirmed and favored preexisting beliefs over anomalies and the multiple sources that argued that the Baghdad regime was in general compliance with international treaties. The U.S. administration was overconfident that the intelligence community had reliable information; and leading administration officials have repeatedly and honestly testified that the War on Terror gave Iraqi WMDs a new sense of urgency and made a qualitative difference in the decision-making process. However, if we rank the reasons into a chain of evidence, the *blind spot hypothesis* describes the dominant narrative.

> Before 9/11, Saddam was a problem America might have been able to manage. Through the lens of the post-9/11 world, my view changed. I had just witnessed the damage inflicted by nineteen fanatics armed with box cutters. I could only imagine the destruction possible if an enemy dictator passed his WMD to terrorists. (Bush, 2010, p. 229)

The preexisting belief that Saddam was toying with the international community, that he was still pursuing WMD capabilities, carefully concealed those efforts, and was willing to deploy them against his enemies, was so strong that it tended to marginalize evidence to the contrary. Opponents of forceful action against Iraq would concede as much in the long debates that preceded the war, and the issue of the *smoking gun* would become increasingly academic to the proponents of such action. Even the cautious head of the UNSCOM at the time, Hans Blix, talked about the Iraqi behavior in this way, although arguing that there was no detection of the proverbial smoking gun (Blix, 2004, p. 151). Cheney, Rice, and others in the Bush administration would answer that the "smoking gun might be a mushroom cloud" (Blitzer, 2003).

In addition, there was a strong sense in the top circles of the Bush administration that being successful is being right, and that as long as regime change would be swift, comprehensive, and stabilizing to the region, the international and domestic criticism would be mild. This disregard of the long-term legitimacy problem is a central part of the ethical failure of the U.S. Iraq policy.

The U.K.

In Britain, the Iraq policy was strongly buoyed by that of the United States, and the intelligence process followed a similar trajectory. The intelligence cooperation between the two states is far-reaching, and British intelligence agencies have become growingly dependent upon the larger resources and the longer reach of their American colleagues. Nevertheless, British intelligence has some comparative advantages in their remaining ties with their former colonies and other (commercial) spheres of interest around the globe that U.S. organizations sometimes have a hard time penetrating. If the Valerie Plame controversy was a defining incident for the relationship between the intelligence community and the political leadership in the United States, the leaked identity and suicide of WMD expert Dr. David Kelly in July of 2003 was the British equivalent.

The Kelly affair cut right to the heart of the Blair government's handling of dissenting voices in the civil service and in the media regarding the war. The controversy started with BBC radio reporter Andrew Gilligan claiming on national radio that Downing Street had doctored intelligence reports to strengthen the case for war against Iraq, and that the government knew that the *45-minute claim* was false when they stated it. Blair's team immediately went on the offensive and took action against the BBC, forcing a showdown that shook the public service broadcaster to its foundation. The Ministry of Defence (MoD) released a statement on the unauthorized sharing of information to Gilligan that was phrased in a way that made it possible to guess Kelly's identity. When confronted with Kelly's name, the MoD confirmed it, and Dr. Kelly was thrown into the public eye. In June, he appeared before two parliamentary committees, one of them public and televised. Kelly was interrogated quite harshly, and his employer informed him that he might be subjected to legal action. On the afternoon of July 17, Kelly left his home to take a walk, during which he committed suicide (Hutton, 2004).

Kelly's suicide brought to light the aggressive communication tactics of Blair's Downing Street operations. In order to contain the public outrage,

Lord Hutton was appointed to lead a judicial inquiry into the death of government employee Kelly and the events that had preceded it. When Lord Hutton released his report in 2004, he basically exonerated the government from driving Dr. Kelly to his actions, but in the testimonies that had been delivered, several troubling issues had surfaced. For the prime minister himself, it was damaging that his former Permanent Secretary, Sir Kevin Tebitt, had pointed to Blair as chairing the meeting that was instrumental in the strategy of naming Dr. Kelly (Hutton Inquiry, 2003b). Blair had denied this in the media, but was let off conspicuously easy when he appeared before the Hutton inquiry (Hutton Inquiry, 2003a). The immediate victim of this controversy was Alastair Campbell, Blair's belligerent communications director, who had been such a central figure in the conflict with the BBC and in the preparation of evidence of the Iraqi breach of UN resolution 1441. The ethical controversy in the Kelly affair finally boiled down to whether Alastair Campbell forced the *45 minute claim* on the Joint Intelligence Committee (JIC), which was in charge of drafting the so-called *Iraq Dossier* (Hutton, 2003b).

The *45-minute claim* had been the account of a single source. According to the chairman of the JIC, John Scarlett, "This was a report from a single source. It was an established and reliable line of reporting; and it was quoting a senior Iraqi military officer in a position to know this information" (Hutton Inquiry, 2003c). According to senior intelligence officials, this disputed fragment had remained in the intelligence flow because of its significance for potential military action against Iraq. If such action was to take place, the deployment time for WMDs was of the utmost importance, and any piece of intelligence that could shed light on strategies for conflict initiation was of some value. In fact, there seems to have been a slow merger going on between a classified assessment of Iraq's WMD capacities and the infamous public dossier that was being prepared for the prime minister to state his case against Iraq. The classified text talked about deployment times for biological weapons by Iraq's army in terms of 20–45 minutes (Hutton, 2003c). These assessments were based on scenarios with input variables that were speculative at best for the purpose of preparing the British military for an invasion.

The JIC team that was in charge of preparing the intelligence matter of the dossier was called to Alastair Campbell's office at 10 Downing Street on several occasions to discuss *presentation*. The dossier for the use of the prime minister was to have a foreword that used a looser and more suggestive language than the intelligence-based text body. The body of the report, however, recounted testimonies by individual Iraqi citizens in order to strengthen the argument that Saddam Hussein was a cruel dictator that needed to be disposed of. The communications staff had, through this arrangement, a reason to get involved in the drafting process, and to give advice. In an odd passage of Alastair Campbell's published diary, Manchester United manager Alex Ferguson called Campbell, "really worried about Iraq, said he thought it was a very dangerous situation for [Blair]. I said that TB had a real sense of certainty about this one." (Campbell, 2007, p. 639) The influence by the prime minister's staff on the process of crafting the dossier increased exponentially as the moment of presentation drew closer. In an e-mail from one of the British prime minister's press office employees, David Pruce, strong suggestions were made regarding the wording in the dossier:

> In the public's mind the key difference between this text and the IISS [International Institute for Strategic Studies] text will be the access to intelligence material. I like the idea of the history of JIC assessments. Might we also include a general statement on the nature of the intelligence services and their role. This could be drawn from material that is already in the public domain. Its inclusion might help underline the fact that the services have contributed to the report, often in ways which, for perfectly fair reasons, are imperceptible. (Hutton Inquiry, 2003d)

This is the scheming of an overeager junior staffer and not hard evidence of tampering with the JIC process. However, it is revealing of the mentality of the press office staff and the way that they wanted to present a *slam dunk case*, to paraphrase CIA Director Tenet. Blair's own position was set with the decision to join forces with the United States. His foreign policy adviser, Sir Stephen Wall, recalls, "He didn't ask a lot of crucial questions about the extent of Saddam's nuclear capacity, for example. Partly because he didn't want to ask the questions" (Rawnsley, 2010, p. 115). But the real problem at the cabinet level was the lack of high-level quality control. The MoD and the Foreign Office were excluded from the work on the dossier, and Defence Secretary Geoff Hoon first laid eyes on the full document only hours before its presentation. The other cabinet members were sent to see Head of MI6 Dearlove and JIC Chairman Scarlett one by one and were presented with evidence that "there was nothing speculative about it" according to Culture Secretary Tessa Jowell (quoted in Rawnsley, 2010, p. 115).

In Blair's own account of his thought process leading to the conclusion that an invasion was called for, there is a strong emphasis on Saddam's track record of defying sanctions and engaging in human rights abuses. This underscores the idea that the possession of WMDs was not the primary reason for the decision on either side of the Atlantic (Blair, 2010, pp. 383–387). At the political level, for which the integrity and credibility of the intelligence community was not the overriding concern, the behavior and the duplicity of the Iraqi regime was evidence enough of the ambition to retain and develop WMD capabilities. However, there is strong evidence to suggest that the idea that Saddam possessed WMDs was intimately linked, by cognitive consistency, to the image of Saddam Hussein as a highly motivated and politically reckless leader. There was nothing in the behavior of the Iraqi regime that suggested he had forfeited the WMD option after the Gulf War, and his consistent uncooperative behavior toward the UN weapons inspectors was considered further proof that this was an option he was still pursuing. As mentioned earlier, the U.S. administration imbedded the *smoking gun* debate in the *Saddam Hussein as reckless villain* narrative, and many accounts reflecting a similar attitude can be found among the U.K. leadership.

Finally, we need to address the fact that the two cases in this study are closely linked, and that they, in a sense, contaminate or spill over to one another. When studying the meetings between the leaders and their senior advisers, it is clear that there is a mutually reinforcing air of certainty, not only about the correct strategy to deal with Iraq, but also about the existence of Iraqi WMDs. According to a declassified diplomatic telegram that was sent from the British embassy to the Foreign Office, the following was said between Bush and Blair in their April 5–7 meeting in Crawford, Texas: "They agreed that Iraq's WMD programmes were a major threat to the international community, particularly when coupled with Saddam's proven track record on using these weapons. Letting that programme continue unhindered was not an option" (Iraq Inquiry, 2002).

The bolstering of one another's attitudes on Iraq and WMDs was an ongoing process between Bush and Blair, causing British senior advisers great worry. Foreign Secretary Jack Straw wrote Blair a letter days before Blair left for the Crawford meeting with Bush: "the rewards from your visit to Crawford will be few," and he urged Blair "to beware of elephant traps," stating that "regime change per se is no justification for military action" (Straw, quoted in Rawnsley, 2010, p. 93). U.S. officials, too, pressured Blair to hold back the seemingly relentless movement toward a war that originated in Washington. Colin Powell had long conversations with Jack Straw to devise a strategy to get the leaders to tone down their war rhetoric and appealed personally to Blair to be firm with Bush, especially concerning a second UNSC resolution in 2002. "Blair would express his concerns, but he would never lie down on the railroad tracks. Jack and I would get him all pumped up about an issue. And he'd be ready to say 'Look here, George.' But as soon as he saw the President he would lose all his steam" (Powell, quoted in Rawnsley, 2010, p. 104; see Schaefer & Walker, 2006). The two cases are thus intimately intertwined, and the initiation of the Iraq war and the intelligence failure that preceded it constitute a unique mix of personal interactions between national leaders, not only on strategy, but also on the worldviews that informed their respective foreign policies.

One overriding theme of these encounters was the nature of the War on Terror that they both saw themselves as the leaders of. Blair, who prided himself on having understood and successfully mitigated the infected conflict in Northern Ireland, had a natural authority on the subject (Seldon, 2007, pp. 535–541). But when it came to the global terrorism, represented by al-Qaeda, he saw the problem as having deeper roots and requiring violent action in a way that had not been the cure for Northern Ireland. "Back in the instant following the cataclysmic act of terrorism that stunned, shocked and appalled the world, the issue was clear: the madmen had declared war. They would be rooted out and eliminated" (Blair, 2010, p. 349). The connection between 9/11 and Iraq was made in similar terms: "the issue of Saddam and his ten-year obstruction of weapons inspection was not upfront, but from then on, it was there in the background. There was no decision at that point as to how to deal with him; nevertheless, that he had to be confronted, brought into line or removed was, on any deeper analysis, fairly obvious." (Blair, 2010, p. 357)

The worldviews of the two leaders were highly compatible, and the main difference seems to have been the means by which to further the end of regime change in Iraq: unilateral action or multilateral? Blair's appeals for Bush to be more patient with the UN Security Council process ultimately fell on deaf ears, and Bush entered the Iraq war a believer in regime change as the one remaining option. The only way forward in justifying this course of action was to argue material breach of UNSC 1441, and Blair, more than Bush, needed the intelligence to prove it.

The U.K. Modus

The British case is different from the American in the sense that the U.K. intelligence apparatus never overestimated their own intelligence capacity regarding Iraq nor, for any longer time spans, that of the United States or other services. The JIC process that produced the public Iraq dossier failed primarily because of political pressure. Blair's own involvement was not motivated by a will to consciously distort intelligence, but his strong conviction on the facts and the way forward made his close advisers realize that in order to keep up with his thinking, and to protect him from future political fallout, they needed to influence the process in terms of *presentation* to the general public. This was the reaction of party officials in an environment that was threatening to be politically disastrous and to wipe out political support for their boss.

The result of this strong emphasis on presentation was the deterioration of responsibility and quality control, and ultimately a breakdown in political-administrative relations, as political appointees ended up influencing what was generally perceived as intelligence material. The long debates about the doctoring of intelligence and the integrity of the JIC cannot significantly alter this general finding. One reason for the ethical failure was the erased boundaries between the public dossier and the material prepared for operational planning.[8] This all points to support for the *breaking eggs hypothesis,* which suggests a strong top-down pressure to conform to the official line and deselect anything that would contradict it. There is little to suggest that this was part of a declared strategy, but rather that the interpretation of the preferred process hardened as it descended from the prime minister down the ranks of the British government.

CONCLUSIONS

The two cases of this study are different in a number of core aspects. The U.K. security apparatus was subject to a much more temporary breakdown as the combined impact of political pressures caused a short-circuiting of its quality control mechanisms and its separations of products aimed at evidence collection and those aimed at tactical intelligence. The U.S. system, on the contrary, was suffering from a long-standing lack of trust between representatives of major institutions for foreign policymaking. It is a fact that the outcome of these two national processes was similar, and that we would need further evidence (over a longer time period) to fully substantiate this claim. However, there is little evidence on the British scene of the first three patterns under investigation (hypotheses 1–3; see "Ethical Failure: Four Hypotheses" above), which would suggest a more systematic imbalance in the intelligence cycle and political assessments of intelligence analysis.

The specific breakdown of the British system is one of political-bureaucratic relations, and it only occurred in a combination of extreme uncertainty, scarcity of validated information, and great political momentum. We described the outcome of a *breaking eggs* scenario (hypothesis 4) as predetermined in the sense that there are too many converging policy incentives for the system to absorb, thus forcing a disintegration of the analytical process. In fact, British intelligence organizations had avoided the *blind spot* trap (hypothesis 3), as well as the *shortcut* (hypothesis 2) by discrediting a number of sources early on, only to have them creep back into the process as the pressure mounted in 2003. The other greatly influential factor in explaining the British outcome was the influence of the American intelligence services and the cooperation between the two states' leaders. The MI6 and the JIC operated in an environment that slowly, but surely, converged around cherry picking from the highly dubious stories of defected Iraqis. We should not overstate their attempts to discredit this information, but a central vehicle for doing so would have been political support. As Jack Straw lost Tony Blair's ear and was marginalized in the cabinet, and Colin Powell seemed to drop his objections and jump aboard his administrations push for war, that avenue was closed.

The U.S. case seems much more deep-seated and systemic in its origins for ethical failure. The intelligence community was operating in a credibility deficit with the administration, which forced them to deviate from professional standards and, on a number of occasions, to report findings it knew to be false. The idea of actionable intelligence and the notion of the usefulness of the intelligence agencies had acquired a political dimension that was impossible to ignore. George Tenet's personal position as a survivor from the Clinton administration, and the elevation of his office following 9/11, seemed to further reinforce the need to capitalize on the proximity to power and turn it into political legitimacy.

The infighting in the Bush foreign policy team was detrimental to critical debate. Powell was shut out of important processes regarding the Iraq policy and war planning, and the mentality that produced the Valerie Plame incident illustrated a perception of the administration as being under siege by *appeasers* and *containment* advocates. Bush wrote in his memoir about his phone call to Bush Sr. after reading the op-ed article of his father's former security adviser, Brent Scowcroft, in the Wall Street Journal, entitled, "Don't Attack Saddam" (Scowcroft, 2002). "'Son, Brent is a friend,' he assured me. That might be true. But I knew critics would later exploit Brent's article if the diplomatic track failed" (Bush, 2010, p. 297).

The ethical challenge that was in focus for both these governments was one of standing up to a tyrant versus the international legal aspects of the cause for war. The first dimension remained more important and would, in the main actors' own minds, legitimize the gentle fabrication of the second. Besides, "everybody knew" that Saddam had WMD programs; only the weakness of the inspection regime prevented evidence from being on the table. Also, both governments considered the breach of UNSC resolution 1441 as the foundation for the cause for war, and a second resolution based on findings of Baghdad's material breach of UNSC resolution 1441 was to shore up international support. To this day, the main representatives of both governments argue that UNSC resolution 1441 was enough to justify an intervention (Blair, 2010; Bush, 2010). The failure of the intelligence system in this view is secondary, and coupled with the laurels-of-victory theory that success breeds legitimacy, presentation of evidence was allowed to take precedence over actually proving the case.

The false WMD claim came to be a *white lie* rather than a *blatant lie* in these deliberations, and the ethical deficiency in the formal causes for war was, in the eyes of the U.S. and U.K. governments, amply justified by the *secondary* legal arguments regarding human rights abuses, previous aggression, and poor compliance with existing resolutions. The weakness, however, of this position is manifested when the long-term effects materialize. It is hard for the former leaders to justify their previous statements in the absence of WMD discoveries, and the ability to sustain a policy in line with the principles stated at the outset of the campaign is greatly weakened. In their autobiographies, published two months apart in 2010, both Bush and

Blair blame the intelligence services for overstating their case (Blair, 2010; Bush, 2010). As we have seen, that is a highly dubious approach, and it would serve future governments much better to take a long hard look at how the political level interacts with these agencies, and which pitfalls and quagmires lurk when the relationship is compromised.

NOTES

1. "Ethical failure" is here taken to mean a failure to balance the values relevant to the main arenas of scrutiny in a way that hinders a sustainable justification strategy.
2. Justification can have two distinct connotations: to found a claim in law and thus argue that an action that is generally deemed illegal is rendered legal by specific circumstances; or to explain by reference to values that are politically expedient and thus produce political support for the action. These connotations will coexist in this text, as the distinction rides not on theoretical conceptualization but on empirical examination.
3. *Breaking eggs* refers to the tendency to allow the ends to justify the means when it comes to matters that are relevant to leaders' worldviews.
4. http://daccess-dds-ny.un.org/doc/UNDOC/GEN/N02/682/26/PDF/N0268226.pdf?OpenElement
5. http://www.guardian.co.uk/world/2002/aug/27/usa.iraq
6. http://whitehouse.georgewbush.org/news/2003/012803-SOTU.asp
7. http://www.guardian.co.uk/world/2003/feb/05/iraq.usa
8. This includes incorporating the *45-minute claim* in the list of evidence presented to the world.

REFERENCES

Berkowitz, B. (2003). Failing to keep up with the information revolution: The DI and "IT." *Studies in Intelligence* (unclassified version), *47*(1), n.p.

Blair, T. (2010). *A journey*. London: Hutchinson.

Blitzer, W. (2003). Search for the "smoking gun." *CNN*. Retrieved October 19, 2010, from http://articles.cnn.com/2003-01-10/us/wbr.smoking.gun_1_smoking-gun-nuclear-weapons-hans-blix?_s=PM:US

Blix, H. (2004). *Disarming Iraq*. New York: Pantheon Books.

Bush, G. W. (2010). *Decision points*. New York: Crown Publishing.

Campbell, A. (2007). *The Blair years*. London: Hutchinson.

Garthoff, D. F. (2005). *Directors of central intelligence as leaders of the U.S. intelligence community, 1946–2005*. Washington, DC: CIA Center for the Study of Intelligence.

Heimer, C. A. (1988). Social structure, psychology, and the estimation of risk. *Annual Review of Sociology, 14*(1), 491–519.

Hersh, S. M. (2005). *Chain of command*. London: Penguin.

Halverscheid, S., & Witte, E. H. (2008). Justification of war and terrorism: A comparative case study analyzing ethical positions based on prescriptive attribution theory. *Social Psychology, 39*(1), 26–36.

Herrmann, R. K., Voss, J. F., Schooler, T. Y. E., & Ciarrochi, J. (1997). Images in international relations: An experimental test of cognitive schemata. *International Studies Quarterly, 41*(3), 403–433.

Hutton, Lord (2004). *Report of the inquiry into the circumstances surrounding the death of Dr David Kelly, C.M.G.* London: House of Commons.

Hutton Inquiry. (2003a). *Testimony of Mr Anthony Charles Lynton Blair (Called).* Retrieved October 5, 2010, from http://www.hutton.softblade.com/transcripts.php?action=transcript&session=22&witness=35#wit35

Hutton Inquiry. (2003b). *Testimony of Sir Kevin Reginald Tebitt (Called).* Retrieved October 5, 2010, from http://www.hutton.softblade.com/transcripts.php?action=transcript&session=14&witness=16#wit16

Hutton Inquiry. (2003c). *Testimony of Mr John McLeod Scarlett (Called).* Retrieved October 5, 2010, from http://www.hutton.softblade.com/transcripts.php?action=transcript&session=18&witness=29#wit29

Hutton Inquiry. (2003d). *E-mail from Daniel Pruce to Mark Matthews.* Retrieved October 6, 2010, from http://www.hutton.softblade.com/mirror/evidence/cab_11_0025.pdf

Iraq Inquiry. (2002, April 5–7). *Diplomatic telegram about meeting between Prime Minister Blair and President Bush.* Unclassified. Retrieved October 4, 2010, from http://www.iraqinquiry.org.uk/transcripts/declassified-documents.aspx

Kay, D. (2004). Weapons of mass destruction: Lessons learned and unlearned. *Miller Center Report, 20*(1).

Khong, Y. F. (1998). *Analogies at war: Korea, Munich, Dien Bien Phu and the Vietnam decisions of 1965.* Princeton, NJ: Princeton University Press.

Krasner, S. D. (1993). Sovereignty, regimes, and human rights. In V. Rittberger & P. Mayer (Eds.), *Regime theory and international relations.* Oxford, UK: Oxford University Press.

March, J. G., & Olsen, J. P. (1998). The institutional dynamics of international political orders. *International Organization, 52*(4), 943–969.

Preston, T. (2001). *The president and his inner circle: Leadership style and the advisory process in foreign affairs.* New York: Columbia University Press.

Putnam, R. (1988). Diplomacy and domestic politics: The logic of two-level games. *International Organization, 42*(3), 427–460.

Rawnsley, A. (2010). *The end of the party: The rise and fall of new labour.* London: Viking.

Renshon, J. (2008). Stability and change in belief systems: The operational code of George W. Bush. *Journal of Conflict Resolution, 52*(6), 820–849.

Rosati, J. A. (2000). The power of human cognition in the study of world politics. *International Studies Review, 2*(3), 45–75.

Seldon, A. (2007). *Blair unbound.* London: Simon & Schuster.

Schaefer, M., & Walker, S. (2006). Democratic leaders and the democratic peace: The operational codes of Tony Blair and Bill Clinton. *International Studies Quarterly, 50*(4), 561–583.

Scowcroft, B. (2002, August 15). Don't attack Saddam. *Wall Street Journal,* p. 4.

Suedfeld, P., Tetlock, P. E., & Jhangiani, R. (2007). The Bush doctrine and the psychology of alliances. In S. A. Renshon & P. Suedfeld (Eds.), *Understanding the Bush doctrine: Psychology and strategy in the age of terrorism.* New York: Routledge.

Tetlock, P. E. (1982). Attribution bias: On the inconclusiveness of the cognition-motivation debate. *Journal of Experimental Social Psychology, 18*(1), 68–88.

Tetlock, P. E. (1985). Integrative complexity of American and Soviet foreign policy rhetoric: A time-series analysis. *Journal of Personality and Social Psychology, 49*(6), 1565–1585.

Tsebelis, G. (1991). *Nested games: Rational choice in comparative politics.* Berkeley: University of California Press.

UNSCOM. (1995, August 22). *Notes on a meeting between Hussein Kamal and UNSCOM and IAEA, Amman, Jordan.* Retrieved September 13, 2010, from http://www.un.org/Depts/unmovic/new/documents/hk.pdf

U.S. Senate. (2004). *Report on the U.S. intelligence community's prewar intelligence assessments on Iraq* (Report). Washington, DC: Select Committee on Intelligence.

United States of America v. I. Lewis Libby. (2005, October 28). *Indictment.* Washington, DC: United States District Court for the District of Columbia.

Vertzberger, Y. (1998). *Risk taking and decisionmaking: Foreign military intervention decisions.* Stanford, CA: Stanford University Press.

Walzer, M. (2000). *Just and unjust wars: A moral argument with historical illustrations* (3rd ed.). New York: Basic Books.

Weiner, T. (2007). *Legacy of ashes: The history of the CIA.* New York: Anchor Books.

Woodward, B. (2006). *State of denial.* London: Simon & Schuster.

Woodward, B. (2008). *The war within.* London: Simon & Schuster.

CHAPTER 4

INTERNATIONAL HUMANITARIAN ASSISTANCE

Legitimate Intervention or Illegitimate Interference?

Lieuwe Zijlstra, Andrej Zwitter, and Liesbet Heyse

ETHICS AND CRISIS MANAGEMENT IN HUMANITARIAN EMERGENCIES

International humanitarian organizations—be they intergovernmental such as the United Nations' agencies for refugees (UNHCR), children (UNICEF) and food (WFP), or nongovernmental, such as Médecins sans Frontières, Oxfam, or Medical Corps—can be considered experts in humanitarian crisis management. These organizations have a worldwide mandate to reduce the suffering of those in need, irrespective of race, religion, or political belief. Whenever humanitarian emergencies occur, these organizations are prominently present to mitigate the effects of natural disasters, conflicts, hunger, and illness by building refugee camps for shelter, providing medical and psycho-social care, distributing food, and assisting in rebuilding livelihoods.[1]

Ethics and Crisis Management, pages 57–74
Copyright © 2011 by Information Age Publishing

57

The work of international humanitarian organizations is fundamentally ethical by nature, if only because they constantly need to decide about who to help and who not, what to do and not, and when to start and stop, given their limited monetary and human resources. Consequently, the work and decisions of these organizations have great impact upon the lives of those they aim to help. The presence of humanitarian organizations, and the way they work, can mean the difference between life and death for those who are struck by disaster or conflict.

In addition, the moral and normative foundations of international humanitarian organizations—whose headquarters are predominantly based in the Western world—implicitly or explicitly reflect a specific interpretation of humanitarianism (see Calhoun, 2008 for a historical overview). It is this particular interpretation that influences the work methods and actions of international humanitarian organizations in such a way that it might create even more (difficult) ethical challenges, especially within particular cultural contexts, as we will argue in this chapter. Hence, this chapter discusses the ethical ramifications of the normative foundations and resulting behavior of a particular group of crisis managers (international humanitarian organizations) in a specific type of crisis (humanitarian emergencies) in certain cultural (non-Western) contexts.

The Challenge: Perceptions of Illegitimate Interference

One important challenge of international humanitarian organizations is related to the observation that the work of these organizations is regularly perceived as illegitimate by the recipients, despite the ethical imperative of these organizations to reduce suffering neutrally, impartially, and humanely. The increase in attacks on aid workers is one of many signals that this perception of illegitimate interference by humanitarian actors is becoming more common. In 2008, for example, 260 humanitarian workers were killed, kidnapped, or injured on the job, compared to 143 in 2003 (Stoddard, Harmer, & DiDomenica, 2009, p. 3).[2] This violence against humanitarian workers predominantly occurred in Somalia, Darfur, and Afghanistan; areas that are characterized by conflict due to a lack of state power or will to impose order. Consequently, other groups, often related to radical Islam, have found room in these areas to pursue their political aims. What followed was an increase in politically motivated attacks on humanitarian workers in these areas from 29% in 2003 to 48% in 2008 (Stoddard et al., 2009, p. 5).[3]

Other examples hinting at perceptions of illegitimate interference by international humanitarian organizations include the destruction of girls' schools financed by the international community in Afghanistan (Donini,

2009), the Sudanese government expelling international humanitarian NGOs from Darfur after the International Criminal court demanded that Sudan's president be arrested (Eckroth, 2010), and empty shelter facilities built by international organizations because they are perceived to be cultural inappropriate (Rodriguez, Wachtendorf, Kendra, & Trainor, 2006).

Perceptions of illegitimate actions by humanitarian actors can cause serious impediments to successful aid provision and ultimately result in violent responses to humanitarian organizations and their employees, as illustrated above. Beyond that, humanitarian actors are often the first Western actors on the ground when conflicts or disasters occur. If these humanitarian actors are already resented by the local communities because of their Western approach, every other Western actor might face the same lack of legitimacy when trying to resolve conflicts or mitigate disaster. It is therefore important to look at how Western humanitarians can prepare the (good or bad) ground for future crisis management.

The Explanation: The Philosophical Roots of Western Humanitarianism

The questions at the heart of this chapter are how and why international humanitarian assistance becomes perceived as illegitimate. We argue that the explanation for these perceptions of illegitimate interference should be sought in the different historical and philosophical backgrounds of Western societies and those societies in which Westernized humanitarian aid operations take place. It is these backgrounds that illuminate our understanding of the roots of humanitarianism, the nature of international law, the international system, as well as the activities of humanitarian organizations in the field. We illustrate how understanding the differences between Western and other historical and philosophical traditions help explain the fine line between perceptions of international humanitarian action as legitimate intervention or illegitimate interference.

In the following section, we further elaborate on the philosophical background of Western humanitarian intervention. This is followed by a section on the roots of international humanitarian action and the differences between and problems resulting from needs-based and rights-based approaches to humanitarianism, as developed in the international arena. In the last two sections, we demonstrate how these problems (as theoretically elaborated upon) relate to international developments and create ethical challenges in the daily practice of humanitarian action on the ground. Based on these theoretical elaborations and empirical illustrations, we conclude that humanitarian actors preparing the ground for succeeding crisis management actors balance on a fine line of beneficiaries' perception between illegitimate interference and legitimate intervention.

HUMANITARIANISM AND ITS
WESTERN PHILOSOPHICAL ROOTS

The most important reason why the provision of humanitarian assistance is perceived as interfering in domestic affairs has to do with the historical and philosophical roots of Western societies as compared with non-Western societies. The Western idea that states have a right to intervene in other states on humanitarian grounds dates back to 1625 when the Dutch legal expert Hugo Grotius (1925) published his influential treaty *On the Law of War and Peace.* Hugo Grotius argued that when the rights of individuals are violated in other nations, a statesman has the right to wage war against these nations to protect their citizens. This right to intervene is based on the idea that individuals possess natural rights. Natural rights belong to every individual, are not contingent upon laws or customs, and are considered to be universal. These ideas of universal rights belonging to each individual, combined with the idea of the right to intervene on humanitarian grounds, are deeply entrenched in Western societies.

Other related ideas that form the historical and philosophical roots of Western societies result from 18th-century European Enlightenment. This revolution in philosophical thought brought along ideas of progressive social change, individual autonomy, democratic equality, and the emancipation of minority groups. Enlightenment philosophers such as Hobbes, Spinoza, Locke, Voltaire, and Montesquieu argued in favor of individual rights, the protection of private property, individual autonomy, and additional rights, which were to ensure protection against the power of the authoritarian state. Immanuel Kant laid the moral foundation of these individual rights in the 18th century in his rationalized moral philosophy. On the basis of his famous *categorical imperative,* he even formulated the humanitarian imperative to help others in need (Kant, 2008; Rawls, 1999; see also Slim, 2002a). In his work *To Perpetual Peace,* of 1795, Kant argued that we are obliged to strive for a just world order that is based on shared values. It is ideas like these that lie at the base of the social, political, and economic institutions in Western societies and, of course, also at the base of Western humanitarian assistance (Calhoun, 2008).

Enlightenment values and the concept of human rights represent fundamentally Western values. These values belong to the core of Western society and constitute the guiding principles of the basic structure of Western society. Moreover, many contemporary Western philosophers and politicians argue that these values should be applied universally. For example, John

Rawls (1999), one of the most influential thinkers in political philosophy of the past century, wrote that he believes that "a liberal constitutional democracy is, in fact, superior to other forms of society" and because of this, we have to teach other societies to recognize "the advantages of liberal institutions and take steps toward becoming more liberal on its own" (p. 62). Therefore, Rawls argues, we have a duty to provide humanitarian assistance to societies that are less well off and help them to eventually attain liberal institutions and respect human rights. This idea reverberates in the opinions of many Western intellectuals such as Francis Fukuyama, who argued that liberal democracy will eventually become the universally defining form of government (1992).

The tendency of Western intellectuals to praise the worth of Western social and political values at the expense of non-Western values, and the tendency to impose these values on other countries has been opposed by many other scholars. For example, Asian philosopher and public intellectual Kishore Mahbubani argues that Western policymakers suffer from feelings of moral superiority. Mahbubani demands that they should refrain from imposing their view of society on the rest of the world; leave them free to make their own choices, Mahbubani exclaims. Western values are not superior to Asian values, which have their own merits. Asian values, such as attachment to the family, deference to societal interests, thrift, conservatism in social mores, and respect for authority are, according to Mahbubani, of equal worth to Western values (Mahbubani, 2004). Because of this, humanitarian organizations have to be careful about what ideas about social change and human rights they bring with them in their work.

The question is not, however, whether Western values are really superior to other values. Rather, what we would like to point out is that Western organizations are perceived as bringing with them a set of Western values that they impose on local communities.

THE INTERNATIONAL SYSTEM: HUMAN RIGHTS AND HUMANITARIAN PRINCIPLES

Ideas about the duty to intervene in order to reduce suffering, and ideas about natural and universal rights are reflected in international law and in the conduct of actors in the international system. The adoption of the Universal Declaration of Human Rights by the UN General Assembly in 1948, for example, represented a mark in history with major implications for Western societies and their relations to non-Western societies. Although the Universal Declaration of Human Rights purports to have universal applicability, this applicability has not been acknowledged by all states. In fact, only 56 nations worldwide were represented in the UN General Assembly in

1948 and, of the total votes, there were 48 in favor of the declaration and 8 abstentions. In addition, the majority of the present-day Asian and African member states in the United Nations were still colonies in 1948 and thus had no right to vote (see also Leary, 1990). As a result, while the Universal Declaration of Human Rights has played a major role in international relations since its adoption, its founding was an essentially Western endeavor.

The Western roots of the international system become even more pronounced given the relatively recent idea that humanitarian action should be rights based, instead of needs based or related to humanitarian principles (Maus, 2011; Zwitter, 2010). The principles of humanitarian aid form the original basis of humanitarian action and are first and foremost based on the moral principle of humanity. *Humanity*, the humanitarian imperative, compels us to alleviate suffering wherever it is found. This approach to humanitarian action is also referred to as a needs-based approach. "Its purpose is to protect life and health and to ensure respect for the human being. It promotes mutual understanding, friendship, co-operation and lasting peace amongst all peoples" (Pictet, 1979). Accompanying this prime principle of humanitarianism are two narrower principles: *neutrality* and *impartiality*. These principles have also been recognized by the international community and many nongovernmental organizations (NGOs) as foundational in humanitarian action (Good Humanitarian Donorship,[4] 2003; General Assembly Resolution 46/182;[5] IFRC Code of Conduct[6]). Neutrality means not taking sides in a conflict in operational terms, and impartiality means giving aid independently from religious as well as cultural and political opinions, thereby reflecting a principle of nondiscrimination. In conjunction with independence, in particular independence from national authorities, the International Committee of the Red Cross and Red Crescent (ICRC)—one of the leading organizations in the field of humanitarian action and human rights—regards these principles as a prerequisite to accessing beneficiaries. This access is based on the trust of every party of the conflict that the ICRC will not shame or blame perpetrators of crime, thereby ensuring a humanitarian space of operational freedom and access to beneficiaries for humanitarian organizations (Thürer, 2007).

However, present-day perspectives on humanitarian action have also incorporated human rights and have now formed a new rights-based approach to humanitarian aid. In accordance with this approach, recipients of aid are not merely seen as needy victims, but as rights bearers and active stakeholders in the conduct of humanitarian action. This approach, supporters argue, will lead to accountability among the humanitarian actors. The development of the rights-based approach was the result of a call for the strengthening of participatory approaches involving local communities in giving aid, the increasing professionalization of aid work, and a need to hold humanitarians accountable for their actions (see Anderson, 1999; Slim, 2002b).

Humanitarian principles focusing on needs and a human rights-based approach are not necessarily compatible, however. Two lines of argument pertain to the two approaches' incompatibility: (a) introducing rights leads to the introduction of violators of rights and contradicts the principle of neutrality, (b) a rights-based approach might contradict other culturally developed systems of community survival that are not based on individual rights, thereby violating the principle of impartiality. These two fundamental arguments of contradiction need further elaboration.

Incompatibility with Neutrality

The system of human rights is an inclusive system granting the same rights to everybody based on the idea of universality and the notion of natural rights. The system is inclusive because the same rights are granted to both victims and perpetrators of human rights violations alike. However, the notion of rights also introduces the idea that if these rights are not met, they are violated either by commission or omission. A violation of rights, therefore, immediately raises the question of who the violator of these rights is, accompanied by international (criminal) legal and political consequences. In armed conflicts, large-scale human rights violations can amount to international crimes, which are sought to be punished by the international community. In other words, rights that can be violated automatically lead to a values-based judgment, the introduction of a dichotomy of victims and violators, of good and evil. As a consequence, the system of human rights does not, in fact, reduce the perception of beneficiaries as victims, which was originally assumed, but rather reinforces it. The conception of a violator of human rights can, in this light, be seen as incompatible with the idea that humanitarian organizations should remain neutral toward the parties in a conflict. With a human rights perspective in mind, it is easy to see how parties might be treated differently, and whether or not they receive aid might not be based on needs alone.

A striking example of this relates to the crisis in Rwanda in the 1990s, as violence erupted between the Hutu and Tutsi populations. In 1995, Médecins sans Frontières (MSF) provided aid to battle cholera in Goma, Zaire, which had received over 1,000,000 refugees from the Rwanda crisis. The organization discovered that they were treating perpetrators of violence who, after having been treated, would return to continue to mass killing (Calhoun, 2008). Heated debates in the organization followed: should MSF continue providing medical aid to both victims and perpetrators, thereby strictly adhering to *neutrality* and *impartiality*, or withdraw their support and adhere to the human rights convention? This example shows that the language of human rights creates a discourse in an organization about good and evil, about victims and perpetrators. The original idea of neutrality, as promoted by the ICRC, would in this case mean providing aid to both sides of a conflict, whereas from a human rights point of view, humanitarian organizations are forced to take the side of the victim. That there was no easy solution to the dilemma in this case was illustrated by the decision by the Belgian and the French section of MSF to withdraw, while the Dutch section decided to stay in Zaire.

The requirement of humanitarian NGOs to report human rights violators might not mean that they necessarily take sides consciously, but the effect is the same as if they did. The introduction of the principles of neutrality and impartiality aimed to keep humanitarian organizations unaffected by power politics and free from discriminating biases that could restrict access to vulnerable populations and thereby violate the humanitarian imperative. Humanitarian actors introducing concepts of rights holders and rights violators might have the same consequence as not remaining neutral, and might result in those accused of human rights violations denying these humanitarian actors access to beneficiaries. This is not to say that human rights do have not a place in humanitarian work, however, their place is not in the delivery of relief aid, provided that the aim is to gain access to all in need of aid. Humanitarian actors should be aware of the fact that the introduction of a rights-based approach can lead to the perception among beneficiaries that humanitarian actors are not as impartial as they claim to be. Rather, their work could be viewed as illegitimate interference.

Incompatibility with Impartiality

Let us assume that as humans we all share the same basic needs, be they physiological needs, love needs, or needs for self-fulfillment (see Maslow, 1943). When looking at different cultures, it immediately becomes apparent that love needs can be institutionalized culturally in different ways (monogamy, polygamy, marriage, or living community, being just superficial examples). Similarly, self-fulfillment in individualistic societies more often takes the meaning of putting oneself ahead of others, while in communitarian societies it often means serving the community as well as possible. Even with basic physiological needs, we see differences in how communities safeguard and fulfill these needs. As argued before, the international human rights system is intrinsically Western, not because the physiological needs are different, but because the way these rights are safeguarded is inherently cultural. The discussion regarding Asian and Westerns perspectives on individualism and communitarianism exemplifies these cultural-specific mechanisms of community survival in the question of universal human rights (Brems, 2001; Tharoor, 1999/2000). The first thing to be raised by Asian proponents in this debate is that human duties toward the community are absent in the Western perspective on human rights. Many African natives likewise struggle with the assumption that an individual's rights trump the community's rights and well-being. According to these African advocates, human rights are more about a complex relationship between the duties of the individual toward the group, and the corresponding duties of the group toward the individual, than it is about *rights* per se (Tharoor, 1999/2000). African values stress the dignity of membership and one's prescribed social role in the family, kinship, or tribe (see Howard, 1990). These communitarian values stand in contrast to Western values of individual autonomy and equality. African philosopher Fasil Nahum argued, for example, that Western values alienate the individual from society, seeing him as an entity all by himself and as having an existence independent of society. Nahum argues that African Humanism does not make this mistake of isolating the individual from society but rather sees the individual as part of society (see Howard, 1990, p. 162). Similar criticisms come from intellectuals who defend Islamic values against the supposed superiority of Western values. Islamic law, although compatible with human rights, as agued by some scholars (Baderin, 2003), presents a clear structure of individual and community duties in the relationship between the two.[7]

In the Western tradition, duties arise only with regard to limitations of rights, that is, my rights end where another person's rights begin. Humanitarian actors introducing international human rights in local communities with the intent of entitling the community member assumes, to put it bluntly, that their previous cultural systems were wrong to begin with. It suggests that individuals had been violated in terms of their natural rights before the humanitarians showed up. This can easily lead to a rejection by local communities, not only of the newly introduced system but of the humanitarian actors themselves (as representing a first instance of an illegitimate Western view, which might reflect on other actors of crisis management). Putting it differently, obliging communities to implement the Western view of how they have to ensure their survival by introducing the concept of individual rights might objectify beneficiaries in a cultural sense (even if, legally speaking, they are becoming entitled rights holders). If humanitarians do this, they are not impartial with concern to local values, cultures, and beliefs, but active political (sometimes even discriminating) players. This shift in roles often occurs in humanitarian disasters without the organizations realizing it, because they assume that the idea of human rights is universal.

In conclusion, when looking at the international human rights regime, one must be aware of its inherent assumptions: (a) a priority of the individual over the group, and by claiming universality (b) the definition of a "right" way for communities to ensure their survival and that of their members. The degree to which local communities resent such an approach depends on how different the traditional, cultural ways of community survival and support systems are from the Western idea of ensuring survival and needs fulfillment through individual human rights. As a result, a human rights discourse in humanitarian assistance can become perceived as a form of cultural imperialism (Katsui, 2008) and a further departure from the more neutrally and impartially based humanitarian principles that humanitarian organizations used to base their humanitarian disaster work on.

INTERNATIONAL DEVELOPMENTS STRENGTHENING THE IMPERIALIST IMPRESSION

Specific developments during the 1990s and onwards have intensified the impression of humanitarian disaster relief as cultural imperialism. First of all, humanitarian organizations themselves started to advocate in favor of humanitarian interventions in countries where gross human rights violations were taking place (see Foley, 2008). For example, in 1991–1992, a humanitarian crisis was unfolding in Somalia. Different humanitarian organizations such as CARE, the International Rescue Committee, and Oxfam America were publicly calling for military intervention in the country. Save the Children UK was the only humanitarian organization to speak out against this approach. Similarly, in 1994, as the Rwandan genocide took place, several humanitarian organizations such as MSF and Oxfam tried to convince Western governments to intervene militarily. As Conor Foley notes, MSF ran a series of adds proclaiming that "one cannot stop a genocide with medicines" (Foley, 2008, p. 62).

Furthermore, recent humanitarian interventions have been justified by political leaders as proceeding on humanitarian grounds. Especially former U.S. president George W. Bush and former British prime minister Tony Blair used this motivation during the military interventions in Afghanistan and Iraq. Blair (2004) argued in a speech on March 5, 2004, that "we surely have a responsibility to act when a nation's people are subjected to a regime such as Saddam's." Despite the controversy in international law about whether or not the United States and the U.K. had the right to intervene in Iraq and Afghanistan, these political leaders proceeded with their course of action. It is precisely these kinds of humanitarian interventions, based on just a thin layer of justification and legitimacy, that are perceived as a form of cultural imperialism in non-Western countries (see also Abbott, 2005).

The fact that in Iraq and Afghanistan humanitarian organizations soon followed after the military intervention to provide aid led to local perceptions of humanitarian organizations as partial, dependent allies of Western nation states. What made things even more problematic was that during these humanitarian interventions, the distinction between humanitarian organizations providing relief and the coalition forces performing military actions became blurred (Zwitter, 2008). In large part, this can also be attributed to the performance of military and political officials. For example, U.S. Secretary of State Colin Powell stated that humanitarian NGOs "are such a force multiplier for us, such an important part of our combat team" (Barnett & Weiss, 2008, p. 25) when he spoke at an assembly of humanitarian aid organisaties in the War against Terrorism in Afghanistan. Andrew Natsios, head of USAID, added to this in 2003 by stating that humanitarian NGOs are "an arm of the U.S. government" (Natsios, 2003). The result of the blurred distinction between humanitarian organizations and the coalition forces in the Afghan war was a deteriorating perception of humanitarian assistance in the eyes of local people and increasing violence toward relief workers (Dijkzeul & Salomons, 2009).

Hence, developments in the international arena (as sketched above) further strengthen the impression that humanitarian assistance is not neutral, impartial, or independent, but rather represent Western values and interests. This has serious consequences for humanitarian organizations, as we will argue and illustrate below.

ILLEGITIMATE INTERFERENCE AND CULTURAL IMPERIALISM ILLUSTRATED

In the previous sections, we have discussed the Western philosophical roots of the concept of humanitarianism, their reflection in international law and in the international system, as well as recent developments in humanitarian action strengthening the breeding ground for perceptions of illegitimate interference or even cultural imperialism by international humanitarian organizations. These features and developments all have an impact on the work of humanitarian organizations and the way they are perceived by the people these organizations aim to help. The consequences of these influences can be placed into two main categories: the consequences of taking an individualistic approach, and the consequences of explicitly addressing human rights issues.

The Consequences of an Individualistic Approach

The work methods of humanitarian organizations mirror notions of universalized individual rights resulting from developments since the Enlightenment Era. Consequently, humanitarian organizations often have a strong individualistic focus in both their needs assessments and their aid provision. This is illustrated by the worldwide initiative to develop so-called Sphere Standards. Many NGOs participated in developing universal minimal standards for humanitarian assistance; standards that, it has been argued, reflect Western, not local, norms (Batt, 2000, p. 15; Dufour, Maury, De Geoffroy, & Grünewald, 2004).

For example, some of the minimum standards for water supply are the following (Sphere Handbook, 2011, p. 60) (a) Average water use for drinking, cooking and personal hygiene in any household is at least 15 liters per person per day; and (b) "The maximum distance from any household to the nearest water point is 500 meters." Next to the formulation of the standards on a per-person basis and the underlying assumption that these standards are universally applicable, one could question the chosen content of the standards. The standards have been argued to be particularly technical in nature, based on insights from Western academic thinking and experiences from Western humanitarian organizations (Dufour et al., 2004). This is particularly salient, for example, in the second water standard, as there are many people in the developing world who have to walk more than 500 meters in order to collect safe water. Application of these standards in sites such as refugee camps bears the risk of creating higher living conditions within the camps than in the surrounding villages. This can easily lead to the local population resenting the presence of humanitarian organizations, especially if the refugee group is very different from the local population. Unintentionally, humanitarian organizations might signal a preference for specific groups in societies, which makes them partial in the eyes of some, even though this choice is based on needs (see Anderson, 1999).

Similar dynamics have been observed in the case of food aid distributions. An individualistic needs-based approach to food aid would lead humanitarian organizations to target the neediest individuals with food aid (i.e., children, the sick, and breastfeeding women). However, the effect of this strategy is often low(er) because of local practices of sharing food in the family and community. Taking local cultural norms into account, it could even be considered inappropriate to exclude the leaders of families and communities from the distribution process and to provide food directly to those lowest in the hierarchy. Save the Children argued on the basis of an evaluation of food aid projects in Southern Africa that individually focused distribution practices might even undermine community cohesion and cooperation as well as threaten indigenous support and coping mechanisms (ALNAP, 2004, pp. 92–94). Such individually based aid distribution practices, based on an ambition to provide aid according to need, could thus unintentionally lead to perceived illegitimate interference. However, letting go of the individualistic approach to food aid distribution is incompatible with the human rights perspective, since the human rights perspective sees beneficiaries as subjects with individual rights. This stems, as we have argued above, from the idea that every human being has inalienable natural rights. If NGOs accept collective food aid distribution methods in the communities they target, they bear the risk of not fulfilling the individual rights of the most needy, since family or community leaders could decide to distribute the food not on the basis of need and rights, but on the basis of status and hierarchy. They could thus be accused of wasting donor money by giving food to those who do not need it, which could lead donors to withdraw their funding.

Consequences of Explicitly Addressing Human Rights Issues

Next to the focus on the individual and its unintended consequences, some humanitarian organizations explicitly emphasize human rights in their operations, which can even further strengthen opinions of illegitimate interference and an organizational reputation of cultural imperialism.

This especially holds for humanitarian organizations promoting women's rights in countries where these are not part and parcel of reality. A pressing example in this respect is the case of female genital circumcision. Whereas this is a widely respected local tradition in some parts of the world, the practice means a breach of the human rights of women in the eyes of international humanitarian organizations. Some humanitarian organizations even forbid their employees to assist with or provide care after female genital circumcision, even if this is done from a purely medical point of view in order to prevent disease and death as a consequence of the practice (see for an example Hilhorst & Schliemann, 2002). Hence, the human rights perspective sometimes leads humanitarian organizations to withhold care from people in need in order to avoid becoming linked to the breaching of human rights themselves. This contributes to the impression that humanitarian organizations provide aid on their own terms, pressing for their Western beliefs and values, and not solely on the basis of need.

A related example is the humanitarian assistance effort in war-torn Afghanistan. In addition to the fact that humanitarian organizations need military protection to operate, which strengthens local perceptions that these organizations represent a Western agenda, there are other mechanisms at work that further enhance the imperialist impression. For example, the humanitarian sector is enthusiastically assisting in the building of schools for girls, which fit their human rights agenda for equal rights for men and women. However, this clashes with traditional views and more conservative groups in Afghanistan who perceive these activities as illegitimate (Donini, 2006), resulting in attacks on both girls and schools.

All in all, the Western philosophical roots of the concepts of humanitarianism and human rights are clearly reflected in the daily practices of humanitarian organizations. Through their activities, they may (re)affirm local recipients' perceptions that humanitarian organizations have a Western agenda and thus contribute to feelings of illegitimate interference, either by explicitly advocating human rights issues or by more subtle messages sent when providing aid with an individualistic focus.

BETWEEN LEGITIMATE INTERVENTION AND ILLEGITIMATE INTERFERENCE

In this chapter, we have argued that notions of international humanitarianism are closely related to Western philosophical thought. These influences are reflected in international law, the international system, and the humanitarian sector. This makes the business of humanitarian aid an inherently Western-biased type of crisis management, characterized by a strong focus on the individual and his or her rights. This focus shapes the methods of aid distribution and can unintentionally contribute to perceptions of illegitimate intervention, even if humanitarian aid is given on the basis of need. A strong explicit emphasis on human rights can add to these dynamics, generating impressions of cultural imperialism. All in all, there is a fine line in humanitarian assistance being perceived either as legitimate intervention or illegitimate interference as humanitarian organizations try to mitigate the consequences of humanitarian disasters. A lack of understanding of local cultures, traditions, and norms can cause humanitarian organizations to cross this fine line without even realizing it.

The observations presented in the chapter leave us with the question of what we should take away in terms of managing humanitarian crises ethically? Should "de-Westernize" humanitarian aid. Or can humanitarianism not exist without Western values? What does this mean for the debate between rights-based and needs-based approaches to humanitarian aid? What we can conclude is that humanitarian organizations would be wrong if they assume that either one of these approaches are going to be compatible with any one local culture. Adopting a rights-based approach is perfectly understandable from a Western point of departure, but actors in the field should be aware of the intrinsically Western nature of this approach, which could lead to perceptions of illegitimate interference in non-Western cultures, instead of perceptions of legitimate intervention for humanitarian purposes. Hence, there is also no easy way out here, we would argue, with regard to the individualistic needs-based approach. Having knowledge of local traditions and cultural norms is important, but does not solve the ethical dilemmas that evolve when two fundamentally different cultural systems meet. For example, if international humanitarian organizations would de-cide to completely adapt to the local culture by solely distributing their aid through local channels and allowing aid to be distributed on the basis of other criteria than individual need, so that this would be perceived as local-ly appropriate by recipients, this would probably not be understood by their Western donors. On the contrary, it might lead to accusations of corrupted or partial aid, which could lead to cutbacks in funding. However, one can also not ignore the potentially harming effects of a purely individualistic approach. Some humanitarian organizations, therefore, opt to distribute aid through community leaders while stressing the importance of giving it to the neediest and then purposefully give more aid than strictly needed according to an individualistic approach. In other words, they anticipate that the distribution of food will also be based on status and hierarchy. With regard to the rights-based approach, some organizations pursue their hu-man rights agenda by means of silent diplomacy or by financing particular projects without making public who paid for them. However, these prag-matic solutions do not provide a final answer to the ethical question of how to help others on the basis of your own values without breaching the ones of the other to the extent that your assistance is not welcomed anymore.

In conclusion, the mandate of international humanitarian organizations requires them to work in areas of the world with fundamentally different cultural systems than those of the West. Being aware of, on the one hand, what aspects of humanitarian work and thinking are inherently Western-based and biased, and on the other hand, how some cultural contexts of aid provision fundamentally clash with these biases helps international hu-manitarian organizations become aware of the fine line between legitimate intervention and illegitimate interference. This, however, will not prevent international humanitarian organizations from being confronted with ethi-cal challenges as to what to do next. Pressing questions will remain as to whether intervention is always better than no intervention, and if one in-tervenes, how to minimize the potential damaging effect of a Westernized approach to humanitarian action as discussed in this chapter.

The baseline for all thinking about this topic is that international humani-tarian organizations can only continue to do their work if their presence and methods are perceived legitimate by their recipients. Humanitarian actors are the first actors on the ground when armed conflicts occur or disaster strikes, and most of these actors are Western. Humanitarians, therefore, prepare the ground for future crisis management by establishing an environment where basic needs are not threatened anymore. If these first actors are already reject-ed by local communities because they are perceived as imposing norms and values foreign to them, there is a good chance that any other Western actor will face the same resentment and therefore lack legitimacy. Without legiti-macy, humanitarian aid provision becomes an impossible job. It can therefore be argued that humanitarian actors are not only first-aid providers but also actors preparing the ground for other external crisis management players. As such, they should not cause perceptions of cultural imperialism and illegitimate interference well before other Western actors of crisis management have the chance to even start, because it could limit the success of aid provision.

NOTES

1. This is not to say that international humanitarian organizations are the sole or most important actors in humanitarian crisis management. On the contrary, local communities and organizations often provide the majority of aid, especially in the first moments after disaster strikes. However, for the purpose of this chapter, in which we explore the tension between a Westernized perception of humanitarianism within non-Western cultural contexts, the focus is on international humanitarian organizations.
2. In other words, in 2008, approximately 9% of 10,000 aid workers in the field were confronted with violence compared to 4% in 2003 (Stoddard et al., 2009, p. 3).
3. It has been argued that, especially in Afghanistan, where humanitarian organizations often have to work under the auspices of international military troops, there is an increase in politically motivated attacks. In 2008, almost two thirds (66%) of the attacks were of this nature, compared to 40% in 2007 (Stoddard et al., 2009, p. 5; Zwitter, 2008).
4. International Meeting on Good Humanitarian Donorship, "Principles and Good Practice of Humanitarian Donorship" Endorsed in Stockholm, June 17, 2003 by Germany, Australia, Belgium, Canada, the European Commission, Denmark, the United States, Finland, France, Ireland, Japan, Luxemburg, Norway, the Netherlands, the United Kingdom, Sweden, and Switzerland.
5. A/Res/46/182 of 1991, "Strengthening of the coordination of humanitarian emergency assistance of the United Nations," Annex para. 2: "Humanitarian assistance must be provided in accordance with the principles of humanity, neutrality and impartiality."
6. This Code of Conduct counts more than 450 signatories, including NGOs as well as the ICRC and the IFRC. See http://www.ifrc.org/publicat/conduct/index.asp
7. Individual duties would be, for example, the five pillars of Islam: profession of faith (shahada), praying regularly, fasting during Ramadan, being charitable, and performing the hajj (the pilgrimage to Mecca). Particularly, charity in Islamic law is enforced by a poor-due tax (zakat) for Muslims, to be paid at the end of fasting with a reciprocal community entitlement of classes such as, for example, the needy, the destitute, and the collector of the poor-due (Bakhtiar 1996, pp. 229–241).

REFERENCES

Abbott, C. (2005). Rights and responsibilities: Resolving the dilemma of humanitarian intervention. *Global Dialogue, 7*(1–2), 1–15.

Anderson, M. B. (1999). *Do no harm.* London: Lynne Rienner Publishers.

Baderin, M. A. (2003). *International human rights and Islamic law.* Oxford, UK: Oxford University Press.

Bakhtiar, L. (1996). *Encyclopedia of Islamic law—A compendium of the major schools.* Chicago: ABC International Group.

Barnett, M., & Weiss, T. G. (2008). *Humanitarianism in question: Politics, power, ethics.* Ithaca, NY: Cornell University Press.

Batt, M. R. (2000, October). Sphere in India: Experiences and insights. *Humanitarian Exchange, The Magazine of the Humanitarian Practice Network.*

Beck, T. (2004). Field Level Learning, Synthesis of Findings of Evaluation Reports from 2003. In *ALNAP Review of Humanitarian Action in 2003* (pp. 85–132). Retrieved May 16, 2011, from http://www.alnap.org/publications/RHA2003/pdfs/FCh301b1.pdf

Blair, T. (2004). *Speech on the threat of global terrorism.* Retrieved November 12, 2010, from www.pm.gov.uk/output/Page5461.asp

Brems, E. (2001). *Human rights: Universality and diversity.* The Hague: Martinus Nijhoff Publishers.

Calhoun, C. (2008). The imperative to reduce suffering: Charity, progress, and emergencies in the field of humanitarian action. In M. Barnett & T. G. Weiss (Eds.), *Humanitarianism in question.* Ithaca, NY/London: Cornell University Press.

Dijkzeul, D., & Salomons, D. (2009). De politieke economie van humanitaire ruimte. In D. Dijkzeul & J. Herman (Eds.), *Humanitaire bewegingsruimte: Hulp tussen politiek en onpartijdigheid* [Humanitarian Space: Aid Caught between Politics and Impartiality]. Gent, Belgium: Academia Press.

Donini, A. (2006). *Humanitarian agenda 2015: Afghanistan country study.* Briefing paper, Feinstein International Center, Tufts University, Boston.

Donini, A. (2009). *Afghanistan: Humanitarianism under threat.* Briefing paper, Feinstein International Center, Tufts University, Boston.

Dufour, C., Maury, H., De Geoffroy, V., & Grünewald, F. (2004). Rights, standards and quality in a complex humanitarian space: Is Sphere the right tool? *Disasters, 28*(2), 124–141.

Eckroth, K. R. (2010). Humanitarian principles and protection dilemmas: Addressing the security situation of aid workers in Darfur. *Journal of International Peacekeeping, 14,* 86–116.

Foley, C. (2008). *The thin blue line: How humanitarianism went to war.* New York: Verso.

Fukuyama, F. (1992). *The end of history and the last man.* London: Hamish Hamilton.

Grotius, H. (1925). *De jure belli ac pacis* [On the Law of War and Peace]. (F. W. Kelsey, Trans.). Oxford, UK: Clarendon Press.

Hilhorst, D. & Schiemann N. (2002). Humanitarian principles and organisational culture: Everyday practice in Médecins Sans Frontières-Holland. *Development in Practice, 12*(3&4), 490–500.

Howard, R. E. (1990). Group versus individual identity in the African debate on human rights. In A. A. An-Naim & F. M. Deng (Eds.), *Human rights in Africa: Cross cultural perspectives.* Washington, DC: Brookings Institution.

Kant, I. (2008). *Fundering voor de metafysica van de zeden.* (T. Mertens, Trans.). Amsterdam: Boom.

Katsui, H. (2008). *Downside of the human rights-based approach to disability in develop-ment.* Working Paper Series of IDS at Helsinki University 2/2008. Available from https://www.umail.utah.edu/owa/redir.aspx?C=9567f53888fb4b4c8da 39678d5b8c9c7&URL=http%3a%2f%2fblogs.helsinki.fi%2fkatsui%2ffiles%2f 2008%2f11%2fdownside-of-hrba.doc

Leary, V. A. (1990). The effect of Western perspectives on international human rights. In A. A. An-Naim & F. M. Deng (Eds.), *Human rights in Africa: Cross cultural perspectives.* Washington, DC: Brookings Institution.

Mahbubani, K. (2004). *Can Asians think?* Singapore: Marshall Cavendish Editions.

Maslow, A. (1943). A theory of human motivation. *Psychological Review, 50,* 370–396.

Maus, S. (2011). Human rights in UN peacekeeping missions: A framework for hu-manitarian obligations? In H.-J. Heintze & A. Zwitter (Eds.), *International law and humanitarian assistance.* Munich: Springer.

Natsios, A. (2003). *Remarks by Andrew S. Natsios, administrator, USAID.* Retrieved De-cember 9, 2010, from http://www.usaid.gov/press/speeches/2003/sp030521. html

Pictet, J. (1979). *The fundamental principles of the Red Cross: Commentary.* Retrieved November 15, 2010 from http://www.icrc.org/eng/resources/documents/ misc/fundamental-principles-commentary-010179.htm

Rawls, J. (1999). *The law of peoples.* Cambridge, MA: Harvard University Press.

Rodigruze, H., Wachtendorf, T., Kendra, J., & Trainor J. (2006). A snapshot of the 2004 Indian Ocean tsunami: Societal impacts and consequences. *Disaster Pre-vention and Management, 15*(1), 163–177.

Slim, H. (2002a, February 21–22). *Claiming a humanitarian imperative: NGOs and the cultivation of humanitarian duty.* Paper presented at the 7th annual Conference of Webster University on Humanitarian Values for the Twenty First Century, Geneva, Switzerland.

Slim, H. (2002b). *By what authority? The legitimacy and accountability of non-governmen-tal organisations.* The International Council on Human Rights Policy Interna-tional Meeting on Global Trends and Human Rights, *Before and after September 11.* Retrieved November 12, 2010, from http://www.jha.ac/articles/a082.htm

The Sphere Project (2011). *Humanitarian charter and minimum standards in hu-manitarian response.* Rugby, UK: Practical Action Publishing. Retrieved May 16, 2011, from www.sphereproject.org/component/option,com.../task.../ lang,english/.

Stoddard, A., Harmer, A., & DiDomenica, V. (2009, April). *Providing aid in insecure environments: 2009 update. Trends in violence against aid workers and the opera-tional response.* Humanitarian Policy Group (HPG) Policy Brief 34.

Tharoor, S. (1999/2000). Are human rights universal? *World Policy Journal, 16*(4), 1–6.

Thürer, D. (2007). Dunant's pyramid: Thoughts on the "humanitarian space." *Inter-national Review of the Red Cross, 89*(865), 47–61.

Zwitter, A. (2008, October 26). Humanitarian action on the battlefields of the global war on terror. *Journal of Humanitarian Assistance.* Retrieved November 15, 2010, from http://jha.ac/2008/10/25/humanitarian-action-on-the-battlefields-of-the-global-war-on-terror

Zwitter, A. (2010). Neutrality and impartiality in implementing human rights: A framework for measuring human security. In W. Benedek, M. Kettemann, & M. Möstl (Eds.), *Mainstreaming Human security in peace operations and crisis management.* London: Routledge.

CHAPTER 5

DROWNING IN DISCRETION

Crisis Management Ethics and the Problem of Aporia

Arjen Boin and Paul Nieuwenburg

INTRODUCTION: TRAGIC CHOICES
FOR FIRST RESPONDERS

A growing body of research on crisis and disaster management has been documenting just how hard it is to manage sudden manifestations of adversity (Boin, 't Hart, Stern, & Sundelius, 2005; Rodriguez, Quarantelli, & Dynes, 2006). This literature explains why it is hard to recognize and understand impending crises in time; why it is hard to collect and analyze the information needed to make sense of an evolving crisis; why it can be excruciatingly difficult to make the right calls under immense pressure; why it is nearly impossible to coordinate a dense network of response organizations; why it is surprisingly hard to mobilize resources; and why it always is a challenge to effectively communicate with an angst-ridden public. Crisis management, to summarize, is somewhat akin to an *impossible job* (cf. Hargrove & Glidewell, 1990).

These research findings have, over time, led to something of a paradigm shift. The traditional *command and control* approach has been gradually re-

---

Ethics and Crisis Management, pages 75–95

placed by a more nimble and decentralized approach. Planning and central command structures have made way for response networks in which decision-making authority is increasingly shifted to the lower levels of the response chain.

While there are perfectly sensible reasons to shift authority down the chain to first responders (cf. 't Hart, Rosenthal, & Kouzmin, 1993), it does create one often overlooked problem. The shift of authority down the chain is accompanied by a shift in agonizing dilemmas, which fall from the rooms of policymakers into the lap of first responders. In Srebrenica, for instance, Dutch forces had to implement a dilemma-ridden UN mission: protect the local population through the use of a limited defensive force in the face of overt Serbian aggression. A tragedy ensued with heavy ethical overtones, as the Dutch forces allowed the Serbs to take away the male population (the Serbs would proceed to murder them).

The literature on crisis management ethics tends to focus on tragic choice situations that play out at the highest levels of government (think of crucial decisions like those in the Cuban missile crisis). This chapter considers what happens at the other end of the response chain.

In this chapter, we describe and analyze one such case. We revisit the tragic choices that first responders faced in the Memorial Medical Center of New Orleans during the aftermath of Hurricane Katrina.

We begin this chapter by defining the problem in more precise terms. To this effect, we draw on a classic concept—*Aporia*—to describe the unintended outcome of pushing policy dilemmas down the response chain. When dilemmas sink to the bottom and first responders by necessity become *policy leaders*, a development warmly welcomed if not advocated by many academics (Vinzant & Denhardt, 2000), a policy twilight zone is created from which unforeseen and often rather undesirable consequences can emerge. We explore the prospects of deliberation as a way to deal with the challenge of crisis-induced *Aporia*.

A CLASSIC PROBLEM RESTATED: DISCRETION, DILEMMAS, AND APORIA

To understand the plight of first responders, it is helpful to rephrase it in terms of administrative discretion. Discretion is defined here as the "legitimate right to make choices based on one's authoritative assessment of a situation" (Feldman, 1992, p. 164). This is a classic topic in public administration, but scholars have rarely studied the use of administrative discretion in crises.

Discretion is an inevitable feature of the policymaking and policy-delivery process (Hawkins, 1992; Lipsky, 1980). This appears to be especially true for those at the end of the policy line, the so-called street-level bureaucrats (Lipsky, 1980). It is important to distinguish between two types of discretion. Forms of *authorized discretion* occur when policymakers design decisionary room into the implementation instructions for street-level bureaucrats. Policymakers do so because they think it will benefit policy outcomes (often it does). Forms of *rule-compromise discretion* occur when "the legislature or other rule-making body cannot agree on appropriate rules and consequently passes the responsibility on to individual decision-makers" (Hawkins, 1992, p. 4).

In both forms, discretion provides lower-level administrators with room to make decisions that work *against* intended policy outcomes. This piece of conventional wisdom tends to worry policymakers, public managers, and politicians who, after all, bear formal responsibility for what lower-level bureaucrats do. Here we run into one of the classic problems of bureaucracy (White, 1990; Wilson, 1992).[1]

Most field organizations and street-level bureaucrats possess implementation discretion, because policymakers cannot or will not specify behavioral guidelines for every possible situation. Without such specification, street-level bureaucrats have room to choose between alternative courses of action. There are several reasons why specification is inherently difficult.

The most commonly recognized source of discretion is the inability of policymakers to program the actions of street-level bureaucrats. Policymakers simply do not possess the intellectual capacity required to prioritize conflicting and ever-changing goals, weigh the various alternative courses of action, and formulate understandable and feasible directives (Hood, 1976).[2] It is very hard to predict the outcomes of the various alternative courses of action, as patterns of human interaction are not fully comprehensible and always changing. The stream of incomplete information further impairs rational capacity. The available information cannot always be fully understood, due to organizational and cognitive limitations (Wilensky, 1967). In short, policy quality might suffer from the bounded rationality of policymakers (Cook & Levi, 1990; Simon, 1945).

Policymakers cannot monitor all the behavior of their field personnel, because complete and unambiguous feedback is seldom available (Kaufman, 1973). But even if policymakers could detect field deviation from prescribed courses of action, their means for intervention are limited. In most public systems, civil servants cannot be easily fired or replaced. Moreover, coercive tactics to ensure compliance tend to provoke resistance (Gouldner, 1954; Lipsky, 1980). The costs of compliance may be high: "The use of coercion . . . is an invitation to sustained sabotage . . . and leads to disaster" (Landau & Stout, 1979, pp. 151–152).

If street-level discretion is hard to limit or control in normal times and in routine policy processes, it might well be inevitable during crises and disasters. These situations are sometimes characterized as *ill-structured messes*. In these situations, crisis managers never have sufficient information to instruct first responders in any detail, and they often lack even the means to communicate with them, which makes monitoring very hard. In such situations, different perceptions and ideas with regard to the task at hand might well arise (Hill, 1979).

Aporia

An important consequence of ambiguous and inconsistent policy is that street-level bureaucrats are left with the difficult job of solving dilemmas: "situations in which it is impossible to move toward one goal without moving away from another" (Hood, 1976, p. 152). Rein and Rabinovitz (1978) observe that the arena of decision making shifts to a lower level. The everyday practitioners become the ones who resolve the lack of consensus through their concrete actions.

Decision making shifts quite naturally in times of crisis ('t Hart et al., 1993). The first responder is expected to use his judgment and make decisions in such a way that both victims and the multiple goals of the organization are served. But first responders are not always enabled with knowledge, solutions, interpretations, and sufficient resources to make this happen. They are aware, however, of the many rules and constraints that may be used to evaluate their behavior after the crisis (cf. Wilson, 1989). Discretion may thus give rise to an uncomfortable situation. We surmise that this situation can be, to put it mildly, very unpleasant.

We use the Greek term *Aporia* to capture this very specific state of anxiety.[3] In his relatively unknown *Topics*, Aristotle provided what is perhaps the best characterization of the term. Strictly speaking, Aporia is a state of equilibrium between two alternative courses of action structuring a choice situation, in which the arguments or considerations adduced in favor of either alternative cancel each other out in such a way as to render rational (or deliberate) choice between them impossible (Aristotle, 1958, p. 145a).[4] The choice is *rationally* underdetermined (Crowder, 1994).

The thought-experiment of Buridan's donkey may help to understand this notion of rational underdetermination. Imagine a hungry donkey, idling in front of two absolutely identical haystacks. A rational choice between these haystacks would involve comparison with respect to certain features: Is one bigger, cheaper, or more nutritious? From a rational perspective, there is thus no *reason* for the donkey to choose. In other words, the hungry animal's choice will not be determined by the haystacks' *objective* features justifying that choice. This does not mean that the donkey would be incapable of choosing at all (only rational choice theorists can make him starve in front of two haystacks), but it demonstrates that the objective features of a choice situation do not always allow for *rational* choices between the two alternatives.

In a true case of real-life Aporia, a public official is habitually confronted with situations in which arguments in favor of available courses of action hold each other in check. This can happen, for instance, when a prison guard observes a minor rule infraction (like teachers and police officers, prison guards see them all the time). The clearly formulated and widely supported goal of maintaining order and security dictates that the violator is booked and punished. The equally valued goals of providing a humane environment, allowing inmates some room to develop themselves, tells the prison guard to ignore the violation. The prison guard cannot begin to analyze each of these situations in rational detail, but a decision has to be made (even if it is a decision to look the other way).[5]

Or take the case of the police officer. On patrol, the police officer has to negotiate between the goals of maintaining order and enforcing the law (Wilson, 1968). A barroom fight violates both the law and public order. Making an arrest could help to enforce the law, but may very well present a renewed threat to public order. What to do? Formal goals expressed in laws and policy statements cannot help the officer, "thus he approaches incidents that threaten order not in terms of enforcing the law but in terms of 'handling the situation'" (Wilson, 1968, p. 31).

These examples suggest that Aporia can be a structural component of a street-level bureaucrat's task environment. In a way, the repetitive occurrence of such situations is built, sometimes even designed, into the institutional context. In routine situations, Aporia is therefore likely to be a collective experience, shared by those populating the same pigeonhole of the organizational configuration (Searle, 1995, pp. 23–26).[6]

In crisis situations, which by definition produce unique threat situations, the context of Aporia is typically much less institutionalized. New configurations of undersourced organizations provide a fragmented context that offers little if any help in coping with Aporia. Apart from what their training and colleagues provide, first responders will have to deal with crisis-induced Aporia all by themselves.

Effects of Aporia

If these situations are reliably painful, one might expect street-level bureaucrats to organize their activities in such a way as to forestall, deny, or circumvent them. The practical thinking fed into making rational choices between incompatible courses of action may deflect into practical thinking designed to avoid such underdetermined choice situations. An official habitually facing a rationally underdetermined choice between x and y, might thus invest his practical reasoning into contriving strategies that enable him to evade such choices.

The research on street-level bureaucrats appears to bear this out. When street-level bureaucrats by necessity become street-level politicians, they tend to solve policy dilemmas in a way that suits them best (Lipsky, 1980). For instance, they will emphasize one particular aspect of the policy, usually the one that is easiest to measure and to uphold. In our prison example, order will prevail over resocialization considerations, for the simple reason that prison guards know how to maintain order, whereas they don't have a clue how to rehabilitate a criminal. If the officers cannot maintain order by sheer force, they might try to do so by cooptating inmate leaders (Sykes, 1956). Either way, unguided discretion is more than likely to result in sub-optimal policy effects.

The consequences might, in fact, be more than just unpleasant or subop-timal. In prisons, for example, a far more serious consequence arises from the uncertainty that comes to govern the relations between officers and in-mates. In situations of Aporia, officers are not sure how to resolve particular problems. Furthermore, they do not know how their colleagues will resolve the same problems. Inmates then become confused as to what is expected from them and what type of behavior will be tolerated. Inmates will play individual guards off against each other, in the same vein as kids can play their parents. Experienced guards often cite this type of uncertainty as hav-ing a negative impact on guard-inmate relations (Fleisher, 1989; Kauffman, 1989). Uncertainty with regard to guard behavior may rapidly translate into frustration and aggression (DiIulio, 1991).

Lawrence Sherman (1978, p. 132–133) explains how conflicting aims in policing may set the stage for wide-scale corruption. When police chiefs set arrest quotas that are all but impossible to achieve by legitimate means and subsequently evaluate their subordinates on these standards of *productivity*, the typical result is perjury in trial testimony and in affidavits for search war-rants. Sherman found that this *institutionalized lying* paved the way for lying to cover up corruption, a precondition for a deviant organization. "Given the absence of any clear direction for the field commanders on what they were supposed to do in order to reduce crime, this corrupt response . . . was quite predictable" (Sherman, 1978, p. 133).

Aporia might well be an inevitable feature of public bureaucracies. Most public policies consist of multiple and mutually incompatible goals (Wil-son, 1989). The underlying tensions or dilemmas remain invisible as long as policymakers do not specify or *translate* these policy goals into understand-able, workable, and publicly acceptable instructions. But considerations of political feasibility make it rationally attractive to refrain from specification. For political-administrative elites, delegation is a time-honored way of solv-ing hard choices (cf. Simon, 1945, pp. 64, 141).

When the repetitive rational underdetermination of policy decisions becomes a habit and is exposed to further institutionalization, then *institutional* Aporia becomes a likely outcome. Institutional Aporia can therefore be interpreted as the result of an institutionalized practice of dodging political responsibility; not by denying that responsibility *ex post*, but by organized devolution of practical perplexity. In other words, street-level bureaucrats become tasked with solving dilemmas that have been passed down the line.

While we have at least an informed idea of how street-level bureaucrats tend to cope with routinized occurrences of Aporia, the same cannot be said for situations of crisis-induced Aporia. We know that first responders encounter tragic choice situations. Very little research has attempted to document how first responders deal with these situations. As their response to these situations clearly has ethical repercussions for the entire response operation, we want to take a first cut at exploring how first responders deal with Aporia. For this, we turn to one of the most complex disasters in recent U.S. history: Hurricane Katrina.

A CASE STUDY OF CRISIS-INDUCED APORIA: THE MEMORIAL HOSPITAL TRAGEDY[7]

On Monday morning, August 29, 2005, Hurricane Katrina lashed the coastal areas of Louisiana and Mississippi. The largest city in the hurricane's path, New Orleans, had seen most of its citizens evacuate before the arrival of the storm. A sizeable part of the population had decided to stay, however. Due to a variety of reasons (congestion of the routes leading out of the city, the lack of hospitals for accommodating patients, the frailty of many patients), hospital officials considered it safer to stay in place rather than expose their patients to the possible consequences of a badly organized, hasty, and chaotic evacuation.

Hundreds of people (most family of staff) had decided to ride out the storm in Memorial Medical Center, which in the past had proven safe from hurricane-strength winds. Nearly 2,000 people (including 200 patients and 600 staff) had hunkered down in the massive building.

The hospital was located in one of the lower parts of the city. When the city flooded after the hurricane had moved on and the levees gave way, many were caught by surprise in one of the largest disasters in recent U.S. history. What happened during the anxious 3 days after the levees broke would later turn out to be one of the most heart-wrenching and disturbing dramas in a city rife with desolation. In the final hours before the hospital was finally completely evacuated before nightfall on Thursday, September 1, thirty-five patients had died. A substantial number of those patients were euthanized by two or three doctors who injected the weak patients with a deadly mix of morphine and benzodiazepine sedative.

One of the physicians, Dr. Anna Pou, and two nurses were subsequently arrested for murder. A Grand Jury refused to issue an indictment. While there appears to have been little doubt among the jurors that Dr. Pou had administered lethal injections, the jury members (New Orleanians) reportedly weighed the circumstances in her favor. This prompts the question that we seek to answer: how did a couple of physicians who were known for their caring and professional attitude toward patients sit down next to patients, administer a lethal mix, offering a prayer before moving on to the next patient? Or, to use the words of one patient's son, "Who gave them the right to play God?"

In the following section, we describe and analyze this situation in terms of Aporia. We describe the key decisions and critical circumstances that helped set the scene for this tragedy. We highlight the painful dilemma that confronted an exhausted staff in several different guises and with increasing urgency: *Which patients should get a share of limited resources, and who decides?*

The Water Rises: Three Crucial Decisions

In the early morning of Monday, 4:55 a.m., the city's power failed as hurricane winds took power lines down across the city. The Memorial suffered damage to the windows, but the auxiliary generators worked. As the hurricane slowly moved away, all seemed to have gone well by the end of that long Monday. New Orleans dodged the bullet, or so the news wires told the nation.

Tuesday morning, water began to rise in the streets of New Orleans. The leadership of the hospital understood immediately that evacuation of patients would be necessary. The auxiliary generators were located on the ground level and were not submergible. It would be, in other words, only a matter of time before the electricity would be gone. In a building that is designed to keep heat out and cool air in, the absence of air conditioning quickly leads to stifling heat in the building.

The medical department chairman, Richard Deichmann, called the physicians together to discuss how the evacuation would be handled. The 246-page emergency plan "offered no guidance for dealing with a complete power failure or for how to evacuate the hospital if the streets were flooded" (Fink, 2009a). The first critical dilemma that physicians faced (and they had to make the decision) was how to triage the 180 patients. In the absence of an accepted triage system, the physicians had to come up with their own.

The doctors agreed that women, children, and babies should go first. The weakest patients would go last. These are the patients with so-called Do Not Resuscitate (DNR) orders: patients that are so weak that they or their family decided that they should be allowed to slip away if their time comes. But these DNR orders were never drawn up with a disaster evacuation in mind, nor did DNR stand for *Do Not Evacuate*. While at this point in time everybody expected a rapid evacuation, this decision would have far-reaching repercussions. The 52 patients on the seventh floor of the hospital would especially feel the brunt of this decision. The seventh floor was leased out to LifeCare Hospitals, a company that specializes in the treatment of elderly patients.

Tuesday afternoon, the first helicopters arrived across the street. The pilots were in a hurry and evacuation was not easy as patients have to be moved to the helicopter pad via the parking garage. In the hospital, few people were aware of how bad the situation across the city was. The helicopters left with 50 patients. The incident commander of LifeCare, Diane Robichaux, who was 7 months pregnant, realized that her patients on the seventh floor would not be evacuated that day.

At this point, the hospital staff is exhausted. They have been holed up in the hospital since Sunday. Limited power, little sleep, and no relief enhance their worries about the fate of loved ones. The situation is chaotic: patients have been moved to the second floor from where the evacuation will take place. All but the most critical treatments have been discontinued. But the end is in sight, as evacuation should be near.

But the crisis is about to escalate. At 2 a.m. (Wednesday morning), the backup generators quit working and the hospital is without power. The lives of some of the LifeCare patients (the weakest ones) are threatened as the breathing machinery stops working. An immediate evacuation is ordered, and patients have to be moved down the stairs (elevators are no longer working) while nurses frantically hand-bag air into the lungs of the threatened patients. That night, two patients die and several are evacuated.

Wednesday morning it is decided to move all remaining 100 patients to the second floor (the staging ground for the evacuation). Triage begins—who should be carried out first? Now a second crucial decision is made. Three groups are created. The healthiest will go first (even if they need attention the least); patients in the third group, some who are close to death, are kept apart. Dr. Pou, who has no training in triage, takes charge of this process. Pou would later say she was trying to do the most good with a limited pool of resources.

Wednesday is a bad day. The evacuation stalls as few helicopters are coming. Rumors reach the hospital: helicopters are focusing on the *roof toppers* (survivors who are waiting on their roofs to be evacuated). They are being shot at. The staff face new dilemmas. Desperately sick people somehow make it to the hospital (one family floats on a mattress). Most are turned away. On the eighth floor, a 350-pound woman with advanced cancer and sedated by morphine cannot be brought downstairs. Four nurses attend her. Dr. Cook, a Memorial administrator, tells the nurses to increase the morphine and come downstairs where their help is needed.

That afternoon, the idea of euthanizing patients begins to take hold. Cook later reported that he saw only two choices for the hopeless cases: quicken their deaths or abandon them. While Cook and Pou must have realized it was illegal, they wanted to relieve the suffering of their patients (some of whom they knew well). The contours of Aporia are becoming quite sharp.

Dr. Pou is working a third night on one hour's sleep. Thursday morning, a flotilla of boats arrives to move patients. Helicopters land. But the evacuation proceeds very slowly. This creates a new sense of crisis for the staff as the Louisiana State Police have made it clear that their officers will not guard the hospital after 5 p.m. The rumors of armed gangs roaming the streets have created an atmosphere of fear. As one staff member described his perception of the situation, "the laws of man had broken down" (Fink, 2009a). The evacuation operation is perceived in the hospital as a last chance. It is within this context, in the middle of the final straw operation, that Dr. Pou discovers nine patients who are still left on the seventh floor.

The crucial third decision, then, comes almost naturally. Dr Pou has already been informed by Dr. Cook how to administer a combination of morphine and benzodiazepine sedative that is sure to hasten death. The remaining patients on the seventh floor receive an injection. In the triage area, Dr. Pou continues to administer doses to the category 3 patients who she thinks will not be part of the evacuation (or, as all participants later convince themselves, would not have survived the evacuation). Dr. Pou does not work alone. Dr. Thiele assists, as does Karen Wynn (who was in charge of the hospital's ethics committee). Thiele defends his actions:

> This was totally against every fiber in my body. But we were abandoned by the government, we were abandoned by Tenet [the company that owned the hospital], and clearly nobody was going to take care of these people in their dying moments. I did what I would have wanted done to me if the roles were reversed. (Fink, 2009a)

It is not clear how many patients died as a result of these injections. But we do know that a tragedy unfolded behind the walls of Memorial. Closed off from the rest of the world and suffering from rapidly deteriorating conditions, temperatures rising quickly above 100 degrees, breakdown of essential equipment, deplorable hygienic conditions (Gray & Hebert, 2006, pp. 5–8), the medical staff faced what they perceived as a horrifying dilemma: quicken the deaths of dying patients or abandon them. In the aftermath, Dr. Pou was vilified by many when it became clear what had transpired in those frantic days. Intriguingly, the people of Louisiana refused to indict her. It leaves us with a pressing question with ethical dimensions: What should we make of the actions of Dr. Pou and her colleagues?

Analysis

What we have described is a situation of crisis-induced Aporia. Unexpected and painful dilemmas had to be resolved by individuals who were not trained to deal with these dilemmas. This particular case provides an insight as to just how painful these dilemmas can be. They also give us an idea as to how people may cope with such extreme dilemmas. Two prominent observations can be made. First, it is clear that initial decisions can have strong path-dependency effects: they set the stage for crucial decisions down the line. Second, it appears that a denial of ethical implications of first decisions (when the ethical implications might not be clear) may set the stage for ethical transgressions down the line.

With the benefit of hindsight, we can easily see how the first triage decision was guided by a crucial misconception that would have huge ethical implications.

Memorial's medical department chairman proposed to evacuate patients with a DNR order last. But a DNR order is not a living will. Under Louisiana law, patients can request that life-sustaining procedures be withheld from them when they are in a terminal or irreversible condition. By contrast, a DNR order does not require the patient to be in such a condition. It is an order, signed by a doctor, supported by the informed consent of the patient or a health care proxy, that in the case of a ceasing of heartbeat or breathing, the patient not be revived.

It is not clear whether the doctors fully understood the nature of the DNR order. One doctor surmised that those patients who had signed a DNR would not have wanted to be saved at the expense of others. In terms of moral philosophy, we see here a utilitarian calculus (the greatest good for the greatest number of people) at work: those whose lives are worth less receive less care. The first decision set the staff on a utilitarian course, which had immediate but unforeseeable consequences (several patients died when the auxiliary power gave out).

The staff's initial deliberations and the subsequent adoption of the utilitarian criterion would have repercussions all the way down to the third decision (to euthanize patients). Dr. Pou, a surgeon untrained in triage, would let this utilitarian calculus inform her triage decisions, which, under intense conditions, would ultimately lead to a death verdict for more than a few patients.

In hindsight, the level of ethical error is baffling. It is not only that the technical skills for performing an adequate triage were lacking; much more important is that the question of killing patients should never have arisen in the first place. There was no way that the doctors could properly assess whether the patients in category 3 suffered from an irreversible or terminal condition.

Dr. Pou took it upon herself to "save" category 3 patients from further suffering, although there was no adequate warrant or reason for doing so. This becomes poignantly clear in the language used as reported in interviews with the Louisiana Justice Department investigators and journalists. In testimonies, the emphasis is not so much on euthanasia, but on the peaceful way of dying (comfortableness). People were told that the cocktail administered would make them feel better: "I'm going to give you something to make you feel better." According to one witness, the goal of administering the cocktails was "death: our goal was to let these people die." According to another, all the staff could offer was "comfort, peace *and dignity*" (Fink, 2009a).

These testimonies reveal the complete lack of ethical consciousness of the parties involved. A Do Not Resucitate order presupposes informed consent by the patient. This is so for a very specific ethical reason: the fact that only decisions that are autonomously made, in full awareness of the implications and consequences, provide a manifestation of *human* dignity. Administering a painless death is not part of that notion.[8] Nevertheless, those involved in the operation described a dignified death in terms of painlessness. The fact that people were lied to before receiving the lethal cocktail does little to make things better.

But we want to make a bigger point: this situation of Aporia should have never occurred in the first place. It is unfair, or rather *unethical*, to let people who are coping with an intense, scary, and life-threatening disaster make decisions over who should be evacuated. Alan Levine, Louisiana's Secretary of Health (2008–2010), made a good point when he observed that "the time to have the discussion [on triage standards] is not when the wheels are coming off" (Fink, 2009b). If only that would have happened—but the hospital's management left the hardest decisions to the staff.

This misunderstanding of the situation at the highest level in the hospital's hierarchy created an *Aporetic* situation for those who were in charge of the evacuation procedure and the triage operation that was part of it. The case is tragic twice over: the worst possible option in a perceived dilemma was chosen, while there should not have been a perceived dilemma in the first place. It is, in short, a case of moral failure at the higher level, with devastating consequences for first responders and those who were placed in their care.

PREVENTING APORIA

Crisis-induced Aporia may cause ethical problems, we have argued. To say that Aporia is problematic is not to say that we should do away with discretion, however. There is no doubt that discretion is both necessary and inevitable in the process of policy implementation (Feldman, 1992). It increases the policy's effectiveness by tapping the problem-solving abilities of those working closest to the problem (Elmore, 1979; Sabatier, 1986; Sabatier & Mazmanian, 1983). This is even more true for crisis situations.

But as they become the receptor of inherent or emerging dilemmas, street-level bureaucrats look for norms and values that can guide the decisions they have to make. Discretion works best when it is accompanied by some *mental map* or *technology* that assists street-level policymakers in their decision-making process.[9] The question is, then, if and how first responders can be equipped with this type of mental technology. The literature suggests two approaches: incentives and trust.

The rational choice approach at first sight seems to offer a simple and elegant solution. In this approach, by supplying the right mixture of incentives to insure compliance with central intentions, street-level bureaucrats are induced to select the prescribed use of discretion as their rational choice (cf. Edwards & Sharkansky, 1978). This is typically done by negotiating a contractual agreement between central policymakers and implementing agents, in which benefits and outcome measures are specified. As Miller (1990) demonstrates, it is generally impossible to construct a correct set of incentives for shaping *agent* behavior. The control problem looms large, as it is impossible for most policymakers to monitor street-level bureaucrats at acceptable costs. The problem is exacerbated by civil service personnel protection, which makes it impossible for principals to detect and penalize deviant workers. Crisis conditions only make the problem worse.

A second approach prescribes the *empowerment* of street-level bureaucrats (Peters & Pierre, 2000, p. 9; cf. Kernaghan, 1992). In recent years, more and more public employees have become *empowered* in the sense that they get to make more decisions on their own. This is supposedly a good thing, because "discretion gives the bureaucrat the maneuvering space needed to be able to conduct this work according to professional norms and standards, rather than organizational rules and procedures" (Peters & Pierre, 2000, pp. 18–19). Not only do they like their work better and become more "enthusiastic" (Borins, 1995, p. 125), but public servants are said to become more effective as well.

Yet mere trust in street-level bureaucrats is an insufficient condition for avoiding undesired consequences of unchecked discretion from an effectiveness, democratic, or ethical point of view.[10] In the terms of our earlier analysis, this advice can only result in a *lack* of central guidance on how street-level bureaucrats should apply their increased discretion. When guidance is forsaken in the name of trust, the street-level bureaucrat will spend his energy to avoid drowning in the complexities and demands of boundary management (cf. Gawthrop, 1984).

Exploring the Potential of Deliberation

If centralization is not an option, and the empowerment of bureaucrats results in undesirable behavior or decisional paralysis, what then can be offered as a solution? We argue that the solution lies in a balanced combination of both centralization and empowerment.

To use more precise terms, we make a case for *cross-hierarchical deliberation* as means of providing guidance to the use of street-level discretion. We start by adopting two principles of public administration and policymaking. The first principle accepts street-level discretion both as inevitable and potentially beneficial to policy outcomes. The second principle is that the responsible politicians and policymakers should be actively involved in policy setting.

Deliberation refers to a process of interaction, which enables policymakers to make informed decisions that prevent Aporia. Through a process of collective practical reasoning, potential dilemmas are identified, and actionable guidelines are designed to negotiate these dilemmas.

Deliberation is, first and foremost, *practical reasoning.* It is practical in the sense that it is reasoning about what to *do* (Richardson, 1994). Typically, but not exclusively, deliberation amounts to a weighing of considerations for or against a certain course of action. This provides the link with Aporia: for one way to redescribe the rational underdetermination involved in Aporia is in terms of deliberative deadlock. Deliberation does not refer to noncommittal *discussion* about practical problems. Phenomenologically speaking, there is a qualitative difference between, on the one hand, merely discussing a practical or even moral problem (say, discussing abortion at a birthday party), without there being any need to act and, on the other, reasoning about such a problem because one has to act (discussing abortion because one, or one's partner, is pregnant). It is a fact well-attested to by experience that principles are much easier professed in noncommittal discussion than adhered to in truly practical reasoning.

One of the functions of deliberation is heuristic: while deliberating, we may discover that an end that motivates our deliberation cannot be achieved by any conceivable or practicable means. In that case, we might say that our deliberations are abortive from a narrowly practical point of view, but that they retain a certain diagnostic value. As Thomas Hobbes has it: "Every Deliberation is then sayd to End, when that whereof they Deliberate, is either done, or thought impossible" (Hobbes 1968, p. 127).

Second, deliberation is *collective* practical reasoning. Deliberation and practical reasoning are ambiguous terms. They refer to either the practical *thinking* that occurs in the mind of one and the same individual, or to the exchange of ideas taking place between more than one person (Goodin, 2000). Because deliberation is collective, it is an expedient instrument to pool resources, bringing different kinds of experience to the fore.

A common misunderstanding is that deliberation is deployed to forge some kind of consensus. Since one of the functions of collective interpersonal deliberation lies in the clash of (sometimes fundamentally) different conceptions of ends and its power to generate better decisions, consensus cannot be the sole end of the deliberative procedure itself. The aim of consensus would (and frequently does) put a mortgage on the productivity of the deliberative process. This is not to say that consensus is bad, or that it should be prevented. Consensus, of course, is a most convenient outcome of a deliberative policymaking process, but it should not be the *aim* of such a procedure. One of the heuristic functions of deliberation, namely, drawing up an inventory of positions, will be impaired when consensus is tolerated as a (formal) aim of the process, because participants will tend to anticipate positions that can be accommodated more easily by others.

The worst thing that can happen to the effectiveness of deliberation is its graduation into a self-contained end—deliberation for deliberation's sake. Turning the road into a destiny (in a Habermasian way) is all too likely to deprive it of its credibility and to foster skepticism about deliberation as an instrument of decision making.

Third, a little-noticed function of deliberation is the *identification* of Aporia. Policy ends and values frequently are stated in too abstract or general a way and therefore obscure possible conflicts between such ends and values in situations in which actual decisions have to be made by street-level bureaucrats. Deliberation not only serves to get means-end reasoning going, by providing adequate specifications of the ends of a public institution, but also to *detect* possible tracks to institutional Aporia. Just as specification of end(s) requires feedback in terms of conceivable means, cross-hierarchical deliberation, to discharge its important heuristic function, requires the experience of street-level bureaucrats to feed into the process.

From a perspective of institutional design, the creation of venues for cross-hierarchical deliberation in order to detect Aporia presents an attractive alternative to the dialectic of centralization and decentralization. What is more, it takes seriously the concept of discretion as a real power to exercise practical reason in making decisions at all levels of the institution. Moreover, it accords a place to the experiential knowledge of those to whom the benefits of discretion are supposed to accrue.

Organizing Deliberation

Deliberation should happen *before crises occur*. The process of deliberation takes time, which, by definition, is not available in a crisis. Moreover, during a crisis, communication and thus deliberation often becomes impossible. From the literature on deliberation, we can distill three simple conditions that must be satisfied if Aporia is to be avoided.

First, an informed debate between crisis authorities and first responders should be organized (preferably institutionalized) in which the ends of crisis and disaster management are discussed in terms of feasibility on the ground. It should be noted that deliberation is a rule-governed activity, the exercise of which requires a certain level of competence. In other words, the capacity to collectively deliberate, and thus to exercise practical reason to meaningfully use one's discretionary powers, is to an important extent learned.

Second, there has to be a suitable measure of involvement or commitment among deliberators. The leaders of a crisis response should take the time and demonstrate the commitment to enter this process.

Third, deliberation has to be transparent. Any decision-making procedure that is deliberative and not transparent is, by our lights, not really a deliberative procedure—or only in a metaphorical, or derived sense. A specification of transparency is *followability*. Anything that is to count as deliberation (or practical reasoning in general) should at least aim to be followable by others for whom it is to count as reasoning. The outcomes of the process should be actively disseminated in the response community. They should become part of the training curriculum.

CONCLUSION: TAKING SERIOUSLY THE ETHICAL DIMENSION OF CRISIS MANAGEMENT

Discretion is both inevitable and potentially valuable in times of crisis. Academics often view street-level discretion as an antidote to the frustrations and impossibilities of large-scale response operations. This chapter highlights the possibility that the benefits of improvisation are sometimes outweighed by the unintended and often unrecognized consequences as played out behind the walls of Memorial Medical Center.

This chapter shows how unsolved policy dilemmas are sometimes delegated down the line. Sometimes this happens in the name of empowerment and job enrichment. If policymakers and street-level officials must cope with dilemmas because these cannot be solved at a higher level, these decision makers are at least entitled to guidance as to how abstract policy intentions should be applied to concrete situations.

An important question, then, pertains to the source of guidance. As centralized dictates tend to be ineffective for all the well-known reasons, we have to look for other solutions. One traditional solution is the reliance on professional norms and standards, which help policymakers and implementers to make the right decisions. Whereas some professions can indeed rely on a well-articulated and widely agreed-upon body of expertise (think of hospitals, accountants, and foresters), it appears to us that the crisis response community cannot. We cannot simply put our trust in professional norms and values as some academics do (Peters & Pierre, 2000).

The real issue is that incompatible policy aims must be reconciled and translated into a clear philosophy that guides the use of implementation discretion. It is clear that political-administrative elites are ultimately responsible for this process of policymaking. Rather than centralizing the decision-making process in their hands, however, we propose the use of deliberation to ensure that street-level expertise is fed into that process. If a process of deliberation supplants the practice of dodging, a state of bureaucratic Aporia is effectively avoided. A positive side effect is that the political-administrative foundations are shored up by this process, thus limiting the prospects of unproductive conflict and ethical transgressions.

NOTES

1. It worries some academics, too. Wilson (1992, p. 209) defines discretion as the opposite of the rule of law: "Discretion allows agencies to constrain the behavior of others while remaining free of clear legislative standards." Wilson fears that discretion is used to empower street-level bureaucrats to achieve policy goals in an illegal fashion.
2. "If perfect knowledge was available, there would be no need for discretion" (Landau & Stout, 1979, p.149).
3. As so many Greek words, the term *Aporia* is difficult, if not impossible, to render in English. Current translations fail to do justice to the anxiety overwhelming someone who, like Hercules at the crossroads, faces a choice as to which of two directions to go (from the verb *poreuô*, "to go"). The English word that comes closest to the original meaning is perhaps "perplexity." Aporia, as we conceive of it, differs from the concept of tragic choice in that the latter is a choice between two morally binding obligations (e.g., Antigone's dilemma of obeying the laws of Thebes or the commands of the gods). The

scope of Aporia is wider than that. It comprises tragic dilemmas, but is not confined to it; it need not have any moral significance at all (Williams, 1980).

4. Of course, there may be more than two alternatives in a choice situation. For the sake of expository convenience, however, we limit ourselves to binary situations.

5. There is a rich literature on guard behavior. For an introduction to the topic, see Johnson (1996).

6. Indeed, the coping behavior of street-level bureaucrats tends to be collectively organized (Baumgartner, 1992; Lipsky, 1980). According to Hasenfeld (cited in Handler, 1992, p. 340), street-level bureaucrats develop "practice ideologies," which are sets of ideas or ideologies that tend to contrast official policies.

7. Unless otherwise noted, all empirics in this section were taken from Sheri Fink (2009a,b).

8. Sigmund Freud famously refused morphine on his deathbed for fear of losing his capacity for clear thinking.

9. When the use of discretion is effectively controlled, the existence of discretion itself becomes quite unimportant. When field administrators think and act like central policymakers, discretion becomes a source of ingenuity and flexibility (Weick, 1993).

10. For some unintended consequences of "empowered" citizens, see Solas (1996) and Nieuwenburg (2004).

REFERENCES

Aristotle (1958). *Topica et sophistici elenchi.* Oxford, UK: Oxford University Press.

Baumgartner, M. P. (1992). The myth of discretion. In K. Hawkins (Ed.), *The uses of discretion* (pp. 129–161). Oxford, UK: Clarendon Press.

Boin, R. A., 't Hart, P., Stern, E., & Sundelius, B. (2005). *The politics of crisis management: Public leadership under pressure.* Cambridge: Cambridge University Press.

Borins, S. (1995). The new public management is here to stay. *Canadian Public Administration, 38*(1), 122–132.

Cook, K. S., & Levi, M. (Eds.). (1990). *The limits of rationality.* University of Chicago Press.

Crowder, G. (1994). Pluralism and liberalism. *Political Studies, 42*(2), 293–305.

DiIulio, J. J., Jr. (1991). Understanding prisons: The new old penology. *Law and Social Inquiry, 16*(1), 65–99.

Edwards, G. C., & Sharkansky, I. (1978). *The policy predicament: Making and implementing policy.* San Francisco: W.H. Freeman & Co.

Elmore, R. F. (1979). Backward mapping: Implementation research and policy decisions. *Political Science Quarterly, 94*(4), 69–83.

Feldman, M. S. (1992). Social limits to discretion: An organizational perspective. In K. Hawkins (Ed.), *The uses of discretion* (pp. 163–183). Oxford, UK: Clarendon Press.

Fink, S. (2009a). *The deadly choices at Memorial.* Retrieved August 8, 2009, from http://www.propublica.org/article/the-deadly-choices-at-memorial-826

Fink, S. (2009b, December 27). Louisiana doctors working on crisis standards for when medical system is overwhelmed. *The Times-Picayune.*

Fleisher, M. S. (1989). *Warehousing violence.* London: Sage.

Gawthrop, L. C. (1984). *Public sector management, systems, and ethics.* Bloomington, IN: University Press.

Goodin, R. E. (2000). Democratic deliberation within. *Philosophy & Public Affairs, 29*(1), 81–109.

Gouldner, A. W. (1954). *Patterns of industrial bureaucracy: A case study of modern factory administration.* New York: The Free Press.

Gray, B. H., & Hebert, K. (2006). *After Katrina: Hospitals in Hurricane Katrina.* Washington DC: The Urban Institute.

Hargrove, E. C., & Glidewell, J. C., (Eds.). (1990). *Impossible jobs in public management.* Lawrence: University Press of Kansas.

't Hart, P., Rosenthal, U., & Kouzmin, A. (1993). Crisis decision making: The centralization thesis revisited. *Administration and Society, 25*(1), 12–45.

Hawkins, K. (Ed.). (1992). *The uses of discretion.* Oxford, UK: Clarendon Press.

Hill, M. J. (1979). Appendix II: Implementation and the central-local relationship. In Social Science Research Council (Eds.), *Central-local government relationships: Report of an SSCR panel to the Research Initiatives Board* (pp. 119–183). London: Social Science Research Council.

Hobbes, T. (1968). *Leviathan.* Harmondsworth, UK: Penguin.

Hood, C. C. (1976). *The limits of administration.* London: John Wiley & Sons.

Johnson, R. (1996). *Hard time: Understanding and reforming the prison.* Belmont, CA: Wadsworth Publishing Company.

Kaufman, H. (1973). *Administrative feedback: Monitoring subordinates' behavior.* Washington DC: The Brookings Institution.

Kauffman, K. (1989). *Prison officers and their world.* Cambridge, MA: Harvard University Press.

Kernaghan, K. (1992). Empowerment and public administration: Revolutionary advance or passing fancy? *Canadian Public Administration, 35*(2), 194–214.

Landau, M., & Stout, R., Jr. (1979, March/April). To manage is not to control: Or the folly of type II errors. *Public Administration Review,* 148–156.

Lipsky, M. (1980). *Street-level bureaucracy: The dilemmas of the individual in public services.* New York: Russell Sage Foundation.

Matland, R. (1995). Synthesizing the implementation literature: The ambiguity-conflict model of policy implementation. *Journal of Public Administration Research and Theory, 5*(2), 145–174.

Miller, G. J. (1990). Managerial dilemmas: Political leadership in hierarchies. In K. S. Cook & M. Levi (Eds.), *The limits of rationality* (pp. 324–348). University of Chicago Press.

Nieuwenburg, P. (2004). The agony of choice. *Administration & Society, 35*(6), 683–700.

Peters, B. G., & Pierre, J. (2000). Citizens versus the new public manager: The problem of mutual empowerment. *Administration and Society, 32*(1), 9–28.

Rein, M., & Rabinovitz, F. F. (1978). Implementation: A theoretical perspective. In W. D. Burnham & M. W. Weinberg (Eds.), *American politics and public policy* (pp. 307–335) Cambridge, MA: MIT Press.

Richardson, H. R. (1994). *Practical reasoning about final ends.* Cambridge, MA: Cambridge University Press.

Rodriguez, H., Quarantelli, E. L., & Dynes, R. (Eds.) (2006). *Handbook of disaster research.* New York, NY: Springer.

Sabatier, P. A. (1986). Top-down and bottom-up approaches to implementation research: A critical analysis and suggested synthesis. *Journal of Public Policy, 6*(1), 21–48.

Sabatier, P. A., & Mazmanian, D.A. (1983). Policy implementation. In S. S. Nagel (Ed.), *Encyclopedia of policy studies* (pp. 143–169). New York: Marcel Dekker.

Searle, J. (1995). *The construction of social reality.* Harmondsworth, UK: Penguin.

Sherman, L. (1978). *Scandal and reform: Controlling police corruption.* Berkeley: University of California Press.

Simon, H. A. (1945). *Administrative behavior: A study of decision-making processes in administrative organization.* New York: The Free Press.

Solas, J. (1996). The limits of empowerment in human services work. *Australian Journal of Social Issues, 31*(2), 147–156.

Sykes, G. M. (1956, March). The corruption of authority and rehabilitation. *Social Forces, 34,* 257–262.

Vinzant Denhardt, J. (2000). Contactambtenaren en Bestuurlijk Vermogen. *Bestuurswetenschappen, 54*(3), 209–226.

Weick, K. E. (1993). The collapse of sensemaking in organizations: The Mann Gulch disaster. *Administrative Science Quarterly, 38*(4), 628–652.

White, O. F. (1990). Reframing the authority/participation debate. In G. L. Wamsley, R. N. Bacher, C. T. Goodsell, P. Kronenberg, J. A. Rohr, C. M. Stivers, et al. (Eds.), *Refounding public administration* (pp. 182–245). Newbury Park, CA: Sage.

Wilensky, H. L. (1967). *Organizational intelligence: Knowledge and policy in government and industry.* New York: Basic Books.

Williams, B. (1980). *Moral luck.* Cambridge, MA: Cambridge University Press.

Wilson, J. Q. (1968). *Varieties of police behavior: The management of law and order in eight communities.* Cambridge, MA: Harvard University Press.

Wilson, J. Q. (1989). *Bureaucracy: What government agencies do and why they do it.* New York: Basic Books.

Wilson, J. Q. (1992). On predicting the bureaucratization of American government. In L. B. Hill (Ed.), *The state of public bureaucracy* (pp. 209–215). New York: M.E. Sharpe.

CHAPTER 6

THE ETHICAL DILEMMAS OF STRADDLING THE PUBLIC–PRIVATE DIVIDE IN ECONOMIC CRISES

Lina Svedin

We thought somehow the hand of Adam Smith would be benign.
—David Freeman, gubernatorial energy advisor,
quoted in Taylor (2002)

INTRODUCTION

This chapter examines how the U.S. government attempted to navigate the public–private division of responsibility in relation to recent economic and financial crises. It addresses some of the ethical dilemmas that arise when the government becomes involved in major private sector crises. In particular, the chapter looks at the idea of a partnering with the private sector in these crises and what the common rationales are for intervention in these kinds of situations. Furthermore, we will look at the implications of the government's decisions and behaviors in two major private sector crises:

Ethics and Crisis Management, pages 97–118
Copyright © 2011 by Information Age Publishing

the failure of Enron and the 2008 Wall Street financial crisis. In its concluding section, this chapter contemplates the crisis strategies governments face—mitigation, management, or mop-up—and evaluates the ethics of the government's crisis management policy and the justifications for its crisis decisions in these two cases.

PUBLIC–PRIVATE PARTNERSHIPS IN CRISES

Most public–private partnerships are formed between government entities and private sector parties as part of a planned project management strategy (Mörth & Sahlin-Andersson, 2006). In the case with the U.S. financial regulatory system, this partnership constitutes the structure of the regulatory system itself (Fooks, 2003, p. 19).[1] Few would argue that this has been an effective and/or happy partnership. The very fact that this system was built on an assumption of private sector collaboration and division of labor between the public and private parties might well have created the larger structural setting that allowed the subsequent crises to occur.[2]

IT IS NOT A MARKET FAILURE

The kinds of crisis decision making and behavior that the U.S. government displayed in the Enron crisis in 2001 and the Wall Street financial crisis in 2008 are by no means obvious or mandated. So what were the government's rationale and its decision-making criteria for market intervention in these situations?

The most common and accepted rationale for government intervention in market economies is to deal with so-called *market failures,*[3] and a number of strategies exist by which a government can address such failures. These include providing the service or good itself, an increasingly unpopular option, or providing the infrastructure for a new market as the United States did with tradable emissions permits (Cordes, 2002, pp. 262–263). Governments can also provide a number of economic incentives, such as loan guarantees, tax expenditures, or allowing asset depreciation on the books to reduce the financial risks companies face if they agree to produce the service or good needed (Howard, 2002, pp. 416–420; Kahn, 1988b, p. 34; Stanton, 2002, pp. 387–390).

What happened around Enron and its subsequent bankruptcy, however, had nothing to do with market failures of the sort described above. While it is true that the company operated in a regulated sector, its demise had nothing to do with a lack of economic viability of the market. Neither could the situation facing Wall Street in September 2008 be characterized as a market failure in the traditional sense. In the case of mortgage-backed loans, consumer credit, and derivatives, there were ample profits to be made and plenty of firms willing to take the risks involved in lending and reselling loans to make a profit. As such, the situation that emerged would not have warranted or legitimized intervention by the U.S. government to address a market failure.

A second rationale that might justify government intervention in a market economy is as lender of last resort. The U.S. government has stated that it is willing to offer loans to large banks and other institutions when no one else will (in financial crises), in order to guarantee the operability (mainly maintaining some level of liquidity) of the financial system (the market) (see for instance Ryssdal & Dimsdale, 2008). Ever since the National Banking Act of 1864 (Federal Deposit Insurance Corporation, 2010), the United States government, through the Federal Reserve, has maintained this emergency power. Since commercial banks lend depositors money in a way that cannot be rapidly reversed into liquidity (only a fraction is kept in the bank to cover withdrawals), but still guarantees that depositors can get all their money out when they want, the federal government (through the FDIC) insures private depositors' accounts up to $250,000 (Federal Deposit Insurance Corporation, 2010). This government insurance is meant to stem the impulse of depositors to take their money out of banks during periods of financial turbulence, thereby preventing a potential run on banks.

Based on these two rationales for government intervention in the market, the question whether or not to intervene would appear rather straightforward. Yet despite this, the U.S. government faced a series of ethical dilemmas during the aforementioned crises; dilemmas that both complicated and, in some instances, motivated their subsequent intervention.

AS A REGULATOR, YOU ARE ALWAYS IMPLICATED IN THE CAUSE OF THE CRISIS

One initial dilemma involved facing the, if not faulty, then woefully inadequate control and supervision of actor behaviors in the marketplace. Such mechanisms exist to regulate the market and market actors under normal day-to-day operations of the economy, mechanisms the government is largely responsible for setting in place and ensuring they work properly. As a consequence, the government has a vital role to play, as well as a responsibility to make sure these crises never come about in the first place. This responsibility brings the public sector into the crisis as a factor in what, if not created, at least allowed the crisis to materialize. To the extent that the regulation and supervision of market behaviors by companies are not adequately pursued by the public agents and structures charged with this mission, the government, in a sense, is a cause of the crisis. Having said that, the case can also be made that both the understaffing and underfunding of regulatory agencies, as well as the sheer inequality in expertise and know-how that exist between the regulators and the private companies they regulate make it extraordinarily difficult for the government to effectively fulfill this mission. Private enterprise is strongly incentivized to push the limits of what can be done in financing and accounting, and to stay one step ahead of regulators to pursue a competitive edge in the launch of new products and revenue generators. The incentives facing bureaucrats and policymakers aiming to regulate free enterprise and the growth of the economy are far less compelling. In general,[4] the American public and the American private enterprises they work for do not want a heavily regulated market because they want to maximize opportunity, innovation, and profitability.

THE RISK OF SANCTIONING BAD BEHAVIOR

A second dilemma for the government is acknowledging and addressing the actual behavior that caused or allowed the crisis to happen. Oftentimes, there is great risk-taking by corporate executives and strategists, even blatant exploitation of the loopholes in regulation, practices that polarize the inability of regulators to keep up with how financial innovations really work and what their consequences are. The ethical dilemmas of the government present themselves in how they choose to respond to the poor, risky and/or unethical decisions by private actors. Regardless of whether the government chooses to become actively involved in the management of the crisis or not, it is imperative that the government hold these individuals accountable. Otherwise, the government is perceived as sanctioning the behavior that was pivotal in bringing the crisis situation about in the first place. The moral implications of helping someone who has endangered, exploited, and deceived the system to a point where their own actions are bringing their companies down are debatable. However, helping these actors manage the consequences of their own bad behavior and *not* holding them accountable for their actions is unquestionably unethical.

VIOLATING THE RULES OF THE GAME

A third dilemma the government faces is blatantly violating the very rules that it has set in place. Regardless of the many very good reasons the U.S. government has for intervening when a large company faces insolvency, it constitutes a gross violation of market principles and the very ideas they rest on (Stiglitz, 2010, Preface). Acting contrary to the logic of the market system violates the expectations of the participants in the market and creates uncertainty. Suspending the rules of the game, which the government has the power to do, requires at least an explanation and might still undermine trust in the system's regular functioning. In addition, acting contrary to or suspending the rules of the game also undermines the fundamental expectation and trust that the rules of the game will be applied to all participants equally and fairly. Stiglitz (2010) even goes as far as to say that it might undermine social cohesion in a country. The undermining of trust that these kinds of action bring about makes the market less viable and opens up the potential for more violations and risk-taking opportunism (the so-called moral hazard). In other words, when the government, as an exceptionally powerful actor in the marketplace, violates or suspends the rules and the operation of the market, that is, acts unethically, it becomes more likely that future crises related to the market will occur. The reasons the government chooses to do this, to violate the principles of the system that it has put in place, is the essence of the *too-big-to-fail* dilemma.

TOO-BIG-TO-FAIL

The primary reason large corporations or banks are viewed as *too-big-to-fail*, is the massive negative effects their sudden bankruptcy would have on both domestic and foreign economies.[5] The *death-by-market-forces* of such companies would produce consequences the government was unwilling to accept. As a result, the U.S. government intervened in a way that violated the basic principles of the free market. As seen in both the Enron and the Wall Street financial crises, the basis for which the government chose whether or not to intervene is far from clear-cut. The outcomes of the cases, however, are remarkably similar.

The Enron Bankruptcy

In the Enron case, the government chose not to step in and take an active part in the management of what was to quickly become a major economic crisis, with repercussions for countless Americans for years to come.[6] Beyond simply the employees and shareholders, the company's bankruptcy produced a dramatic ripple effect across the entire U.S. economy. A large number of investors and employees of Enron lost their life savings, thousands of people also became instantly unemployed, and the stock market plunged into a downward spiral, pulling down several other large firms.

What Caused the Crisis?

How Enron came to lose economical and ethical status has been vigorously debated. Some argue that its very size and effects on the market contributed to its failure (Sims & Brinkmann, 2003, p. 243), while others have argued that its organizational culture led to its downfall (Kulik, 2005; Sims & Brinkmann, 2003).[7] Still others suggest that its deceptive accounting practices, and the lack of understanding of these practices by regulators and professional auditors, prevented fire alarms from going off.[8] There are also those who take a broader view and say that the structure of the financial regulatory system[9] and the domestic political environment in which it was operating facilitated the crisis (Fooks, 2003, p. 18).[10]

Regardless of the underlying reasons, when Enron filed for bankruptcy on December 2, 2001, the bankruptcy examiner argued that "the Tier 1 financial institutions for Enron failed to carry out their fiduciary responsibility" (Cosimano, 2004, p. 179).[11] Subsequent lawsuits by investors that lost money claimed that the Tier 1 banks[12] defrauded them by withholding essential information about "'the true facts of Enron's financial condition, especially its actual amount of debt and its actual debt-to-capitalization ration, and the extent of the improper transactions conducted by Enron with [the Tier 1 banks] and others'" (New York Law Journal, quoted in Cosimano, 2004, p. 181)

What Values Were at Stake and What Criteria for Decisions?

There were a number of key values at stake for the government in the Enron crisis. Among them were understanding and addressing the accounting and auditing problems that the crisis brought to bear, avoiding signaling that the government will bail out private corporations that had engaged in very risky behavior, securing the functioning of the energy market, distancing the problems at Enron from the policy of deregulation,[13] and keeping the ties between top-level politicians and Enron[14] out of the limelight.

When Enron's CEO alerted the U.S. Secretary of Energy and the Secretary of Commerce of Enron's financial trouble in the fall of 2001 (CNN, 2002; Kadlec, 2002; Svedin, 2008),[15] the government chose not to act. The government did not act to mitigate the impending economic disaster that Enron's failure was certain to create. No bail-out package was discussed, nor did the government help Enron negotiate with its creditors.[16] Whereas the U.S. Treasury and the Federal Reserve had worked in tandem to successfully manage other financial crises in the past, providing both political leadership and the technical tools to contain the crisis (U.S. General Accounting Office, 1997), these actors did not get involved in the Enron case. The U.S. government let the chips fall where they may, and approximately 2 months after Enron's plead for help from the U.S. Treasury and the Commerce

Department, on December 2, the company filed for bankruptcy protection (FERC, n.d.).

What Was the Outcome?—An Expensive Bill and Calls for More Regulation

In the aftermath of the crisis, several public actors were also indicated as having contributed to developing the crisis in the first place. The SEC and FERC did not do their job as oversight bodies and did not speak up when Enron's accounting practices exceeded their knowledge and supervisory mechanisms. The U.S. administration had also played a part in advancing Enron's interests and image at very high level political negotiations, which reinforced Enron's near "untouchable" status among U.S. and world corporations. And while the U.S. government effectively avoided actually managing this crisis, the public sector, and to an even larger extent the American public, ended up bearing the brunt of the financial burden.

In July 2002, the Sarbanes-Oxley Act was signed into law with the intent of preventing a financial disaster like the one that stemmed from the Enron crisis from ever happening again. President Bush stated that it was "'the most far-reaching reforms of American business practices since the time of Franklin Delano Roosevelt'" (President Bush, quoted in U.S. Securities and Exchange Commission, 2010). The Act "mandated a number of reforms to enhance corporate responsibility, enhance financial disclosures and combat corporate and accounting fraud, and created the 'Public Company Accounting Oversight Board,' also known as the PCAOB, to oversee the activities of the auditing profession" (U.S. Securities and Exchange Commission, 2010).

However, as early as 2003, Michalowski and Kramer predicted that a "growing complacency about corporate behavior appears to be replacing what proved to be a short-lived consternation caused by the Enron-era revelations.... the time has come for serious and widespread rethinking of the purpose of corporations and the ethics that guide their relationship to the wider society" (2003, p. 37) Sadly, their call went unheeded, but would ring woefully true as the U.S. government was pulled into the 2008 Wall Street financial crisis. The chairman of the SEC, Harvey Pitt, testified before the Senate Committee on Banking, Housing and Urban Affairs 4 months after Enron filed for bankruptcy that,

> nothing that has occurred in recent months should undermine, or be allowed to undermine, investor confidence that our markets, or the regulatory system governing them, are still the best in the world. Our capital markets are still the world's most honest and efficient. Our current disclosure, financial reporting and regulatory systems also are still the best developed, the most transparent, and the best monitored by market participants and regulators. No other system yet matches the depth, breadth and honesty of our markets, and it is important that we not lose sight of that critical fact. (Pitt, 2002)

The consequences of this value statement were to become painfully obvious 6 years later.

The Wall Street Financial Crisis

In the case the Wall Street financial crisis, the government stepped in early and sought an active role in managing the crisis and mitigating the effects of the failure.

What Caused the Crisis?

While analysts and Nobel prize-winning economists are still arguing about what the underlying causes of the 2008 financial crisis, it is possible to say something about how the crisis began to manifest itself and what some of the key malfunctions in the crisis were.

A key structural factor that contributed to the crisis was introduced as early as 1999 with the repeal of several of the provisions in the 1933 Glass-Steagall Act. This act regulated the separation between commercial loan banks and investment banks (Public Broadcasting System, 2003), a piece of Great Depression-era banking legislation that had been set up when it became clear that "individual investors were seriously hurt by banks whose overriding interest was promoting stocks of interest and benefit to the banks, rather than to individual investors" (Public Broadcasting System, 2003).[17] Ironically, the behavior displayed by Wall Street in 2008 perfectly mirrors the behavior the act set out to prevent.[18]

Beginning in 2006, the U.S. economy had begun slowing down. The aggregate consumer demand dropped and unemployment rose. The financial sector represented a disproportionately large part of U.S. GDP, nearly 40%. What profits that the finance sector had been reporting turned out to be based primarily on highly risky speculation where yields were in stock value, not in actual money or products. The banks and mortgage brokers had also engaged in bad or predatory lending based on the assumption that the housing prices in the United States would continue to rise indefinitely. The housing bubble burst as the mortgage giants[19] Fannie Mae and Freddie Mac's stocks plummeted after reported losses, and the companies could no longer borrow money from either private investors or the public markets (Paulson, 2010, p. 3). Many ordinary Americans found that they now owed more on their houses than they were worth. Unemployment continued to rise, and mortgage owners were defaulting on their mortgage payments. Banks became stuck with what they call *toxic assets* or losses in mortgage investments, and due to the abrupt change in the market (the bubble burst), it was difficult for the banks to know just how large their losses were; that is, how much the houses they lent money on were worth on the market—provided that they could sell them, which is at this point was near impossible due to the foreclosure flood of houses on the market. Several large banks with heavy investment portfolios, starting with Bear Stearns in March 2008, indicated to the government that they might not be able to cover their investor obligations (Paulson, 2010, pp. 3–4). One reason they were not able to do this was that they had used their investors' money to aggressively speculate on the decline in value of stocks or the bankruptcy of other banks, through the financial tools of derivatives and hedge funds, in order to increase bank profits on paper.[20] It turned out that most banks could not cover their bets with actual money, and they all owed each other a great deal of money.[21] The week of September 8, 2008, the U.S. paper market froze,[22] making it impossible for regular businesses to get the short-term credit they needed to pay their bills, signaling a cardiac arrest of the U.S. economy.

Values at Stake and Criteria for Decisions

As the U.S. government faced the beginning of the financial crisis in 2008, a number of values were clearly at stake. While primarily political and economical in nature, these values were also philosophical in terms of understanding the role of government in the economy and the U.S. role in the world. Among the specific values at stake were liquidity in the market so that U.S. firms could do their daily business, avoiding short-term investor panic that could create self-fulfilling prophesies about bankruptcies in particular sectors, and maintaining overall investor confidence in U.S. stocks and the U.S. market. Maintaining political stability, voters' and campaign financer's support, limiting the depreciation of the U.S. dollar, discouraging inflation, and minimizing the perception that this was the beginning of a possibly long and deep recession to avoid further shrinking of domestic consumption were also key priorities for the government. Keeping good U.S. relations with other nations, particularly the countries that own U.S. debt was also very important to the government. Furthermore, not disrupting trade or exposing the United States to trade sanctions, considering its precarious position as the global economy's largest trade deficit holder, were also central values at stake.

There were a number of economic and political reasons the government felt it had to intervene to prevent what was to be an imminent market collapse. The economic reasons had to do with corporations that have been given the dubious epithet, *too-big-to-fail*, while the political reasons stemmed primarily from the impact on citizens and the economy that a failure of these firms would entail.[23] The government's role in two of these corporations, Fannie Mae and Freddie Mac, created an additional moral obligation for the government to intervene and try to prevent harm.[24]

In a situation like this, it is impossible to guard all values simultaneously and equally. Clearly, hard decisions have to be made and so-called tragic choices will appear. However, the lack of explanation of (some moral reasoning around) the government's chosen actions in several clinching moments of the financial crisis has generated additional negative consequences. The fact that the government intervened in the market constituted an extraordinary suspension of the normal rules. Yet the failure of the market that required such an intervention was not openly recognized by the government. To not recognize that the market had failed, and with it, the prevailing philosophy of the U.S. economy, while simultaneously stepping in to avoid rampant economic harm, begs the question of the government's reason for intervening in the first place. Moreover, the inconsistency with which the government chose to suspend the market rules,[25] without explanation, left the public and other market participants with the impression that the government was acting immorally, or at least unethically.

In the aftermath of the financial crisis, the U.S. Federal Government currently holds an unprecedented number of positions across a number of sectors, including "becoming the owner of the world's largest automobile company, the largest insurance company, and (had it received in return for what it had given to the banks) some of the largest banks" (Stiglitz, 2010, p. 16). Stiglitz notes that "A country in which socialism is often treated as an anathema has socialized risk and intervened in markets in unprecedented ways" (p. 16). As such, the very intervention of the government in the economy and the nationalization of many of its corporations fundamentally go against the grain of the American value system.

What Was the Outcome?—An Expensive Bill and Calls for More Regulation

The cumulative bailout costs for the U.S. Department of the Treasury had, at the end of 2009, reached $7.2 trillion. The initial bailout package to banks and financial institutions, the Troubled Asset Relief Program (TARP), covered the then-unimaginable sum of $578 billion ("Behind the real," 2009).

On May 20, 2010, the U.S. Senate passed its version of the financial reform bill aimed at correcting the problems that brought about the 2008 financial crisis and imposing stricter regulation on financial actors. This 1,400-plus-page document proposed seven main changes to the regulation of financial markets and actors: (a) introduction of regulation of futures trading and derivatives, (b) a consumer protection agency for financial products, (c) a council of regulators to look for systemic risk, (d) a process for the government to dismantle failing large corporations, (e) executive compensations set by independent directors, (f) restricting proprietary investments (hedge funds and private equity funds) that do not benefit clients, and (g) requiring companies that sell complex financial products like mortgage-backed securities to hold part of the risk themselves and allowing investors to sue credit rating companies (Herszenhorn, 2010).

THE CHOICE: MITIGATION, MANAGEMENT, OR MOP-UP

Mitroff (2004) describes the of crisis leadership as (a) performing crisis audits of strengths and vulnerabilities before a crisis happens and developing appropriate skills and capabilities to manage crises when they do happen, (b) applying these capabilities and skills to work during a crisis, (c) assessing performances in the aftermath of a crisis and, (d) implementing needed changes to create a more effective response to future crises (p. 5). As such, one of Mitroff's key points is that crisis leadership should be anticipatory and preventative rather than reactive. The government has many hard choices to make as it attempts to manage the divide between the public and the private in crises like Enron and Wall Street. However, from a crisis management perspective, it really has three fundamental options for approaching these crises and similar crises in the future: to mitigate, to manage, or to mop-up. As these two cases have illustrated, the U.S. government chose mitigation, but ended up managing and mopping up.

The government claims to value mitigation as a crisis management strategy, yet ultimately chose systemic solutions that decreased its control and increased the risk of critical failure situations with high stakes; that is, crises. Deregulation in the energy and financial sector has exposed society as a whole to unprecedented levels of economic risk. Regulatory agency's acceptance of innovation without risk-testing has created incentives for private sector actors to try and maximize profits through innovation and aggressiveness, not through sustainable growth and ethical business practices.

The outcries and the outrage calling for regulation to prevent what has just happened in a crisis are strong incentives for government to do just that; regulate the *bad* behaviors that seem to have caused the latest crisis, while closing the loopholes in existing regulation and regulatory practices that have been exposed in the postmortem of the crisis. For many reasons already mentioned, such as the lack of public support for a heavily regulated market and regulated enterprise, always being behind the proverbial curve of financial innovation, and a seeming inability to effectively supervise the actions for market actors, the government chooses mitigation though tailored or limited regulation. The problem with designing regulation in the aftermath of a crisis is the same problem facing great generals who are always trying to refight the last war: the 20-20 vision of hindsight is always limited by seeing the problem primarily through the lens of what has already happened.

As a fundamental crisis management strategy, mitigation aims to engineer away blatant risks, incentivize against risky behavior that makes crises more likely to materialize, and to set up mechanisms for early warning so that problems can be addressed before they turn into crises. The regulation designed and put in place after a crisis needs to address these aspects of mitigation in order to be effective in preventing future crises.

Our own culture appears to blind us to the onslaught of the tsunami-size crises that have grown in private businesses. The American love of success, of brilliance, and immense profit generation prevented the public and those who should have known from seeing what was really going on at Enron. In a section titled, "A Lot of Smoke and Mirrors," Sims and Brinkman (2003, pp. 244–245) describe what can be called a bad case of the Emperor's New Clothes.[26] Wishful thinking, or innocence in the face of public and private sector incentives, is not going to give the Emperor new clothes. The fact of the matter is that the baseline ethical problems of business practices in the Enron bankruptcy and the Wall Street financial crisis are almost identical. Mitigation, as a government crisis management strategy, thus seems to be a complete failure in these cases.

This brings to the fore the problems of choosing mitigation as the crisis management approach in the cases we have examined. The public–private divide between the role of the government and the role of private actors in the marketplace has not fundamentally been altered in the regulations put in place after the crises. Because this basic relationship remains unchanged, the government has been unable to engineer away many of the blatant risks inherent in the American market system, even while implementing regulation to address the specific *bad* or *risky* behaviors that played a key role in the last crisis. Regulation, however, does not address the very strong incentives that caused the market actors to try and be one step ahead of regulators and to push the boundaries of rules—the competitive edge to maximize profits. As long as this value remains the primary concern and responsibility of market actors, the incentives discouraging specific behaviors will only lead to new behaviors that serve the same purpose and value.

Finally, the successful establishment of early-warning systems depends on access to accurate, timely information and the ability to discern signals from noise. As long as regulatory agencies simply continue to require more access to the same kinds of information from corporations, delivered in the same manner, information that they often fail to fully understand, their ability to pick up on signals of problems that could become crises will continue to be limited.

The government does not want to manage what are essentially, at least they start out being, corporate crises. However, a number of factors cause the government to intervene and start co-managing the crises that hit major economic and financial actors. The government is implicated in what is going on by its failure to mitigate, and there is often no other lender of last resort. The public consequences of a crisis reaching full-blown proportions are huge, and some of the values involved[27] are fundamentally[28] important. Crises also expose interdependencies built into the relations between the public and the private sector that otherwise do not come to light. The exposure that the crises examined here have given to the political ties between top decision makers and major corporations, the trust that daily debtor and creditor transactions require, and assumptions about the guarantor role the government will play in those interactions, have led to many uncomfortable realizations. The powerful force of the market also makes it frail, and we do not want to pay the price for other people's recklessness, but we often do not have a choice.

THE ETHICAL IMPLICATIONS OF THE GOVERNMENT'S MANAGEMENT OF THE PUBLIC–PRIVATE DIVIDE IN ECONOMIC CRISES

The management of inherent value conflicts that come to the surface in crises, as well as the safeguarding of transparent, just, and fair processes, are key to upholding public trust in government at a time when it matters the most. The public's perception of how crisis managers deal with value conflicts, whether or not they perceive the process by which decision makers make hard and controversial decisions legitimate, form the public's overall assessment of whether the crisis was handled well or poorly.

Looking at the cases we have reviewed, the U.S. government followed legal and social rationales in the formation of its response to Enron's financial troubles. In its policy-forming decision, not to intervene to try and help Enron or bail it out financially, the government could safely rely on the lack of precedents for the U.S. government intervening in the management of large, innovative, and, up until that point, very successful private companies. It was a *laissez-faire* economy (a valued social institution) that had allowed Enron to prosper and innovate (economic prosperity and innovation being other favored social values), and that economic and legal framework prescribed a minimal role to government. The role that government had, according to this same framework, was to ensure that there were accountability mechanisms that could keep corporations' decisions and behaviors in check. In keeping with the trend that prioritizing one value tends to place less value on other competing values, the Enron crisis saw economic and technical rationales essentially sidelined. The consequence of sidelining the economic rationale was a direct hit, cost absorption, by employees of the company and many large retirement funds of the financial cost of the crisis. The effect that the economy felt as Enron collapsed was redirected to the public directly, through job loss, investment loss, and savings and retirement losses. The violation of the social rationale was a violation of the government's fundamental role in protecting the public from harm. By not sharing the financial burden with the people, by having progressively weakened the mechanisms of accountability, and by not addressing the skewed incentives that it had allowed to rule both private and public actors in this case, the government reneged on its responsibility as protector.

Was the government's decision to not intervene on behalf of Enron a good decision? Was it an ethical decision? Judging from the criteria of *effectiveness, efficiency, adequacy, equity, responsiveness,* and *appropriateness,* we get mixed results. Since the government did not see itself as having a problem, the decision to do nothing can be considered to be both *effective* and *efficient* in terms of keeping the government's actions on course and at the lowest amount of effort. Was the decision *responsive?* Not to Enron or its shareholders. Yet if we are generous in our attribution of reasoning, their actions were *responsive* to the interest of the public at-large that supported a *laissez-faire* economy and the government's limited role in it. More importantly, the decision was not *adequate* nor was it *appropriate.* It was not *adequate,* because it failed to recognize the role that government had in protecting the public from undue harm. It also failed to recognize that it had created the conditions that let Enron have such a financially successful, fiscally irresponsible, and incomparably huge impact on the economy of ordinary citizens.

Conversely, in the 2008 Wall Street case, the government seems to have followed economic and technical rationales rather than a legal or social rationality. The very epithet introduced in this crisis, *too-big-to-fail,* was based on an economic rationale. The companies that the government decided to bail out were considered *too-big-to-fail* because the government was not willing to take the negative consequences that their bankruptcy would have had on the economic system. Letting them fail was not considered economically *efficient,* even in a free-market economy. The bail out of these companies, the specific decisions the government took, and the solutions that it presented were a technical solution to the problem defined: that the government would not accept the negative economic effects of letting these companies fail. The bail-out packages presented by the U.S. government prevented the companies from going bankrupt (a technically *effective* solution), despite the fact that many of them were a long way from returning to profitability. The prioritizing of economic and technical rationales is also highlighted by the fact that other rationales, legal and social, were grossly violated. There were no established rules or precedents that would have made the policy chosen either *just* (judged according to a preset objective principle) or *fair* (principle applied equally between and across cases—why bail out Bear Stearns but let Goldmann Sachs fail?). The U.S. government does not customarily work on a principle of corporativism—or in its extreme form, communism—with the state taking over ownership of established private corporations. Ultimately, there was no domestic legal rationale to cover this option. The espoused social value of keeping the economy going really fails to take into account that the economy that the government was *saving* by bailing out these companies was a free-market economy whose fundamental principles the government was grossly violating through its crisis actions and decisions. Likewise, the social rationale of upholding the value of a free economy and stimulating free enterprise was also grossly violated in this case.

Were the decisions in this case *effective?* Yes. *Efficient?* That is harder to say because of the technical expertise required to understand whether another policy option would have been cheaper for the effect sought (to avoid company bankruptcies). If we believe that the government's economists were designing the bail-out packages with a keen eye to the dollars spent, and that they did not want to pay more than necessary for what they bought, then the decisions could be considered *efficient*. Likewise, the decisions were *adequate* (they solved the problem), but the *responsiveness* can be said to have been rather lopsided in favor of Wall Street interests rather than average taxpayers, mortgage owners, and future generations who would have to pay off the bail out. This brings in the criteria of *equity* and *appropriateness*, which it is hard to say the decisions in the Wall Street financial crisis really hold against. The *responsiveness* in favor of big Wall Street firms compared with the interests of the public, future and present, can hardly be said to have been *equitable* (they did not gain equal amounts, nor did they feel, I think, like they both gained *enough* through the government's actions). Were the decisions *appropriate?* Considering the issues of inequitability and the violations of the very principals that the government said it was protecting, the decisions made can, in only a few cases, I think, be considered *appropriate*.

We evaluate the decisions and behaviors of government in crises like Enron or the Wall Street financial crisis; because decisions in crises matter. They matter in consequence at a very practical level to those directly subject to the decisions made, and they matter on a moral level to society at large (see Chapter 1). In Sims and Brinkmann's (2003) discussion of the development of an unethical corporate culture at Enron, they emphasize the role of leadership in the creation and dissemination of this culture. The influence that leadership is generating with those watching the government's decisions and behavior, will be critical in shaping the ethical behavior of the U.S. public and corporate sector going forward. If the U.S. government does not pay attention to questionable behavior by corporations or signals that the regulatory structures set up are not working well, the signal sent is that ethics and regulation are not important. How government reacts to crises, like the Enron bankruptcy and the Wall

Street financial crisis, impresses upon both the public and private sector to question whether the government can be counted on to support, maybe even fix, bad decisions made by individuals and corporations and what repercussion those at fault might face. In the response to crises, the government acts as a role model and tells society something about which values and behaviors are rewarded and which are negatively sanctioned. Consequently, the government's ability to recognize and meet ethical dilemmas and challenges in crises is paramount in how society perceives not only the government's role and performance, but also what behaviors and values it should be striving for as well. If crisis decisions and behaviors are not based on a process of ethical reasoning that is transparent enough for the public to understand, then the government's approach to crisis management is likely to perpetuate unethical behavior and make crises like the one they just managed more likely to occur again in the future.

NOTES

1. "The system of financial regulation in the U.S. is based on a two-tier system of control, comprising the SEC, on the one hand, and a range of unrelated private institutions, on the other. In principle, these private institutions—which include non-executive directors, investment banking firms, commercial lawyers, security analysts, credit rating agencies and auditors—are expected to work in partnership with the SEC to regulate the US's vast capital markets" (Fooks, 2003, p. 19).

2. "Particularly in the context of fraud surveillance, [private institutions] play a far more important role than the SEC. This is because, with only approximately 3,000 employees, the SEC is simply not adequately organised or funded for the purposes of reviewing, inspecting and analysing corporations and their accounts. Its role, in fraud surveillance and detection at least, is therefore peripheral, leaving the actual practice of uncovering corporate fraud to private institutions like securities analysts and investment banks. . . . It is this basic premise of financial regulation in the U.S.—that the detection of fraud can be left to private commercial organisations that are neither positioned nor organisationally motivated to uncover fraud—which ultimately explains the regulatory failure in the U.S." (Fooks, 2003, p. 19)

3. A market failure can be described as a situation where the production or allocation of a good or a service in a free market is inefficient. One type of market failure appears when there is inadequate incentive for private enterprise to provide a service or a good that we as a society deem necessary or needed. It might be that the market for this good or service would not generate enough profit for any one company to provide it, the market is deemed to new and risky for corporations to invest in, or the investments needed to produce the good are deemed to costly by private enterprise (Kahn, 1988a, pp. 3–4).

4. This reflects public opinion in good economic times and in noncrisis situations. The sentiment turns more toward increased and improved regulation when crises hit and the treacherous risks of the system become apparent as it hits average citizens and greater numbers of corporations.

5. At the time they were bailed out by the U.S. federal government in 2009, Fannie Mae and Freddie Mac were the largest corporations in the world, ever. It is appreciated that these companies were, in some way, connected to or had underwritten half of all home mortgages in the United States. Stocks in Fanny and Freddie also constituted the largest foreign capital investment in the United States by foreign governments after U.S. Treasury Bonds. Numerous former finance ministers confirmed that their countries' economies would have been devastated if Fannie and Freddie would have gone bankrupt, because these foreign governments (and pension funds) had invested so heavily in Fannie and Freddie stocks (Davidson, 2008).

6. As Gary Fooks (2003) points out, Enron's bankruptcy, together with four other private sector bankruptcies that year, constituted the largest in U.S. history up to that point. "Moreover, large frauds at other large companies were discovered soon after, as was the need for several major companies to restate their accounts. These included the telecommunications companies Global Crossing, Qwest Communications, and Worldcom (which quickly surpassed Enron as the largest bankruptcy in U.S. history), as well as Tyco International, Adelphia, Dynergy, Rite-Aid, and Xerox. More interestingly, perhaps, Enron's fall had been immediately preceded by a host of other cases, such as Sunbeam, Cendant, and Waste Management, all of which had involved massive frauds and accounting restatements" (Fooks, 2003, p. 18).

7. Enron's corporate culture jockeyed its employees to exploit this opportunity by innovative, independent, and aggressive actions. Pushing the limits was a corporate motto, and an organizational culture of cleverness came to rule the company from top to bottom (Sims & Brinkmann, 2003, p. 244).

8. The evolution of the accounting profession and the role of audits have also been blamed for part of what lead to the Enron crisis. "The evolution of extreme industrial concentration in the accounting profession, and the subsequent unrestrained diversification of the 'Big Five' accounting firms were the sources of multiple conflicts of interest that were unresolved by the time of the Enron debacle" (Boyd, 2004, p. 377).

9. Deregulation, others claim, opened up a window for experimentation by companies in the energy sector (Sims & Brinkmann, 2003, p. 244)

10. "This was especially true given that in most cases the institutions with formal responsibility for regulating the capital markets either did not discover the frauds or did not report them to the Securities and Exchange Commission (SEC), the lead regulatory body in the U.S. Not only, in short, did the watchdogs not bark, but their collective silence suggested systemic failure" (Fooks, 2003, p. 18).

11. Fiduciary responsibility of a financial institution in a business transaction is "to provide information and enforce contracts so that the parties to the business deal act cooperatively" (Cosimano, 2004, p. 179). Financial institutions today "are responsible for the monitoring of investment projects for the in-

vestors so that the firm would not be left to their own devices and possible chat on the investment project. This is why financial institutions are given the fiduciary responsibility to disclose all relevant information about the [investment] project to the investor" (Cosimano, 2004, p. 184).

12. Among the six primary lenders that facilitated Enron's Special Purpose Entities (Cosimano, 2004, p. 180), key accounting entities in Enron's innovative bookkeeping, we find three of the major investment banks that needed to be bailed out by the government in our second crisis case; Citigroup, JP Morgan Chase, and Merrill Lynch.

13. The process of deregulation had allowed Enron to manipulate energy markets and pulled the US government into the center of this crisis. The deregulation of California's energy market in particular created the room for Enron to manipulate the sales of energy and the price of electricity at peak demand.

14. President George W. Bush had often worked to promote Enron internationally. Enron had contributed significantly to Republican representatives' election campaigns. TIME's reporter Daniel Kadlec noted in January 2002 that "the U.S. Justice Department announced last week that it was creating a task force, staffed with experts on complex financial crimes, to pursue a full criminal investigation. But the country was quickly reminded of the pervasive reach of Enron and its executives—the biggest contributors to the Presidential campaign of George W. Bush—when U.S. Attorney General John Ashcroft had to recuse himself from the probe because he had received $57,499 in campaign cash from Enron for his failed 2000 Senate re-election bid in Missouri. Then the entire office of the U.S. Attorney in Houston recused itself because too many of its prosecutors had personal ties to Enron executives—or to angry workers who have been fired or have seen their life savings disappear. Texas attorney general John Cornyn, who launched an investigation in December into 401(k) losses at Enron and possible tax liabilities owed to Texas, recused himself because since 1997 he has accepted $158,000 in campaign contributions from the company" (Kadlec, 2002).

15. "The White House later acknowledged that [Ken] Lay... had lobbied Commerce Secretary Don Evans and Treasury Secretary Paul O'Neill. Lay called O'Neill to inform him of Enron's shaky finances and to warn that because of the company's key role in energy markets, its collapse could send tremors through the whole economy. Lay compared Enron to Long-Term Capital Management, a big hedge fund whose near collapse in 1998 required a bailout organized by the Federal Reserve Board. He asked Evans whether the Administration might do something to help Enron maintain its credit rating. Both men declined to help. An O'Neill deputy, Peter Fisher, got similar calls from Enron's president and from Robert Rubin, the former Treasury Secretary who now serves as a top executive at Citigroup, which had at least $800 million in exposure to Enron through loans and insurance policies. Fisher—who had helped organize the LTCM bailout—judged that Enron's slide didn't pose the same dangers to the financial system and advised O'Neill against any bailout or intervention with lenders or credit-rating agencies" (Kadlec, 2002).

16. The way other financial crises have been solved by other countries during the Asian financial crisis of 1997 (Kim, 2004; Park, 2003; Yum, 2003) but also by the federal government during the Long Term Capital Management crisis (Lacasse, 2004).

17. The repeal came after 25 years and twelve failed attempts at reform, and $300 million spent on lobbying by the banking industry (Public Broadcasting System, 2003).

18. Another factor that seems to have had a significant impact was the extent to which firms were allowed to leverage themselves. Changes to the Net Capital Rule (U.S. Securities and Exchange Commission, 1934) allowed these investment firms to borrow more and more money to make investments with (see U.S. Securities and Exchange Commission, 2004). This way, less of the bank's own money (but more borrowed money) was used in these risky investments. As a consequence, when the investments crash, not only is the investment bank hurt, but also the firm or investors that loaned the money, their investors, and so on. This allowed investment failures to hurt many more actors than before. A final factor that seems to have presented perverse incentives that led to unethical conduct is the role of ratings agencies, like Moody's and Standard & Poor's, which grade risks of investments. These agencies assign risk grades to investments, allowing investors to *know* the risk of what they are buying without understanding all of the company's finances. The perverse incentives stem from the fact that the rating agencies are paid by the creator of the investments. If the rating agencies rate the created investments as high risk, making them harder to sell on the market, the investment bank will shop the various rating agencies to get a better rating. As a consequence, the rating agencies gave better-than-deserved ratings to many investments in order to keep getting business from the investment banks (Genzer, 2010).

19. Together, they owned or guaranteed half of all U.S. mortgages and had issued debt of $1.7 trillion (Paulson, 2010, p. 3).

20. One of the reasons the financial sector, particularly hedge funds, grew so rapidly between the end of the 1990s and 2008 was that pension funds that had been burned by the dot com collapse in 2000 were rushing to hedge funds to secure their investments for their retirement savers (Patterson, 2010, p. 11). Part of the financial crisis in 2008 was the fact that "hundreds of billions of hedge fund dollars marshaled by banks such as Morgan Stanley, Goldman Sachs, Citigroup, Lehman Brothers, Bear Stearns, and Deutsche Bank . . . were rapidly transforming staid white-shoe bank companies into hot-rod hedge fund vehicles fixated on the fast buck—or the trillions more in leverage that juiced their returns like anabolic steroids" (Patterson, 2010, p. 12).

21. Wall Street insiders have called this the Great Hedge Fund Bubble. "[I]t was truly a bubble—was the one of the most frenzied gold rushes of all time. Thousands of fund jockeys became wealthy beyond their wildest dreams. One of the quickest tickets to the party was a background in math and computer science" (Patterson, 2010, p. 12).

22. No one is lending money to anyone. The banks realize they do not know how much they owe and how much their investments are worth and therefore do

not trust that any other bank or firms know their balance sheets either, so they refuse to lend. The paper market freezes.

23. Scholars critical of the deregulation have also argued that these corporations' influence on Washington policy, through campaign contributions and interest group lobbying, had earned them disproportionate political influence, which made it essentially politically impossible for either the Republicans or the Democrats to simply let the market punish these actors to the extent they deserved.

24. The desire by the government to make loans available for more people to own homes in the United States started in the 1950s. In order to stimulate overall growth of the U.S. economy and the liquidity in its market, the U.S. government started Fannie Mae and Freddie Mac as two government agencies that would conform loans to the middle class (Stiglitz, 2010, p. 10). These two agencies were then privatized and run as private corporations while maintaining their overall purpose. The government's role in these corporations initial stage made the corporations' link to the U.S. federal government blurry. Some argue that the government intentionally left it blurry to encourage business with Fannie and Freddie, saying to investors "we support these guys, hint-hint nudge-nudge, do business with them" without actually promising in writing to support investments by Fannie and Freddie with the full force of the U.S. federal government (Davidson, 2008). While banks engaged in subprime lending, which induced the housing bubble and fueled the financial crisis, they argue that they simply did what the government wanted: to lend to poor people so they could buy houses, Fannie Mae and Freddie Mac did not get into subprime lending until well after other commercial banks had entered that market (Stiglitz, 2010, p. 10).

25. Examples of these kinds of inconsistencies were the government's choice to let Lehman Brothers fail, but to bail out Citibank and Goldman Sachs, and letting bank executives get away with getting their annual bonuses even though their banks were clearly in the red, but at the same time requiring workers for GM and Chrysler to take pay cuts due to the companies financial situation. Furthermore, the standard rules of capitalism proscribe that when a company goes bankrupt, shareholders lose everything and the people that own the company's debt or have other claims on the company (bondholders, union health funds, banks) become the new stockholders. This is what happened with the two automakers that were facing bankruptcy. The government (the Obama administration) forced the companies to declare bankruptcy and the government, who had earlier lent money to try and save the companies, then became the largest shareholders in Chrysler and GM. This was not the case, however, in several of the concurrent bailouts, like that of Bear Stearns, AIG, and Citigroup (Stiglitz, 2010, p. 43).

26. Enron can be seen as an Emperor said to be an exemplary dresser with exquisite taste, a leader in innovative fashion that sold like mad, and a corporate revolutionary that only the sharpest people got to work for. And everyone bought it.

27. Such as the care for individual citizens as victims of forces much larger than they are, applying the power of the government to suspend the rules in order to do good or avoid major societal damage, avoiding larger costs down the road.

28. Fundamental in the sense that they relate to the social contract between citizens and the state, the vestige of power in government actors, the role of the government as a lender of last resort, trust in government, and effective governance.

REFERENCES

Behind the real size of the bailout. (2009, December 21). *Mother Jones*. Retrieved December 30, 2010, from http://motherjones.com/politics/2009/12/behind-real-size-bailout

Boyd, C. (2004). The structural origins of conflicts of interest in the accounting profession. *Business Ethics Quarterly, 14*(3), 377–398.

CNN. (2002). *Explaining the Enron bankruptcy.* In CNN (Ed.): CNN. Retrieved February 10, 2004, from http://www.cnn.com/2002/US/01/12/enron.qanda.focus/index.html

Cordes, J. J. (2002). Corrective taxes, charges and tradable permits. In L. M. Salamon (Ed.), *The tools of government: A guide to the new governance.* New York: Oxford University Press, USA.

Cosimano, T. F. (2004). Financial institutions and trustworthy behavior in business transactions. *Journal of Business Ethics, 52*(2), 179–188.

Davidson, A. (Writer). (2008). The economist's nightmare: No bailout [Podcast]. National Public Radio (Producer), *Planet Money.* http://www.npr.org/blogs/money/2008/09/the_economists_nightmare_no_ba.html

Federal Deposit Insurance Corporation. (2006, May 2). *FDIC learning bank.* Retrieved May 4, 2011, from http://www.fdic.gov/about/learn/symbol/index.html

FERC. (n.d.). *The Western energy crisis, the Enron bankruptcy, and FERC's response.* FERC. http://www.ferc.gov/industries/electric/indus-act/wec/chron/chronology.pdf

Fooks, G. (2003). Auditors and the permissive society: Market failure, globalisation and financial regulation in the US. *Risk Management, 5*(2), 17–26.

Genzer, N. M. (2010, April 23). Will reform bill change rating agencies? *Marketplace.* Retrieved May 4, 2011 from http://marketplace.publicradio.org/display/web/2010/04/23/pm-credit-ratings-agencies-reform-bill-change/

Herszenhorn, D. M. (2010, May 21). Bill passed in senate broadly expands oversight of Wall St. *New York Times,* p. A1.

Howard, C. (2002). Tax expenditures. In L. M. Salamon (Ed.), *The tools of government: A guide to the new governance.* New York: Oxford University Press, USA.

Kadlec, D. (2002, January 13). Enron: Who's accountable? *Time.*

Kahn, A. E. (1988a). *The economics of regulation: Principles and institutions* (Vol. II). Cambridge, MA: MIT Press.

Kahn, A. E. (1988b). *The economics of regulation: Principles and institutions* (Vol. I). Cambridge, MA: MIT Press.

Kim, Y. H. (2004). *Daewoo group's crisis settlement.* Unpublished MPA Capstone project, Syracuse University, NY.

Kulik, B. W. (2005). Agency theory, reasoning and culture at Enron: In search of a solution. *Journal of Business Ethics, 59*(4), 347–360.

Lacasse, D. (2004). *The federal reserve and the long-term capital management crisis.* Unpublished MPA Capstone paper, Syracuse University, NY.

Michalowski, R., & Kramer, R. (2003). Beyond Enron: Toward economic democracy and a new ethic of inclusion. *Risk Management, 5*(2), 37–47.

Mitroff, I. I. (2004). *Crisis leadership: Planning for the unthinkable.* Hoboken, NJ: John Wiley and Sons.

Mörth, U., & Sahlin-Andersson, K. (Eds.). (2006). *Privat offentliga partnerskap: Styrning utan hierarchier och tvång?* Stockholm: SNS Förlag.

Park, D. H. (2003). *The currency crisis of South Korea in 1997.* Unpublished MPA Capstone Project, Syracuse University, NY.

Patterson, S. (2010). *The quants: How a new breed of math whizzes conquered Wall Street and nearly destroyed it.* New York: Crown Business.

Paulson, H. M. J. (2010). *On the brink: Inside the race to stop the collapse of the global financial system.* New York: Business Plus.

Pitt, H. (2002). *Written testimony concerning accounting and investor protection issues raised by Enron and other public companies.* United States Senate.

Public Broadcasting System. (2003, May 8). The long demise of Glass-Steagall. *Frontline: The Wall Street Fix.* Retrieved September 16, 2010, from http://www.pbs.org/wgbh/pages/frontline/shows/wallstreet/weill/demise.html

Ryssdal, K., & Dimsdale, J. (2008). Fed becomes "lender of last resort." In K. Ryssdal (Ed.), *Marketplace:* American Public Media. http://marketplace.publicradio.org/display/web/2008/10/07/fed/

Sims, R. R., & Brinkmann, J. (2003). Enron ethics (Or: Culture matters more than codes). *Journal of Business Ethics, 45*(3), 243–256.

Stanton, T. H. (2002). Loans and loan guarantees. In L. M. Salamon (Ed.), *The tools of government: A guide to the new governance.* New York: Oxford University Press, USA.

Stiglitz, J. (2010). *Freefall: America, free markets, and the sinking of the world economy.* New York: W. W. Norton & Company.

Svedin, L. (2008). *Pressured partnerships: Public and private sector cooperation in crises.* Paper presented at the Midwest Political Science Association Annual Conference. Palmer House Hotel, Hilton, Chicago, IL, April 3–6.

Taylor, C. (2002, May 12). California Scheming. *Time.*

U.S. General Accounting Office. (1997). *Financial crisis management: Financial crises in the 1980s* (Staff Study). Washington, DC: United States General Accounting Office.

U.S. Securities and Exchange Commission. (1934). *Net capital requirements for brokers or dealers.* Retrieved May 4, 2011 from http://taft.law.uc.edu/CCL/34ActRls/rule15c3-1.html

U.S. Securities and Exchange Commission. (2004). *Alternative net capital requirements for broker-dealers that are part of consolidated supervised entities.* Retrieved May 4, 2011 from http://www.sec.gov/rules/final/34-49830.htm

U.S. Securities and Exchange Commission. (2010). *The laws that govern the securities industry.* Retrieved May 4, 2011 from http://www.sec.gov/about/laws.shtml

Yum, B. R. (2003). *The 1997 Hanbo scandal as an initial trigger of the Korean financial crisis.* Unpublished MPA Capstone project, Syracuse University, NY.

CHAPTER 7

CHASING EVIL, DEFENDING ATROCITIES

Blame Avoidance and Prisoner Abuse During the War in Iraq

Sanneke Kuipers, Kasia Kochańska, and Annika Brändström

INTRODUCTION

In 2004, the world witnessed in horror, through a series of pictures that were leaked to U.S. media, how U.S. soldiers stationed in the Abu Ghraib prison had physically, sexually, and psychologically abused Iraqi prisoners (Hersh, 2004). The pictures instigated a heated debate on blame and accountability regarding the atrocities American troops had exposed their prisoners of war (POWs) to. The focus of criticism soon shifted up the chain of command to Secretary of Defense Donald Rumsfeld and the Bush administration's decision to disregard the Geneva Convention and apply the term *illegal* combatants in Iraq and Afghanistan.

Around the same time, U.K. soldiers stationed in Iraq were accused of similar practices: torturing prisoners and even killing one of their detain-

Ethics and Crisis Management, pages 119–140

ees.[1] Investigations disclosed that the body of the deceased suspect, who had never received a fair trial, sustained 93 separate injuries caused by severe physical abuse at the hands of his British captors.[2] The British army was quick to frame the situation as an "isolated, tragic incident," that every member of the regiment "bitterly regrets" (Stevenson & Weaver, 2009, para. 7). The case received much media attention within the U.K. and led to the conviction of a low-ranking army official but did not spark much of a debate on British army institutions nor did it seriously compromise the British Minister of Defence or other politically responsible actors.

That media accounts of unethical behavior in crisis situations lead to politicization and blame avoidance among responsible actors is hardly surprising. But why do blame game outcomes differ when violations of core values seem to be so similar? This chapter aims to shed new light on the relationship between unethical behavior in times of crisis and the accountability and blaming processes that follow. Does the ethical dimension by nature lead to a truth finding dialogue, and does it influence the debate on accountability and the outcome of blaming?

BLAME AVOIDANCE THEORY

Blame avoidance research identifies three strategies for officeholders trying to avoid responsibility for their own or subordinates' wrongdoings (Hood, Jennings, Dixon, Hogwood, & Beeston, 2009). These three strategies are (a) agency strategies: avoiding blame by limiting formal responsibility through delegation (cf. Hood, 2002); (b) policy strategies: avoiding blame by designing policies that obscure the causal relationship between officeholder and outcome of his or her decisions (cf. Pierson, 1994, Weaver 1986); (c) presentational strategies: avoiding blame by framing events and manipulating public and media perception (Brändström & Kuipers, 2003; Hood et al., 2009; McGraw, 1990). This study will focus on presentational strategies, after the blameworthy event has occurred. Presentational strategies constitute actual crisis management strategies as they aim to mitigate the (possible) eruption of a firestorm of criticism after a major public service mistake has taken place.

When things are perceived to have gone wrong in government, office holders will try to avoid responsibility. They can resort to rhetorical strategies to escape blame, including moves to deflect blame onto others. In defense, their opponents do the same. And so a *blame game* develops: a verbal struggle about the allocation of responsibility for policy mistakes or negative events. We claim there are three core components to the framing[3] strategies in blame games:

1. *Constructing severity*: depicting events as violations of core public values;
2. *Constructing agency*: depicting events as operational incidents or as symptoms of endemic problems;
3. *Constructing responsibility*: depicting events as caused by a single actor or by "many hands."[4]

A blame game is a staged process. It involves deliberate choices by actors to frame a particular failure and its causes. The selective adoption of framing strategies by political elites and their skills in adopting them will result in different outcomes of political blaming (Brändström & Kuipers, 2003). Let us first examine each of these strategies in turn.

Constructing Severity

The degree to which an event is framed as a violation of core public values (security, integrity, social justice, etc.) determines whether that event becomes "politicized"—subject of a critical political and societal debate. Actors will struggle to dominate this debate with their interpretations of the event. Personal, political, and organizational gains and losses are at stake in this process (Boin et al., 2008; Edelman, 1977, 1988; 't Hart, 1993). Media are explicitly biased toward negative events (good news is no news). Voters are also punishing officeholders harder for negative actions than rewarding them for good behavior. The negativity bias in electoral behavior instructs politicians to duck accountability whenever possible (Bloom & Price 1975; Lau 1985). Highlighting governmental failures is a powerful weapon in the hands of political opponents. Therefore, officeholders will seek to deprive their opponents of this opportunity by denying or reframing failure or by passing the buck to others (Brändström & Kuipers, 2003).

Following McGraw (1991), we distinguish blame avoidance from blame management.[5] Blame avoidance refers to the denial of blameworthiness or "severity": incidents are framed as inconsequential, not negative in their social implications, or as lacking political ramifications.[6] In the domain of misfortune, expert judgment, or confidentiality/secrecy, the blame game is likely to fade out. By contrast, if wrongdoings are framed as a violation of substantive values such as justice, democracy, liberty (Nelkin, 1975) or national security (Bostdorff, 1994; Buzan et al., 1998; Edelman, 1977), a blame firestorm may erupt. When a story about negative political performance does catch on, attempts at blame avoidance have run their course and give way to blame management strategies, which accountable actors employ to avoid being pinpointed as culpable and/or responsible for the problems that have been identified (McGraw, 1991, p. 1135).

Constructing Agency

Once journalists, interest groups, or oppositional politicians have detected a potential scandal, they will put questions about responsibility on the table. Whereas officeholders attempt to point at incidental, ad hoc causal factors in an otherwise sound system, their critics will portray any wrongdoings as epitomizing a much larger systemic failure (Brändström, *Kuipers, & Daléus,* 2008). So, in temporal terms, incumbent elites trying to manage blame will emphasize the immediate causes, such as *human error* or *rule violations,* by lower-level operators to explain what went wrong. By contrast, the accused will stress a broader time perspective in order to shift focus to powerful underlying causes, such as the relevant regulations, government cutbacks, organizational routines, and cultures tolerant of rule violation.[7]

Going back in time often means going up the hierarchy, from street-level operators to top-level strategic policymakers (Bovens & 't Hart, 1996). The latter are thus usually keen to narrowly define the scope of investigation and debate, while their critics will want to broaden the time horizon and deepen the scope of postmortems. Operators and middle managers who feel their superiors are trying to frame them as scapegoats will feed the debate by leaking implicating information about their superiors to media or opposition critics (Brändström & Kuipers, 2003). Successfully framing a failure in narrow technical terms decreases the likelihood of escalating blame games in terms of political implications and sanctions. Only if the problem becomes perceived in wider systemic terms will blame games affect political fates.

Constructing Responsibility

When the frame has been established on the agency dimension, the question remains who precisely should be punished. Incumbent policymakers tend to argue that the incident is the result of a network failure—a complex interplay of structures, actors, and decisions. Network causality makes responsibility for failures a matter of the proverbial *many hands.* If causality is dispersed, then any blame will have to be dispersed too, and sanctions are not administered to anyone (Thompson, 1980).

By contrast, pinning down the root of failure to individuals or parts of organizations will facilitate scapegoat solutions (Ellis, 1994; Jones, 2000; Rochefort & Cobb, 1994). When incumbent politicians succeed in defining such a diagnosis of a critical event, they can relieve pressure on themselves by signalling that they are ready to take steps: firing subordinates and implementing additional measures to deal with the problem (Brändström & Kuipers, 2003).

Synthesis: The blaming tree model

A blame game is a staged process, where each stage presents different alternatives, depicted in Figure 7.1 as branches of a *blaming tree*. These alternative options influence the course of the blaming process, resulting in any of four different outcomes. First, the event can be framed as either ad hoc or endemic, depending on the time perspective that becomes the dominant reference frame in the debates. Subsequently, both stand-alone incidents and systemic failures can be attributed to either complex networks or single actors. The resultant locus of blame is (a) the scapegoat, an isolated single actor failure; (b) the organizational mishap, an incident produced by "many hands"; (c) failing policymaker(s), responsible for shaping flawed policies and/or organizational malpractices; and (d) the endemic system failure, a structural problem implicating many actors in a range of organizations (Brändström & Kuipers, 2003).

Now, why and how do accountability processes lead to different outcomes? Comparative research will reveal under which conditions certain framing strategies are likely to be successful in (re)directing the postcrisis media onslaught, to avoid being blamed, to focus blame on others, or to

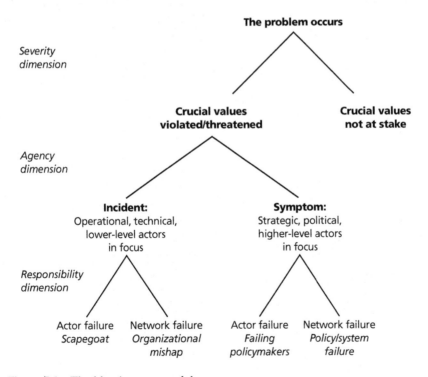

Figure 7.1 The blaming tree model.

successfully disperse blame among many hands. The *blaming tree* serves to analyze the cases and understand how the blame games evolved.[8] Our assumption here is that the behavior of accountable actors in the end defines the public's perception of the crisis as either a *single actor deficiency, organizational mishap, failing governance,* or a *system failure.* The behavior of actors is in turn influenced by a mix of situational, individual, and institutional factors.

Severity of Events: Public Shame and Blame?

The cases discussed here are the type where the severity of events seems beyond dispute, and in this chapter we will have a closer look at how actors managed blame and to what results. Pictures of abused POWs and the autopsy report of the tortured body indicate we are dealing with severe unethical behavior committed by American and British soldiers and possibly sanctioned by their governments.

Figure 7.2 portrays the critical attention by the *New York Times* and the *Guardian* on the abuse of the Iraqi prisoners from 2004 to 2010. The negative publicity toward the United States seems disproportional to that directed at the U.K., though from 2006 onward, attention to the British case in the *Guardian* shows an upward trend.

Given the fact that the allegations were similar, the question arises as to why these blame games took a different course and to what extent the countries' political leadership was held responsible.

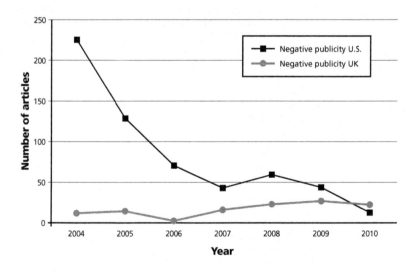

Figure 7.2 Negative publicity in the *New York Times* and the *Guardian.*

Before moving to an analysis of the blame management strategies that were employed in the two cases, we first need to substantiate our core claim that blame was attributed differently in the two cases. At the international level, criticism (including *naming* and *shaming*) of the United States and U.K. by intergovernmental organizations (IGOs), and nongovernmental organizations (NGOs) will indicate the level and direction of blame attribution. At the national level, we look at national public inquires performed after 2004 and to what extent these inquiries attributed responsibility to the U.S. and U.K. governments.

Blame on the International Arena: IGOs and NGOs

The International Criminal Court (ICC) provides 341[9] entries on the Abu Ghraib case (ICC Advanced Search Engine, 2010). The United States is a nonmember of the ICC, and therefore the court does not have legal rights to interfere with the country's affairs. Regardless, the ICC provides information (such as newspaper articles, the reports of NGOs, and democratic inquiries) regarding the cases of abuse of the Iraqi prisoners performed by the American soldiers as a form of "shaming." The ICC has no references to the British abuse case[10] and therefore does not intentionally shame the U.K. for the cases of POW abuse.

The United Nations search engine yields 29 entries on U.S. involvement in the abuse of Iraqi prisoners in Abu Ghraib and also links the Abu Ghraib events to other instances of U.S. torture. High Commissioner for Human Rights Navi Pillay depicted Abu Ghraib as an example of the United States violating the Convention against Torture (CAT), saying, "The Guantanamo and Abu Ghraib prisons...became high-profile symbols of the practice of torture. New terms such as 'water-boarding' and 'rendition' entered the public discourse, as human rights lawyers and advocates looked on in dismay" (UN News, 2009). The UN did not produce any documents regarding British abuse of Iraqi detainees. This indicates that the UN did not apply any sanction on the country in regard to that matter.

Table 7.1 presents the number of references to the U.S. and the U.K. cases of torture made by four different NGOs during the same time period.

TABLE 7.1 Number of References to the U.S. and U.K. Cases of Abuse as Reported by NGOs

Name of the NGO	# of entries U.S.	# of entries U.K.
Amnesty International	196	11
International Committee of the Red Cross	8	1
Centre for Research on Globalization	9	0
Human Rights Watch	213	3

Many more entries surfaced criticizing the United States than the U.K. during the same time period. NGOs recognized that the British offenses took place, but overall, they did not criticize British institutions, policymakers, or their positions. Criticism directed at the United States focused, apart from the specifics of Abu Ghraib, on bad leadership, long-standing malpractices, and the fundamental flaws in the U.S. War on Terror.

Blame on the National Scene: Public Inquiries

In order to identify culpable parties and assess the severity of their wrongdoings, national governments can appoint inquiries (by court procedures, parliamentary inquires, or other public audits) to hold individuals and organizations accountable.

Inquires in the United States

Between 2003 and 2008, the U.S. Army conducted five investigations into the interrogation methods applied to detainees by U.S. soldiers. In July 2003, Amnesty International had informed the U.S. Department of Defense (DoD) of the abuse.[11] The DoD asked General Ryder to investigate the allegations. On November 5, 2003, Ryder reported problems with all U.S.-held Iraqi prisons. Ryder's report (2003), however, focused only on recommendations, not on establishing culpability.

In January 2004, Lieutenant General Ricardo Sanchez, the senior officer in Iraq, appointed Major General Antonio Taguba to open an investigation into the cases of abuse performed by the 800th Military Police Brigade in the Abu Ghraib prison. They concluded that the Abu Ghraib units run by the military police "lacked discipline, had no training whatsoever and lacked leadership presence"[12] (Burlas, 2004, para.7). Furthermore, the abuse was framed as "systematic and illegal and suggested that the problem might be far reaching" (Lobe, 2004, paras. 10–11). Taguba requested legal action against the members of the U.S. Army and the two civilian contractors involved (Lobe, 2004, para. 8).

Army reports provided by Major General George R. Fay (2004) and later Lieutenant General Anthony R. Jones (2005) focused mainly on the role of intelligence units in the abuse of prisoners.[13] According to these reports, high-ranking officials knew of the abuse at Abu Ghraib but had failed to stop it. Fay's report concluded that the primary cause of the maltreatment was misconduct by a small number of soldiers, made possible by lack of leadership.

A bipartisan U.S. Senate report released in December 2008 concluded that Donald Rumsfeld and other senior Bush administration officials were responsible for the interrogation techniques performed in Guantánamo

Bay, Abu Ghraib, and Afghanistan (Morgan, 2008). In the executive summary of the report, General David Petraeus, commander of the U.S. forces in Iraq, stated that "the abuse of detainees in U.S. custody cannot simply be attributed to the actions of 'a few bad apples' acting on their own. The fact is that the senior officials in the United States government solicited information on how to use aggressive techniques, redefined the law to create the appearance of their legality, and authorized their use against detainees" (Senate Armed Services Inquiry Committee, 2008, p. xii).

Inquiries in the United Kingdom

The death of British captive Baha Mousa triggered three different inquires: by the royal military police, a court martial, and the Parliament. The royal military police investigation into Baha Mousa's death was completed in April 2004, but its findings never reached the public eye.

The U.K. army conducted their own investigation, which resulted in the detention of seven soldiers (Stevenson & Weaver, 2007, para. 7). The soldiers were charged with offenses of "inhuman treatment, battery and assault, manslaughter, perverting the course of justice, and, in the case of the three senior officers, negligently performing a duty" (Rasiah, 2009, p. 178). Only one soldier was convicted (Stevenson & Weaver, 2007).

Mousa's family demanded an independent inquiry (Norton-Taylor, 2004). In December 2004, the British High Court decided that an independent inquiry should be conducted. In May 2008, the Minister of Defence, Des Brown, finally ordered such a public inquiry into Mousa's death. He argued that the inquiries by the royal military police and the court martial had created more questions than answers about the incident (Baha Mousa Inquiry Committee, 2010).

Attributing Agency

As soon as the initial struggle over severity is over, and the perception of a crisis has taken hold, the question how this could have happened becomes highly relevant to political actors, institutional watchdogs, and other critics. The policymakers held responsible are more likely to downplay the scope of the events, whereas their opponents will try to present the crisis as a part of a bigger problem.

Abu Ghraib as a Structural Problem

The U.S. involvement in the Iraq war and the overall dissatisfaction with policies of the Bush administration (which had divided the country ever since its photo-finish victory in the 2000 elections) increased the belief that Abu Ghraib was part of a larger systemic failure. Additionally, Bush's second term lasted from right before the scandal in 2004 until 2008, allowing the opposition to collect near-complete evidence that the Abu Ghraib abuses were part of an endemic failure.

After the Abu Ghraib pictures were revealed, the Bush administration tried to portray the issue as a stand-alone incident caused by a few rotten apples. In reaction to the pictures, Defense Spokesman Larry DiRita said that "no responsible official of the Department of Defense approved any program that could conceivably have been intended to result in such abuses" (U.S. Department of Defense, 2004).

Former Vice-President Al Gore declared that the Bush administration "shamed America" with its policy on Iraq, and called for the resignations of Secretary of Defense Rumsfeld, CIA Director George Tenet, and National Security Adviser Condoleeza Rice, "What happened at that prison, it is now clear, is not the result of random acts of a few bad apples" Gore said. "It was the natural consequence of the Bush administration policy" (Gore, NYU speech, May 24, 2004).

It soon became public that the International Red Cross and Amnesty International had informed U.S. officials about abuse already taking place in 2003 (Lewis, Lichtblau, & Fleck, 2004; Schmitt, 2004). In response to this information, the U.S. Army conducted two separate investigations, resulting in contradictory guidelines on the interrogation of Iraqi detainees. The Miller Inquiry (September 2003) suggested that prison guards (who later became the offenders in the Abu Ghraib pictures) should be given the task of setting conditions for interrogations. The investigation led by General Ryder (November 2003), on the contrary, stated that the military police (prison guards) should not take part in interrogation procedures. A further problem in portraying the matter as an ad hoc incident was the Taguba Report (2004). The fact that crimes against the U.S.-held prisoners were being investigated and sanctioned even before the Abu Ghraib pictures reached the public eye added suspicion to the case.

The issue was fully politicized on June 22, 2004, when information about the so-called 2002 Secret Memos was made public. The memos signed by George W. Bush justified torturing al-Qaeda members as one way to reach the objectives of the War on Terror. Meanwhile, the President insisted repeatedly that "the U.S. does not torture and that's important for people around the world to realize" (Sullivan, 2009, p. 10)

From that moment on, the opposition and media searched for evidence that Abu Ghraib was another indicator of unethical behavior at the highest level of government. New facts supporting such claims started piling up. In July 2006, the U.S. Congress decided that the Third Geneva Convention indeed applied to members of al-Qaeda. Yet in 2007[14] and 2008,[15] the world learned that the Bush administration had continuously approved harsh interrogation methods on alleged al-Qaeda members.

High ranking officials' involvement in creating secret memos was finally confirmed in 2009 when President Barack Obama (elected in 2008) decided to make those documents public. As a newly elected Democratic president, Obama, who opposed the Iraq war and Bush's politics in general, had no interest in hiding the information. He could safely release the documents without being held accountable and had no interest in protecting his predecessor. Thus, together with the revealed torture memos, the case ended. The Secret Memos signed by representatives of the Bush administration (Attorney General Roberto Gonzalez and Department of Justice attorney John Yoo) confirmed full implication of high-level government officials and firmly supported that the Abu Ghraib case was a symptom of structural failure.

Baha Mousa as a Technical Error

The scope of discussion on the death of Baha Mousa has been stretched over the past years. Great Britain has had six different Ministers of Defence and a similar political turnover as the United States (welcoming Conservatives into office in May 2010). The number of high-level officials involved in the case, a broad time-frame, and a change in governing powers affected the accountability process and helped to frame the Baha Mousa case as a technical error.

When officials could no longer ignore the case of Baha Mousa, the reaction of long-term Minister of Defence Geoff Hoon was to portray the event as a one-time incident, framing it as a technical error. When presenting the case before Parliament in May 2004, Hoon insisted that "the unauthorized actions of a very few must not be allowed to undermine the outstanding work of tens of thousands of British soldiers and civilians" ("Iraqi families win," 2004). Until the end of his incumbency in 2005, Hoon opposed an independent inquiry into the Mousa case and the application of the European Convention of Human Rights (ECHR) (and therefore questioned that central public values have been violated), stating that: "the security situation [in Iraq] does not permit all deaths to be investigated in the same way as would happen in peacetime Europe" ("UK must investigate," 2004).

By the time John Reid was appointed Minister of Defence and the British High Court ruled that the ECHR applied to British troops in Basra, the opposition called for an independent inquiry into the Mousa case, and evidence that the unethical practice was common started piling up.[16] Following the steps of his predecessor Hoon, Reid claimed that the abuses were a technical error committed by a few rotten apples. Defending British soldiers' actions in Iraq, he questioned the decision by the High Court.

By contrast, Des Brown, who succeeded Reid in 2006, acknowledged that the ECHR applied to Basra and admitted that the British, although involving only a few soldiers, violated human rights of the Iraqis when applying their interrogation methods. Brown's nonaggressive, apologetic stance proved successful and finally, the creation of an independent inquiry diminished the opposition's argument that the government tried to cover up the case.

On May 12, 2010, the Labour Party passed the power to the Conservatives. Once in power, the members of the Conservative party had no interest in digging deeper into the matter and awaited the conclusions of the public inquiry.

Overall, the Labour cabinet managed to portray the Baha Mousa case as a technical, one-time error. The opposition did not succeed in framing the abuse as a bigger and more complex problem where the political system, rather than individual actors, would have been blamed. The constant changing of Ministers of Defence and a broad time-frame made it difficult to present the Baha Mousa case as an outcome of fundamental problems within British politics. Until the Baha Mousa inquiry presents it findings, the case will still be perceived as caused by a few rotten apples without system implications. The findings have not yet been published.

Assessing Responsibility: Single Actor or Many Hands?

After the frame has been established at the operational or strategic level, stakeholders are left with the question of whom to punish for the unwanted events. Operational incidents direct attention to lower-level actors (easy scapegoats). Alternatively, culprits in defense can always turn to the argument of a network failure, which leads to dispersing responsibility among the so-called *many hands* (Brändström et al., 2008, p. 174). If causality is dispersed, then any blame will have to be too.

If the unwanted event is perceived as a bigger, structural problem, higher level officials are in focus. Rotten apples become a *rotten barrel* in which the most senior leaders should be called to account (Brändström et al., 2008, p. 299). When even punishing top-level officials is insufficient, and events are seen as a systemic failure, painful reforms and drastic policy change are nearly inevitable (Brändström et al., 2008, p. 303).

Abu Ghraib: A Systemic Network Failure

Eleven lower ranking officials were charged with crimes in relation to the Abu Ghraib abuse. Charles Graner, a former Private First Class in the U.S. Army and the ringleader in Abu Ghraib was disciplined with the longest punishment delivered: 10 years in prison (Zernike, 2005, p. 1). Ex-Private Lynndie England, known also as *the lady with the leash*[17] received 3 years of detention (Mestrovic, 2006, p. 188).

By immediately sentencing the *few rotten apples* in court martials, the Bush administration intended to close the Abu Ghraib case and label it an isolated *ad hoc* failure. Nevertheless, scapegoating can be effective only when critical events are not (yet) widely perceived as endemic, structural problems. The discussion on Abu Ghraib had already moved from the people to the controversial policies of the Bush administration. When government's memorandums authorizing implementation of *enhanced interrogation techniques* were revealed in June 2004, the buck could no longer be passed.

To reallocate the blame, the White House pointed at Janis Karpinski, the Brigadier General responsible for the Abu Ghraib prison, who was relieved of her post as a commander of the 800th Military Police Brigade and demoted to the rank of colonel (Zagorin, 2006, para. 2).

When accused, the ex-general told the media of the administration's involvement in creating controversial policies resulting in torture practices. Karpinski explained that during a visit to the Abu Ghraib prison, General Geoffrey Miller[18] had said, "Look, you have to treat them like dogs. If they ever feel like anything more than dogs, you have effectively lost control of the interrogation" (Democracy Now, 2007, p. 5). Additionally, Karpinski stated, "It was clear the knowledge and responsibility goes all the way to the top of the chain of command to Secretary of Defense Donald Rumsfeld" (Zagorin, 2006, para. 2).

These accusations from Karpinski came on top of the Secret Memo's revealing government's involvement in authorizing the torture techniques. Critics therefore further zoomed in on the actions of Rumsfeld. Additionally, various investigations[19] into the Abu Ghraib scandal indicated the active involvement of officials at all levels in the hierarchy, including the very top.

In an attempt to stop further accusations, Rumsfeld apologized to the U.S. Congress, taking full responsibility for Abu Ghraib in May 2004. Rumsfeld offered his resignation to President Bush twice, but was on both occasions asked by the president to stay in office (BBC News, 2006, para. 17). "Bush believed that Mr. Rumsfeld was doing a 'fine job' at a very difficult time—when the nation was at war and the military undergoing major restructuring" (BBC News, 2006, para. 22).

In December 2008, the U.S. Senate found Rumsfeld responsible for the cases of abuse performed by American soldiers abroad. A bipartisan Senate report written by senators Levin and McCain concluded that Rumsfeld and other senior officials were to blame for the interrogation techniques used in Guantánamo Bay, Abu Ghraib, and Afghanistan (Morgan, 2008).

When the incriminating pictures were first made public, the primary reaction of the Bush administration had been to blame a few rotten apples and to portray the problem as an operational, one-time occurrence. The policymakers then intended to assign responsibility to General Janis Karpinski, which backlashed at the Bush administration, as the general started implicating the top of the chain of command. Additionally, the media found evidence that the Bush administration structurally permitted the use of illegal torture procedures in its detention centers in Afghanistan and Guantánamo Bay. This indicated a systemic failure, a crisis as a product of fundamentally flawed systems of policymaking or service delivery. This outcome makes major policy change hard to avoid irrespective of the political fate of the incumbent elite (Brändström & Kuipers, 2003, p. 303).

Aware of the increasing scope of the problem, the Bush administration felt forced to point at a culpable party within its own political camp. Rumsfeld seemed like the right person for the job. Rumsfeld drew the attention away from others involved in creating the controversial policies, including the President. Rumsfeld, admitting full responsibility to U.S. Congress in May 2004, had to close the case once and for all. However, it did not stop; the discussion on blame for Abu Ghraib did not cease, nor did it stop journalists from digging into evidence for other offenses in other prisons.

The more the evidence pointed to Rumsfeld's involvement in the Abu Ghraib scandal, the more the President seemed willing to keep him in office. Finally in 2006, Bush approved Rumsfeld's resignation after the Congressional elections. Rumsfeld was never convicted in court. After his resignation, more high-ranking officials became linked to the scandal. In December 2008, a few months before the end of Bush's electoral term, a report by the Senate Armed Services Committee into Abu Ghraib concluded that Rumsfeld and other Pentagon officials had created policies, from December 2001 onward, that eventually led to the prisoner abuse in Abu Ghraib (Shane & Mazetti, 2008).

Baha Mousa: An ad hoc Actor Failure

In the U.K., framing the death of Baha Mousa as an ad hoc incident allowed for the scapegoating of lower level officials. Although seven soldiers of the Queen's Lancashire Regiment were charged in a court martial in 2007 for their involvement in Baha Mousa's death, only one of them was convicted. All other charges were rejected due to lack of evidence (Rasiah, 2009).

When asked about responsibility regarding Mousa's death, Colonel Jorge Mendonca, the highest ranking military official to be charged, said, "As the commanding officer of that unit, yes, I do accept that responsibility" (Norton-Taylor, 2010b, para. 5). Mendonca temporarily stopped the buck. He did, however, express his belief that he was hung out to dry by his commanders (Norton-Taylor, 2010b, para. 5). A typical scapegoat for ritual sacrifice in the face of public criticism, he allowed senior office holders to survive scandal and demonstrate resolute crisis management (cf. Brändström & Kuipers, 2003, p. 298).

In the meantime, the lawyers working for Mousa's family managed in 2008 to instigate a public inquiry into his death. The investigation committee is presently (2010) investigating the involvement of the higher level officials (Shiner & Gregory, 2010, para. 1) and the role of the Ministry of Defence as an institution. The Commission concluded its hearings on October 14, 2010, its findings and conclusions are still to be expected at the moment. Only recently has evidence of other instances of abuse surfaced. The current independent inquiry into the Baha Mousa case revealed more indications of structural abuse (Norton-Taylor, 2010a). In 2009, Human Rights Watch launched a report presenting the U.K.'s involvement in torture committed on U.K. nationals suspected of terrorist activities in Pakistan. These abuses took place between 2003 and 2006 (Cobain, 2008a, para. 5, 2008b, para. 6).[20]

The British case initially showed a strong relation between the scope of the event and the allocation of blame. For a long time, the death of Baha Mousa seemed to be a stand-alone event and a technical error caused by a few rotten apples, allowing attribution of responsibility for the abuse to lower level officials.

CONCLUSION

The dynamics of the blame games on the two similar cases of detainee abuse by representatives of the government differed considerably. In the first years, the U.S. case seemed to grow bigger and bigger, unveiling more and more indications of endemic system failure. Meanwhile, the British discussion was not fueled by constant news of other instances of abuse. It would take until 2009 before additional evidence of British misconduct leaked out. In retrospect, the British government might have been no less guilty of structural violation of human rights than the Bush administration in the War on Terror. However, by the time the world could see the U.K. case in its true proportion, the responsible politicians had been replaced by their opponents, who had no interest in further escalating the issue. By contrast, the Bush administration took the full blaze of criticism during its incumbency, suffering at the hands of a host of critics who seized every opportunity to hammer another nail into Rumsfeld's coffin.

The analysis on the attribution of agency and responsibility within the respective cases shows an interesting deviation in the rhetorical defense of the accused. The Bush administration continued to insist that it did not torture people in the face of a shower of evidence to the contrary. Unintentionally admitting the widespread involvement of all levels of government, the White House first pointed to military employees on the ground in Iraq (such as Graner and England), then to their superiors (such as Karpinski), and then the top brass (Rumsfeld) in an attempt to contain the case. In the end, Rumsfeld had to hang in front of the White House.

The Blair government representatives initially reacted in much the same way as their U.S. counterparts, pointing to a few rotten apples that had committed specific incidental acts. However, simultaneously, successive Ministers of Defence in the U.K. emphasized that those acts were committed in a situation of war, and that it should perhaps be seen as excessive, but necessary acts in combating terrorism. The crucial difference here is that they managed to maintain credibility with the public and the media by admitting a controversial military approach. Six consecutive incumbent ministers shared responsibility over a 7-year period, which did the rest to disperse blame and avoid political consequences.

Both cases have strong ethical dimensions, and arguably some of the actions by both U.S. and U.K. actors could be judged as highly unethical. Comparative research implies that disregard of ethics in crisis management is likely to lead to bigger problems for government leaders. However, when analyzing the blame games that followed in the United States and in the U.K., there is no clear connection between unethical behavior in the prison abuse cases and the outcomes of the accountability process. Ethical considerations seem to have little place in the blame management strategies by incumbent elites, and ethical arguments cannot explain the difference in blame outcomes in the United States and the U.K.

Independent of how we judge the abuse, the British incumbents were more effective in managing an "ethics crisis" and more strategically reallocated blame compared with their American colleagues. The key to their effectiveness seems to be the proportionality of their reaction: a few British military were scapegoated while allegations were in correspondence with sanctions at that level, whereas the U.S. government tried to scapegoat soldiers when all levels of government were already implicated by the information revealed. Though of little help in making this world a better place in terms of ethical behavior in crisis management, the findings on credibility and proportionality in this study might very well prove insightful in future crisis cases.

NOTES

1. The case of Baha Mousa became public after a video showing the abuse was revealed. Seven Iraqi prisoners died in British detention in the first 2 months after the invasion, leading to an investigation by the military police (The Independent, March 17, 2010, para. 1).
2. Mousa was tortured to death one day after his detention.
3. A *frame* refers to "the production of facts, images and spectacles aimed at manipulating the perception and reaction to a crisis" (Boin, 't Hart, & McConnell, 2005, p. 88) and *framing* can relate to both the *use* and the *impact*

of frames (e.g., D'Angelo, 2002; DeVreese, 2003; Edelman, 1988; Eriksson, 2004; Iyngar, 1996; Kingdon, 1995; Schön & Rein, 1994).

4. The *problem of many hands* was first coined by Thompson (1980).

5. See also Sulitzeanu-Kenan and Hood (2005).

6. That is, beyond the realm of political affairs such as "the free market, the private sphere or matters for expert decision" (Buzan, Waever, & De Wilde, 1998, p. 29).

7. See an overview of such factors in Vaughan (1999).

8. The comparative design of this study allows us to delve deeper into these cases in order to identify specific factors that influenced the blaming process and, consequently, its outcomes.

9. All the information regarding the Abu Ghraib case can be found in the court's two official languages (English and French), where 93 references are to be found in English and as many as 242 are available in French (ICC Advanced Search Engine, 2010).

10. The only keyword yielding four entries is *Basra*, but these entries include no reference to the abuse by the British soldiers. The maltreatment of the Iraqi prisoners performed by the U.K. troops stationed in Iraq is known as the *Baha Mousa Case*. The pictures of Mousa's tortured body triggered the attention of the national media and served as a symbol of abuse of Iraqi detainees by British soldiers. Therefore *Baha Mousa* was used as keyword when searching for information on the abuse performed by British soldiers in Iraq. The supportive keywords when searching for information available on the matter were *Donald Payne* (a convicted soldier), *Basra* (a detention center where Mousa was interrogated), and *abuse/UK soldiers/Iraq*.

11. On July 23, Amnesty International announced that it had received reports regarding prisoner abuse performed by the Coalition forces (Associated Press, 2004).

12. An answer given by Taguba to one of the senators in reply to why Abu Ghraib happened.

13. The previous reports on crimes against Iraqi detainees were mainly focused on the lower ranking officials.

14. On the 4th of October 2007, the *New York Times* revealed new proof of the Department of Justice's 2005 memos serving as proof of harsh interrogation methods approved by Attorney General Roberto R. Gonzales (Rich, 2007).

15. The Justice Department disclosed a memorandum written by John Yoo in March 2003. The document permitted armed forces interrogators to apply torture methods in examining prisoners and stated that "wartime powers largely exempted interrogations from laws banning harsh treatment" (Johnston & Shane, 2008, para.3).

16. As of this writing (summer of 2011), there are 33 cases being investigated in relation to the U.K.'s involvement in instances of brutal behavior against detainees in Iraq (Batty & Percival, 2009, p.1).

17. In one of the pictures portraying the Abu Ghraib abuse, England is photographed with what appears to be a leash attached to one of the detainee's neck (Raleigh, 2004).

18. At the time Miller was sent to the Abu Ghraib detention center by Rumsfeld, he headed the Guantánamo Bay prison. The main purpose of Miller's visit to Abu Ghraib in 2003 was to increase the effectiveness of the interrogation techniques performed by the military intelligence (Pfiffner, 2005, p 314; Schlessinger, 2004, p. 33).

19. The Ryder Report (November, 2003); the Taguba Report (March, 2004); Fay and the Schlesinger Reports (August 2004); Report of the Senate Armed Services Committee (December, 2008).

20. The report, titled "Cruel Britannia: British Complicity in the Torture and Ill-treatment of Terror Suspects" (Human Rights Watch, 2009) describes cases of British individuals subjected to brutal interrogation methods performed by the Pakistani Intelligence Agency in cooperation with the U.K.'s Security Services (MI5) and the U.K.'s Secret Intelligence Agency (MI6).

REFERENCES

Associated Press. (2004, May 7). *Abu Ghraib timeline*. Retrieved from http://www.ap.org/abughraibtimeline/index=58yehe

Baha Mousa Public Inquiry Committee. (2010). Frequently asked questions. *The Baha Mousa Public Inquiry Website*. Retrieved on July 8, 2010, from http://www.bahamousainquiry.org/faqs_may09.htm

Batty, D., & Percival, J. (2009, November 14). Hundreds of uninvestigated Iraqi abuse claims against troops, says lawyer. *The Guardian*. Retrieved from http://www.guardian.co.uk/uk/2009/nov/14/iraq-abuse-claims-british-troops/print

BBC News. (2006, April 15). Rumsfeld resignation calls grow. *BBC News World*. Retrieved from http://news.bbc.co.uk/2/hi/americas/4908948.stm

Bloom, H. S., & Price H. D. (1975). Voter response to short-run economic conditions: Asymmetric effect of prosperity and recession. *American Political Science Review, 69*(4), 1240–1254.

Boin, A., 't Hart, P., & McConnell, A. *(Eds.)*. (2008). *Governing after crisis: The politics of investigation, accountability and learning*. Cambridge, MA: Cambridge University Press.

Bostdorff, D. M. (1994). *The presidency and rthetoric of foreign crisis*. Columbia: University of South Carolina Press.

Bovens, M., & 't Hart, P. (1996). *Understanding policy fiascoes*. New Brunswick, NJ: Transaction Publishers.

Brändström, A., & Kuipers, S. (2003) From "normal incidents" to political crises: Understanding the selective politicization of policy failures. *Government and Opposition, 38*(3), 279–305.

Brändström, A., Kuipers, S., & Daléus, P. (2008). The politics of blame management in Scandinavia after the tsunami disaster. In A. Boin, P. 't Hart, & A. McConnell (Eds.), *Governing after crisis: The politics of investigation, accountability and learning* (pp. 114–147). Cambridge, MA: Cambridge University Press.

Burlas, J. (2004, May 12). Taguba faults leadership for Iraqi detainee abuse. Lessons-learned go to MP schoolhouse. *Army News Service.* Retrieved from http://www.au.af.mil/au/awc/awcgate/army/052704_taguba.htm

Buzan, B., Waever, O., & De Wilde, J. (1998). *Security: A new framework for analysis.* Boulder, CO: Lynne Rienner Publishers.

Cobain, I. (2008a, April 29). MI5 accused of colluding in torture of terrorist suspects. *The Guardian.* Retrieved from http://www.guardian.co.uk/world/2008/apr/29/humanrights.uksecurity1

Cobain, I. (2008b, July 15).Torture: MPs call for inquiry into MI5 role. *The Guardian.* Retrieved from http://www.guardian.co.uk/world/2008/jul/15/human-rights.civilliberties

D'Angelo, P. (2002). News framing as a multi-paradigmatic research program: A response to Entman. *Journal of Communication, 52*(4), 870–888.

Democracy Now. (2007, October 24) Testimony of former Brigadier General Janis Karpinski, the former head of Abu Ghraib, for the French criminal procedure against former American Secretary of Defense Donald Rumsfeld. *Democracy Now.* Retrieved from http://www.fidh.org/IMG/pdf/doc_20_-_Karpinski_Testimony.pdf

De Vreese, C. H. (2003). Framing Europe: Television news and European integration. *Javnost/ The Public, 10,* 116–118.

Edelman, M. (1977). *Political language: Words that succeed and policies that fail.* New York, Academic Press.

Edelman, M. (1988). *Constructing the political spectacle.* Chicago: University of Chicago Press.

Ellis, R. (1994). *Presidential lightening rods. The politics of blame avoidance.* Lawrence: University of Kansas Press.

Eriksson, A. (2004, September 9–11). *The building of a EU military capability—A process of Europeanisation.* Paper presented at the fifth Pan-European conference of the Standing Group on International Relations, ECPR, The Hague, The Netherlands.

Fay, G. R. (2004). *AR 15-6 investigation of the Abu Ghraib detention facility and 205th Military Intelligence Brigade* (pp. 34–176). Report, partly produced by Major General George R. Fay, Investigating Officer. Washington, DC: U.S. Department of Defense.

Gore, A. (2004, May 26) Speech at New York University, see http://pol.moveon.org/goreremarks052604.html

't Hart, P. (1993). Symbols, rituals and power: The lost dimension of crisis management. *Journal of Contingencies and Crisis Management, 1*(1), 36–50.

Hersh, S. M. (2004). *Chain of command: The road from 9/11 to Abu Ghraib.* New York: HarperCollins.

Hood, C. (2002). The risk game and the blame game. *Government and Opposition, 37*(1), 15–37.

Hood, C., Jennings W., Dixon R., Hogwood B., & Beeston C. (2009). Testing times: Exploring staged responses and the impact. *European Journal of Political Research, 48,* 695–722.

Human Rights Watch. (2009, November 24). Cruel Britannia: British complicity in the torture and ill-treatment of terror suspects. *Human Rights Watch*. Retrieved from http://www.hrw.org/en/reports/2009/1/24/cruel-britannia

International Criminal Court. (2010) Advanced Search Engine, see http://www.icc-cpi.int/Menus/ICC/Search?ql=a

Iraqi families win right to challenge government. (2004, May 11). *The Guardian*. Retrieved from http://www.guardian.co.uk/uk/2004/may/11/world.iraq

Iyengar, S. (1996). Framing responsibility for political issues. *Annals of the American Academy of Political and Social Science, 546,* 59–70.

Jones, A. (2005). *AR 15-6 investigation of the Abu Ghraib detention facility and 205th Military Intelligence Brigade* (pp. 6–33). Report, partly produced by Lieutenant General Anthony R. Jones, Investigating Officer. Washington, DC: U.S. Department of Defense.

Jones, D. (2000). *Sultans of spin: The media and the new labour government*. London: Orion Books.

Johnston, D, & Shane, S. (2008, April 3). Memo sheds new light on torture issue. *The New York Times*. Retrieved from http://www.nytimes.com/2008/04/03/washington/03intel.html?scp=2&sq=Mr.+Yoo+torture+memo+2003&st=nyt

Kingdon, J. W. (1995). *Agendas, alternatives, and public policies*. New York: HarperCollins.

Lau, R. R. (1985). Two explanations for negativity effects in political behavior. *American Journal of Political Science, 29*(1), 119–139.

Lewis, N.A., Lichtblau, E., & Fleck, F. (2004, May 7). Outcry: Red Cross says that for months it complained of Iraq prison abuses to the U.S. *The New York Times*. Retrieved from http://www.nytimes.com/2004/05/07/world/struggle-for-iraq-outcry-red-cross-says-that-for-months-it-complained-iraq.html?scp=6&sq=Amnesty+International+Abu+Ghraib+torture&st=nyt

Lobe, J. (2004, May 2). Taguba Report on abuse may be tipping point in Iraq war. *The Albion Monitor*. Retrieved from http://www.albionmonitor.com/0405a/copyright/iraqphotos5.html

McGraw, K. M. (1990). Avoiding blame: An experimental investigation of political excuses and justifications. *British Journal of Political Science, 20*(2), 119–132.

McGraw, K. M. (1991). Managing blame: An experimental test of the effects of political accounts. *American Political Science Review, 85*(4), 1133–1157.

Mestrovic, S. G. (2006). *The trials of Abu Ghraib* (pp.187–192). Boulder, CO: Paradigm Publishers.

Morgan, D. (2008, December 11). U.S. Senate report ties Rumsfeld to Abu Ghraib abuse. *Reuters*. Retrieved from http://www.reuters.com/article/idUSN11414139

Nelkin, D. (1975). The political impact of technical expertise. *Social Studies of Science, 5,* 35–54.

Norton-Taylor, R. (2004, July 29). Iraqi witness tells of torture. Test case of deaths may curb British army abroad. *The Guardian*. Retrieved from http://www.guardian.co.uk/uk/2004/jul/29/iraq.military

Norton-Taylor, R. (2010a, March 16). Baha Mousa inquiry: Eight or more civilians died in British custody. *The Guardian*. Retrieved from http://www.guardian.co.uk/world/2010/mar/16/baha-mousa-inquiry

Norton-Taylor, R. (2010b, June 7). Baha Mousa death "a stain on army's character." *The Guardian.* Retrieved from http://www.guardian.co.uk/world/2010/
jun/07/baha-mousa-death-stain-army-character

Pfiffner, J. P. (2005, Fall). Torture and public policy. *Public Integrity, 7*(4), 313–330.

Pierson, P. (1994). *Dismantling the welfare state?* Cambridge, MA: Cambridge University Press.

Raleigh, N. C. (2004, July 5). Soldier charged with abusing Iraqi prisoners. *NBC.*
Retrieved from http://www.msnbc.msn.com/id/4927273/

Rasiah, N. (2009). The court martial of Corporal Payne and others and the future
landscape of international criminal justice. *Journal of International Criminal
Justice, 7*(1), 177–199.

Rich, F. (2007, October 14). Good Germans among us. *The New York Times.* http://
www.nytimes.com/2007/10/14/opinion/14rich2.html

Rochefort, D., & Cobb, R. (1994). *The politics of problem definition: Shaping the policy
agenda.* Lawrence: University of Kansas Press.

Ryder, D. J. (2003, November 6). *Assessment of detention and corrections operations in
Iraq.* Report produced by Donald J. Ryder, Provost Marshal General. Washington, DC: U.S. Department of Defense.

Schlesinger, J. (2004, August 23). *Final report of the independent panel to review Department of Defense detention operations.* Washington, DC: U.S. Department of
Defense.

Schmitt, E. (2004, January 7). Inquiry ordered into reports of prisoners abuse.
The New York Times. Retrieved from http://www.nytimes.com/2004/01/17/
world/inquiry-ordered-into-reports-of-prisoner-abuse.html

Schön, D. A., & Rein M. (1994). *Frame reflection: Toward the resolution of intractable
policy controversies.* New York: Basic Books.

Senate Armed Services Committee. (2008, December). *Inquiry into the treatment of
detainees in U.S. Custody.* Report 111-345, Executive Summary. Washington,
DC: U.S. Senate.

Shane, S., & Mazzetti, M. (2008, December 11). Report blames Rumsfeld for detainee abuses. *The New York Times.* Retrieved from http://www.nytimes.
com/2008/12/12/washington/12detainee.html

Shiner, P., & Gregory, T. (2010, July 3). This might be Britain's Abu Ghraib. *The
Guardian.* Retrieved from http://www.guardian.co.uk/commentisfree/2010/
jul/03/abu-ghraib-baha-mousa

Stevenson, R., & Weaver, M. (2009, July 13). Timeline: Baha Mousa case. *The Guardian.* Retrieved from http://www.guardian.co.uk/uk/2008/may/14/mousa.
timeline

Sulitzeanu-Kenan, R., & Hood, C. (2005, April) *Blame avoidance with adjectives? Motivation, opportunity, activity and outcome.* Paper presented at the ECPR Joint
Sessions, Granada, Spain.

Sullivan, A. (2009, October). Dear president Bush. *The Atlantic Monthly.* Retrieved
from http://www.theatlantic.com/magazine/archive/2009/10/dear-presi-
dent-bush/7663

Taguba, A. M. (2004, February 26). *Article 15-6 Investigation of the 800th Military Policy
Brigade.* Washington, DC: U.S. Department of Defense.

Thompson, D. F. (1980, December). Moral responsibility of public officials: The problem of many hands. *American Political Science Review, 74*, 905–915.

UK must investigate Iraqi civilian's death. (2004, December 14) *The Guardian.* Retrieved from http://www.guardian.co.uk/world/2004/dec/14/iraq.military

UN News. (2009, June 26). UN officials urge states to put an end to torture on International Day of Victims. *UN News Centre.* Retrieved from http://www.un.org/apps/news/story.asp?NewsID=31277&Cr=Torture&Cr1=

U.S. Department of Defense (2004) Statement from DoD Spokesperson Mr. Lawrence Di Rita, News Release, no 458-04, May 15 2004, see also http://www.defense.gov/releases/release.aspx?releaseid=7372

Vaughan, D. (1999). The dark side of organizations: Mistake, misconduct, and disaster. *Annual Review of Sociology, 25*, 271–305.

Weaver, K. (1986). The politics of blame avoidance. *Journal of Public Policy, 6*(4), 371–398.

Zagorin, A. (2006, November 10). Charges sought against Rumsfeld over prison abuse. *Time.* Retrieved from http://www.time.com/time/nation/article/0,8599,1557842,00.html

Zernike, C. (2005, January 16). Ringleader in Iraqi prisoner abuse is sentenced to 10 years. *The New York Times.* Retrieved from http://www.nytimes.com/2005/01/16/national/16abuse.html_r=1&scp=2&sq=Charles+Graner+sentence+to+10+years+&st=nyt

CHAPTER 8

COMMUNICATION IN CRISES OF PUBLIC DIPLOMACY

The Quest for Ethical Capital

Eva-Karin Olsson

INTRODUCTION

According to Beck and Sznaider (2006), the world society faces four axes of conflict: ecological, technical, terrorist, and moral crises.[1] Despite their initial differences, these axes of conflict share one essential feature in that "they cannot be constructed as external environmental crises but must be conceived as culturally manufactured actions, effects, insecurities and uncertainties" (Beck & Sznaider, 2006, p. 11). Moral crises naturally place the spotlight on ethical dilemmas in crisis management. This chapter will focus on leaders' crisis communication strategies in moral crises that take place in highly complex, religiously and culturally diverse, transnational environments. The multitude of potential stakeholders in the transnational arena place high demands on national leaders' ability to navigate the waters of competing cultural and religious rationales in terms of sense making, decision making, and communication. Whereas traditional theories of public diplomacy have focused on classical information campaigns directed at in-

Ethics and Crisis Management, pages 141–161

fluencing foreign audiences (Tuch, 1990), new public diplomacy emphasizes aspects such as the rise of a new public communication landscape, non-state actors, increased global transparency and interconnectedness, and a domestication of foreign policy (Gilboa, 2006; Melissen, 2005; Wang, 2006). This implies a move from traditional views of public diplomacy efforts focused on the projection of national images through mass media campaigns to a negotiated understanding constructed together with foreign publics; something which requires a dialogue-oriented communication.

Castells (2008) emphasizes the notion of public diplomacy as a dialogue between various social transnational collectives involved in an exchange of social and cultural meaning (p. 91). The diminishing role of nation states can be seen both in the mobilization of transnational organizations as well as in the countermobilization of nation states through various forms of intrastate organizations such as the EU. The transformation of the global public sphere is deeply intertwined with the development of new information technologies, which according to Castells (2008), are a necessary condition for the "emergence of spontaneous, ad-hoc mobilizations using horizontal, autonomous, networks of communication" (p. 86). According to Wang (2006), one of the most intriguing questions posed by new public diplomacy is the role of national governments; do they have enough credibility to be the first communicators in these processes or will the role be taken over by other actors such as NGOs or transgovernmental organizations? In this chapter, credibility is thought of as a form of capital inspired by Bourdieu's (1972) notion of actors competing for positions and power within a given social network or field by accumulating various forms of capital, which is the key asset in that particular field. Capital can then take various forms such as economic, cultural, political, and social. All forms of capitals are composed of an important symbolic dimension (Bourdieu, 1986). The assumption in this chapter is that in order to be able to act as credible communicators in moral crises, actors must not only enter the process by having enough credibility, that is, ethical capital, but also act in a way that makes it possible to maintain and gain ethical capital in the eyes of key stakeholders. One of the intriguing questions from a public diplomacy perspective is then how national leaders gain and preserve the ethical capital needed to function as communicators in moral crises that involve a number of players, among them various transnational movements? The chapter at hand aims to illustrate this process of capital accumulation and/or loss by demonstrating how the Swedish and Danish governments handled their respective Muhammad cartoon crises in terms of message formulation and stakeholder relations.

In terms of stakeholder management, dialogue-oriented communication is essential, which requires the ability for crisis managers to understand the values at stake for various stakeholders. If this is a challenge when managing crises at local and national levels, it becomes more so at the transnational arena. According to Beck and Sznaider (2006), a distinction can be made between cosmopolitanism and globalization. In the former case, actors' capacity for reflexivity is the main focus; that is, the process of globalizations from *within*. Globalization is a phenomenon with a long history, but "what is new is not the forced mixing but global awareness of it, its self-conscious political affirmation, its reflections and recognition before a global public via the mass media, in the news and in the global social movements" (Beck & Sznaider, 2006, p. 10). The core ethical challenge for decision makers at the global level is to understand and master the conflict between universal and heterogeneous values. According to Christians (2005), "communication ethics at this juncture has to respond to both the rapid globalization of communications and the reassertion of local identities. It is caught in the apparent contradictory trends of cultural homogenization and cultural resistance" (p. 12). Beck and Sznaider (2006) stress that what constitutes global norms, ethics, and reflexivity in today's globalized public sphere is an empirical question to be addressed.

The perspective taken in this chapter is that ethical communication ought to be understood as a process in which all stakeholders are being engaged in a fair and open dialogue aimed at reaching consensus (Bowen & Power, 1993; Christensen & Kohls, 2003). Following from this, reflexivity and dialogue at the global level have the capacity to develop increased cultural understanding and resilience where the breakdown of such dialogue might well result in national, social, and cultural tensions. One of the key questions becomes what crisis strategies promote dialogue and under which conditions do they do this? This chapter will explore the preconditions for such a crisis dialogue by focusing on leaders' stakeholder management and the values involved in message formulation.

In order to address the question above, two cases of public diplomacy crises have been selected based on how the communication strategies deployed by national governments escalated or mitigated the crisis at hand. The selected cases are the Danish government's handling of the Muhammad cartoon crisis in 2005, where the actual (mis)management of the crisis made it escalate; and the Swedish government's handling of the so-called roundabout incident in Sweden in 2007, where decision makers managed to mitigate a crisis in the making.[2] The cases are analyzed using a process-tracing approach to crisis management that allows the researcher to disentangle the process by identifying key actors' processes (Stern, 2001). My interest rests primarily with how stakeholder management can, and does, contribute to *crises of management* (see Roux-Dufort, 2007; Smith, 2006), that is, how failed management in the *incubation* period of a crisis can later lead to a full-fledged crisis. In order to examine the interplay between actors' strategic communication and stakeholder interpretations, the developments in each of the two empirical crises, the so-called *crisis escalation phase*, has been distinguished in each case (inspired by Smith, 2006). The notion of escalation is important in order to show how the different types of communication challenges facing the governments at various stages in the process, and how addressing these challenges, raises or lowers the crisis temperature. As noted by Bowen and Power (1993), crisis decisions related to ethical communication ought to be examined through a process-tracing approach, which takes into account the information available to decision makers at the time, rather than the information we have with 20–20 hindsight. This is particularly important in the two cases presented here, since the Swedish government had already witnessed the effects of the Danish mismanagement of the Muhammad cartoon crisis. With the sequencing of these crises in mind, it is important to note that the Swedish management might not have been more ethical in an altruistic sense but might well have been more ethically effective. While pursuing the questions about what crisis strategies promote dialogue and under which conditions, I will draw on scholars advocating that we need to apply communication theories to the study of public diplomacy in order to gain a better understanding of the communication dimension inherent in these processes (Ammon, 2001; Gilboa, 2008; Signitzer & Coombs, 1992; Zhang, 2006). The chapter concludes with a discussion of the implications of the case study results on the potential for effective and ethical/legitimate crisis communication management in the area of public diplomacy.

ETHICS IN CRISIS COMMUNICATION

The bulk of crisis communication theory has developed in corporate settings focusing on issues such as image repair (Benoit, 1997), reputational assets (Coombs & Holladay, 2002) and responsibility framing (Coombs, 1998; Siomkos & Shrivastava, 1993). Studies of political crisis communication have foremost focused on responsibility framing and the development of blame games in the crisis aftermath (Brändström & Kuipers, 2003; Brändström, Kuipers, & Daléus, 2008; De Vries, 2004; Meyer, 1999). Taken together, research in the field of crisis communication has focused more on *what* to communicate, in terms of communication strategies, than *whom* to communicate with, which is focused on stakeholder relations. Even less attention has been paid to the link between stakeholder management and communication strategies (Stephens, Malone, & Bailey, 2005). In this chapter, stakeholder management, message formulation, and the links between the two will be discussed, with the understanding that ethical communication is a process in which all stakeholders are engaged in a fair and open dialogue aimed at reaching consensus (Bowen & Power, 1993; Christensen & Kohls, 2003).

The management of stakeholder relations revolves around how organizations create and maintain strategic relations (Freeman, 1984). Crisis management research focused on stakeholder relations in acute crises depicts the main managerial challenges as associated with sense making and identification. By placing the emphasis on identification of stakeholders, the scope of research moves away from traditional communication management aimed at information dissemination and toward organizational tasks such as observation, interpretation, and choice (Hale, Dulek, & Hale, 2005). In terms of sense making, the challenge consists of the tendency for crises to introduce new and previously unknown stakeholders (Ulmer & Sellnow, 2000). Decision makers are often caught offguard by the demands posed by new stakeholders and by their own tendency to focus on stakeholders with whom they are acquainted and who initially appear the most powerful (Christenson & Kolhs, 2003; Ulmer & Sellnow, 2000). According to previous research in the field, crisis communicators tend to regard stakeholders as a homogenous group, ignoring cultural and religious differences (Falkheimer & Heide, 2006). As a way of circumventing this surprise element, Pauchant and Mitroff (1992) propose a diagnostic model for stakeholder identification in crises based on "emotional, ecological, social, ethical, medical, moral, spiritual, aesthetic, psychological, and existential" (p. 129) criteria.

Acquier, Gand, and Szpirglas (2008) emphasize the link between stakeholders and issue identification, since crises tend to involve a set of often intertwined subcrises. This means that crisis communication has to be conducted simultaneously with a variety of stakeholders involved in these subset issues. Due to stakeholder movements between different issues, failed stakeholder communications in one subcrisis will inevitably affect relations in other subcrises. Furthermore, stakeholders' framings and actions also impact the crisis process, making it impossible to treat stakeholders' interests as external and independent variables (Acquier et al., 2008, p. 111). Stakeholders are not just passive receivers of information but actors in their own right, with a potential to impact crisis developments and outcomes. If we define ethical crisis communication as a process in which all stakeholders are engaged in a fair and open dialogue (Bowen & Power, 1993; Christensen & Kohls, 2003), there is no obvious trade-off between ethical and effective crisis management, since the inclusion of relevant stakeholders makes promotion of both values possible. Rather, as argued by Alpaslan, Green, and Mitroff (2009), normative stakeholder management in crises is intrinsically linked to the pragmatic approach of solving the actual crisis at hand in a way that is beneficial to the organization managing the crisis. The assumption here is that the promotion of universal values is more beneficial to organizations managing crises than advocating particular values. However, moving from single organizations to national governments, we can expect the picture to become more complex, where political actors have to balance different interests or strategically pursuing one interest at the expanse of others. As advocated by Lindholm and Olsson (2011), crises of public diplomacy confront national governments with the challenge of playing a multilevel game. From the perspective of ethical crisis communication, actors have to balance particular and universal values in order to promote dialogue with various key stakeholders.

CONTEXT

Since 2001, Denmark has been governed by a coalition consisting of the Liberal Party (Venstre), the Conservative Party (Konservativ Folkeparti), and the nationalistic party, Danish People's Party (Dansk Folkeparti). Throughout the 2000s, domestic politics in Denmark has focused on taking a tough stance on immigration and asylum (Holm, 2006). Denmark has shown a high degree of intolerance against Muslims in the media in high-level politics during this period. Throughout 2005, there was an ongoing public debate about a cultural clash between European and Muslim norms and values. One of the most influential Muslim organizations in the Muhammad cartoon crisis was the Community of Islamic Faith in Denmark. This organization had for a long period of time been critical of the Danish government for creating a general Islamophobia in the Danish public debate. The background to the publishing of the cartoons was that of the Danish writer Kåre Bluitgen's discussion in the Danish media of the difficulties involved in finding an illustrator for his children's book about the prophet Muhammed. The editors at the newspaper, *Jyllands-Posten,* came up with the idea of giving a number of illustrators the task of drawing their own images of the prophet Muhammad. The challenge was accepted by 12 illustrators, and Kurt Westergaard drew the most well-known of the cartoons, a picture portraying the prophet Muhammad in a turban shaped like a bomb and on which the Muslim confession of faith was written (Lindholm, 2008). According to Hervik (2008), the Danish Muhammad cartoon crisis centered on three main frames in terms of values, where the most dominant frame was the construct of the free press in opposition of censorship and the fear of Islam. The second prominent frame was a construct of freedom of speech with limitations, and lastly, the third frame was a counterreaction to the first, based on a construct of demonization of Muslims as the issue, not free speech (Hervik, 2008, p. 60).

In Sweden, a new government was elected in the fall of 2006. Fredrik Reinfeldt was elected the new prime minister of a right-center coalition consisting of the Liberal party (Folkpartiet), the Liberal party (Centern), the Conservative party (Moderaterna), and the Christian Conservatives (Krist-demokraterna). Sweden did not take part in the coalition invasion of Iraq in 2003, and Prime Minister Göran Persson stated that the invasion violated the UN charter (Axelsson, 2003).[3] Sweden had problems with extreme right groups and segregation in the early 2000s, but did not have a large nationalistic political party like the Danish People's Party. In 2007, Sweden had the greatest number (36,207) of asylum seekers of all EU states, despite its small size. Compared to Denmark, Sweden had on average nine times more applicants in absolute terms or 5.4 times as many asylum seekers per capita between 2002 and 2007 (Migrationsverket, 2009).[4] In July 2007, the management of a local art gallery in rural Sweden decided to remove three drawings of the Prophet Muhammad by artist Lars Vilks that it had had on display. The gallery's management referred to the events in Denmark and its desire to avoid problems for Swedes abroad and trouble for the gallery itself. As the debate intensified, Vilks received an increasing number of threats, including death threats. Vilks also submitted his drawings to an exhibition at a renowned art school in Blekinge, Sweden. In the middle of August 2007, Vilks' drawings were rejected, with the school's management citing that they feared for the safety of their students, teachers, and visitors.

ANALYSIS

Escalation Phase One

The Danish Government: Spinning the Free Speech Frame
 The first indication of the cartoons' offensive nature came at the beginning of October 2005, when a number of Muslim organizations, among them the Community of Islamic Faith, reacted to the publication of the cartoons. The Community of Islamic Faith responded to the publication by sending a protest to the Minister of Culture. He did not respond to their letter until the beginning of February 2006, when he redirected the letter to the prime minister and the Foreign Ministry.[5] The second impetus came September 30, the same day the cartoons were published, as a group of diplomats at a reception in Copenhagen started discussing the cartoons. Following the reception, Egypt's ambassador to Denmark, Mona Omar, with support from the ambassadors from Saudi Arabia and Iran, took the initiative to assemble a number of representatives from Muslim countries[6] and drafted a letter criticizing the publication of the cartoons. They expressed their concern that the publications were a sign of increasing Islamophobia in Denmark, and they requested a meeting with the prime minister (Thomsen, 2006). The letter was received by the prime minister's office on

October 12, but the Danish prime minister was on a trip and did not read the letter until a couple of days later. Prime Minister Rasmussen felt that the ambassadors were interfering with Danish domestic politics, and the Muslim ambassadors' request for a meeting was subsequently rejected in a letter posted on October 21, 2005. In his letter, the Danish prime minister asserted the country's principle of a free press and stated that any criticism regarding the publication should be addressed to *Jyllands-Posten,* not to the Danish government. The prime minister wrote:

> Danish society is based on the respect for freedom of expression, on religious tolerance and on equal standards for all religions. Freedom of expression is the very foundation of Danish democracy. Freedom of expression has a wide scope and the Danish government has no means of influencing the press. However, Danish legislation prohibits acts or expressions of a blasphemous or discriminatory nature. The offended party may bring such acts of expression to court, and it is for the courts to decide in individual cases. (Larsen & Seidenfaden, cited in Hervik, 2008, p. 65)

The prime minister conveyed the message that the Danish government would not interfere with the publication choices of free newspapers and that he did not intend to take action against *Jyllands-Posten.* He further stressed that the Egyptian and Saudi ambassadors had no legitimate right to discuss Danish immigration policy with the Danish prime minister. Egypt continued to put pressure on the Foreign Ministry and indicated that it was considering taking further action on the issue.

The Swedish Government: Remaining Silent

The rejection of Wilk's drawings by the Swedish art exhibition spurred a national debate among artists, cultural journalists, and individual Muslim debaters. On August 18, 2007, the regional Swedish newspaper *Nerikes Allehanda* reacted to the debate by publishing an editorial titled "Rätten att förlöjliga en religion" (The right to ridicule a religion), together with one of the drawings by Lars Vilks, depicting the Prophet Muhammad as a roundabout dog.[7] The publication spurred a group of 60 Muslims to hold a demonstration outside the newspaper's office on August 24. The demonstrators handed a letter to the newspaper's editor demanding an apology for what they perceived as a religious and cultural insult. The editor, however, refused to apologize.

At the end of August 2007, several other newspapers, among them Sweden's largest daily newspapers,[8] had followed *Nerikes Allehanda*'s lead and had also published the drawing. The initial international reaction came in late August as the Swedish *charge d'affairs* in Iran was summoned to Iran's Ministry of Foreign Affairs. Iran officially condemned the publications as offensive. The initial reaction from the Swedish government was not to comment on this protest (Dagens Nyheter, 2007a). In Sweden, two Muslim organizations (the local Islamic Cultural Center in Örebro and the National Islamic Community in Sweden) entered the domestic debate by threatening to take the case to court, claiming that their freedom of religion had been infringed. On August 30, Pakistan summoned the Swedish *charge d'affairs* to receive an official protest. Pakistan also stated that it intended to bring the case before the Organization of the Islamic Conference. The Organization of the Islamic Conference also strongly condemned the publications and urged the Swedish government to take action against the publishers and to make an official apology. Swedish flags and dolls depicting Prime Minister Reinfeldt were burned in Lahore and Karachi, Pakistan (Högfeldt, Sander, & Larsson, 2008). A second demonstration, arranged by the local Islamic Cultural Center in Örebro and the Swedish Muslim Council, was held outside the news office of *Nerikes Allehanda*. However, other Swedish Muslim organizations, including the National Islamic Community in Sweden, were becoming increasingly worried by the international reactions and committed to actively communicate a less radical view to Muslims abroad and stressing that the matter could and should be handled in Sweden.

The National Islamic Community in Sweden is a natural leading body of Muslims and Muslim organizations in Sweden. Following the Danish caricatures crisis, and well before the Lars Vilks incident, the organization called for a meeting aimed at discussing a possible similar event in Sweden. The National Islamic Community in Sweden then set their priorities: a potential crisis should be treated as a national and not international crisis, in order to show solidarity with Sweden's interests at home and abroad. They also decided to insist on the need to take both freedom of speech and freedom of religion into account when communicating with their stakeholders. However, the organization did not get involved at the initial stage, hoping that the incident would be contained at the local level. As international pressure mounted, however, the organization started to communicate through formal and informal channels with Muslim communities around the globe, urging the issue to be left for Sweden to resolve domestically (Benaouda, cited in Edling, 2009).

The Danish and Swedish governments differed substantially in their initial reactions to the crises. The Danish government brushed off requests for meetings from Muslim organizations and foreign ambassadors, referencing the constitutional right to free speech in Denmark. In Sweden, the government remained largely silent and absent from the debate during the first phase of the 2007 crisis.

Escalation Phase Two

The Danish Government: Relying on Traditional Diplomatic Channels

During October and early November, Egypt continued to put diplomatic pressure on Denmark and demanded that the Danish government clarify its standpoint with regard to the cartoons.[9] The Egyptian foreign minister urged all of the ambassadors representing the rest of the Arab world to talk to their respective heads of state about how offensive the cartoons were. The Danish prime minister and the Minister of Foreign Affairs continued to brush off the matter and referred to the situation as a domestic issue of freedom of speech. This was also the message that the government communicated at its press conference on October 30, 2005, which it repeatedly stated to the Egyptian Ministry of Foreign Affairs throughout November and December 2005 (Lindholm, 2008).

The Danish Minister of Foreign Affairs initially received information that Egypt was going to take its complaint to the UN (Møller, cited in Thomsen, 2006, p. 86). In response, he sent a letter to Egypt's ambassador in which he warned of an escalation and, in an attempt to curb such tendencies, proposed a direct dialogue between the two countries. Egypt accepted, and the proposed meeting took place in connection with a conference in Bahrain on November 11, 2005. Denmark considered the issue settled after a meeting, since none of the Muslim representatives from the foreign ministries present had approached Prime Minister Rasmussen or Foreign Minister Møller concerning the cartoons. In mid-November, however, Egypt sent a letter to the Danish Foreign Ministry in which Egypt again demanded an explanation from the Danish government regarding its support of *Jyllands-Posten's* campaign against Islam, as they described it. The Danish Foreign Ministry reacted with surprise to the letter, since they thought the issue had been settled in Bahrain (Lindholm, 2008).

The Swedish Government: Emphasizing the Need for Mutual Respect

In the Swedish debate, there was growing unease with the Swedish prime minister's silence, and domestic criticism was mounting. The government's first official statement came at a press conference on August 31, scheduled to address a different issue, but journalists started to ask questions about the developing crisis. This first government response came 13 days after the Swedish publications of the pictures and 4 days after the formal protest from Iran. In his first statement, Prime Minister Reinfeldt said,

> I think it is important to say two things. Firstly, we are eager to ensure that Sweden remains a country in which Muslim and Christians, people who believe in God and people who do not believe in God, can live side by side in a spirit of mutual respect...We are also eager to stand up for freedom of

expression, which is enshrined in the constitution and comes naturally to us, and which ensures that we do not make political decisions about what gets published in newspapers. (Olsson and Ingvarsson, 2007)

The statement from the Swedish prime minister was more tolerant and open in nature than the Danish reactions. While it is not clear why there was such a delay in addressing the issue, the Swedish prime minister defended his rather sluggish reaction by stating that "there is a risk of signaling that the government has role to play in this when it does not" (Sveriges Radio, 2007). The statement signaled that the government's silence had been a strategic choice aimed at distancing the government from the controversy around the publications.

During this escalation phase, it is clear that the two governments differed in their message formulation, with the Danish government insisting on a free speech frame, whereas the Swedish prime minister also emphasized the value of religious freedom.

Escalation Phase Three

The Danish Government: Initiating a New Communication Strategy

Like in the first escalation phase, the Danish government rejected further requests for dialogue made by the Community of Islamic Faith and the Muslim diplomats. This led representatives from the Community of Islamic Faith in Denmark to contact religious and governmental leaders in Egypt, Saudi Arabia, Lebanon, Syria, and Turkey, and meetings were convened in November and December.[10] The Community of Islamic Faith brought a package of articles, letters, and pictures from Danish newspapers, including the 12 cartoons, to the meetings (Thomsen 2006, p. 82). Except for the official meetings, the Community of Islamic Faith communicated their framing of the event through transnational and personal religious networks (Lindholm, 2008).

The activities prompted a series of meetings in December between the Egyptian and Danish governments, in which the Danish government tried to curb the growing resentments. The intensity of feelings expressed and the heated debates at these meetings made Danish Prime Minister Rasmussen realize that the Danish communication strategy needed to be modified to convey a message that could satisfy both the domestic Danish audience as well as Muslim audiences abroad (Lindholm, 2008). The shift came in Rasmussen's New Year's speech, where, despite any mention of the cartoons, he underlined the importance of tolerance and respect for religious and ethnic diversity.

During the past year, we have witnessed a heated debate about freedom of speech, and limits to freedom of speech. There are some who find that the tone of the debate has become too shrill and unpleasant. I wish to state this very clearly: I condemn any expression, action or indication that attempts to demonize groups of people on the basis of their religion or ethnic background. It is the sort of thing that does not belong in a society that is based on respect for the individual human being. We have a long history of extensive freedom of speech in Denmark. We are to speak freely and present our views to each other in a straightforward manner. However, it must be done in mutual respect and understanding. And in a civilized tone of voice. And fortunately, the tone of the Danish debate is in general both civilized and fair. There have been a few examples of unacceptably offensive expressions. And as a matter of fact, they have come from more than one party to the debate. We must strongly repudiate those expressions. (Rasmussen, 2006)

The prime minister's New Year's speech showed a widening of the problem frame by including not only freedom of speech but also the need for respect when exercising this right. The main message communicated an image of Denmark as a secular society that safeguards the rights of individuals, women, and the freedom of speech.

The Swedish Government: Proposing a Direct Dialogue with Muslim Stakeholders

Afghanistan joined Iran and Pakistan in condemning the Swedish publications. The day Afghanistan expressed its criticism, the Swedish prime minister participated in an interview on Swedish radio and was asked about his late and lame response to national and foreign protests regarding Vijk's published pictures. He responded again by emphasizing the separate roles played by the principle of free speech, him as prime minister, and the need for tolerance and respect with regard to different religions. He also encouraged and thanked the National Islamic Community in Sweden for the initiatives it and other Muslim organizations in Sweden had taken to curb the intensification of moral outrage (Sveriges Radio, 2007). Not everyone agreed with the Swedish prime minister's position, and an editorial in the most influential Swedish newspaper urged the prime minister to take a stronger stand on the principle of free speech (Dagens Nyheter, 2007b). During the days that followed the interview, Egypt and Jordan joined the list of countries that condemned the Swedish publications and demanded legal action. As a response to these developments, a group of Swedish Islamic organizations created a crisis group focused on providing Arabic ambassadors and Arabic media with factual and correct information regarding the unfolding events (Thurfjell, 2007).

On September 4, 2007, Swedish Prime Minister Reinfeldt met with representatives for key Muslim organizations in Sweden. Reinfeldt explained his initiative to meet by saying that "the situation is much more serious than what one can deduce from Swedish media. There is an increasing risk that this will spread. . . . I feel a responsibility to make a stronger effort to mitigate the situation. I want to give my sincere thanks to the Muslim organizations that are acting in a wide area to try to mitigate the risk that reactions escalate further" (Carlbom, 2007). Again, he stressed that "I am the first to regret that people now feel offended and insulted. I would personally never deliberately act in way that would be perceived as provoking or insulting towards other religions" (Regeringskansliet, 2007). The government and the Swedish Muslim communities present decided, out of a joint fear of crisis escalation, to coordinate their communications on the issue. According to Edling (2009), this decision was crucial to the Swedish government's credibility in communicating with Muslim organizations as well states. On September 7, 2007, Reinfeldt, on his own initiative, met with 22 Muslim ambassadors. According to a statement by the government, all parties were pleased with how the meeting went and called for further dialogue (Högfeldt et al., 2008, p. 80).

This was the culmination the Swedish crisis, and negative foreign reactions and foreign media attention sharply declined after this point. In Denmark, the opposite was true. Despite the modification of the government's position introduced in Rasmussen's New Year's speech, the Danish Islamic Faith Community continued to lobby against the Danish government in international arena.

Escalation Phase Four

The Danish Government: Facing a Crisis of Public Diplomacy

In the middle of January 2006, Internet sites and text messages were circulated throughout the Arab world advocating a ban on Danish goods. Furthermore, the Saudi ambassador to Denmark was called home, which finally made Denmark realize that it was facing a diplomatic crisis. The Danish government responded to the situation by arranging an internal meeting on January 29 to discuss possible Danish strategies toward Saudi Arabia. According to one of the civil servants attending the meeting, Denmark had been caught offguard and lacked a clear grasp of the situation (Lindholm, 2008). The Danish strategy was to try to shift the focus from Denmark by making it into a more general international issue concerning the clash of Western and Muslim values. In order for the strategy to succeed, however, Denmark needed the support of the EU. What was troubling to Denmark was that other EU countries had earlier made clear that they did not want to get involved. In addition, it was clear that Denmark needed to change its communication strategies. The crucial problem was how to accomplish this without having the prime minister apologize for his previous stance on the issue. The strategy chosen was to have the prime minister apologize for any potential offense he might personally have made against Islam as a religion (Danish prime minister's office, 2006).

The changes did not have the intended effects, and on January 30, 2006, Danish flags were burned by protesters in the West Bank during violent demonstrations. These incidents made the Danish prime minister realize that the Danish communication strategy needed to be radically revised. He announced a time-out from domestic politics in order to be able to deal with the issue and, in support the domestic opposition parties, kept a low profile during this period. The updated strategy consisted of a media offensive targeted directly at Muslims. An interview was arranged on the Arab-language channel Al-Arabija, and the idea was to use narratives and metaphors that communicated directly with an Arabic-speaking audience, and in doing so, would emphasize the common religious background of Judaism, Christianity, and Islam. Thus, the Danish prime minister still stressed that, even though the Danish government would not support the demonization of people on the basis on religion, neither would the government take responsibility for what a free-standing newspaper published. During the interview, the prime minister underlined that he personally would not have published the drawings, but that the newspaper was free to do so (Olesen, 2007). At the Danish Foreign Office, efforts were made to increase the number of Arabic-speaking staff and to strengthen the Foreign Office's expertise on religious and cultural matters.

The new communication strategy was fruitless, and on February 4, 2006, the Danish, Swedish, and Norwegian embassies in Damascus, Syria, were attacked. The day after, the Danish embassy in Lebanon was burned to the ground, and more than 20,000 people participated in demonstrations against the cartoons. In addition, Iran recalled its Danish ambassador. The attacks created a window of opportunity for the Danish government to advocate a strategic partnership with the EU by referring to the EU Solidarity Clause.[11] The Danish strategy was for the EU to act as a neutral partner and, in doing so, be able to appeal to a sense of belonging and togetherness with the Muslim world. Eventually, Javier Solana agreed to travel to the Middle East.[12] In addition, the Danish government had to rely on support from Danish Imams representing Denmark at the prestigious conference for Muslim religious leaders in Manama, Bahrain, on March 22 and 23, 2006. The aim of the conference was to create a unitary voice on issues pertaining to Islam and to request assurances from the European Union that it would improve the situations of Muslim minorities in Europe (and in Denmark in particular). With these combined efforts, the crisis slowly faded out, and the number of protests and media reports began to decline (Lindholm, 2008).[13]

CONCLUDING DISCUSSION

We now turn our focus to the ethical dimension and its impact on crisis mitigation and escalation. As stated in the introduction, ethical crisis communication is connected to two aspects; first, the ability for crisis managers to engage key stakeholders in a dialogue and second, the communication of universal values and norms. The two cases show how the cartoons caught the Danish and Swedish governments in situations where they had to balance the promotion of universal and heterogeneous values. The two governments chose different strategies, reflected in message formulation and stakeholder management. In short, the Swedish government emphasized universal values, whereas the Danish government initially framed the cartoons as a conflict between Western and Muslim values. Their respective strategies clearly impacted on their ethical capital and, as a result, their ability to resolve the crisis at hand.

In stakeholder management, one of the core challenges to crisis communicators is the very process of identifying stakeholders (Hale et al., 2005; Pauchant & Mitroff, 1992; Ullmer & Sellnow, 2000). In the Danish case, we can see how the crisis escalated mainly due to the government's ignorance of key Muslim stakeholders. Even though the Danish government realized in the second phase that they had to talk to the Muslim ambassadors, the Danish Community of Islamic Faith was not considered a legitimate partner. The Danish government's strategic thinking in terms of traditional diplomatic channels made them underestimate the mobilization potential inherent in transnational networks such as the Community of Islamic Faith. The exclusion of the Danish Community of Islamic Faith resulted in the organization pursuing the issue into the international arena, escalating the incident into a full-fledged public diplomacy crisis. In contrast, the Swedish government was keen on including Muslim stakeholders, with the aim of curbing the growing resentment caused by the Swedish publications.

As argued in the beginning of the chapter, stakeholder management is closely connected to message formulation. If we take message formulation into account, the Danish government exclusion of Muslim stakeholders in their public dialogue becomes understandable. The Danish free speech frame was clearly exclusionary in its dichotomizing of Muslim and Western values at the expense of universal ones. The main goal with the framing was to win voters on the domestic scene, however, in the contemporary communication environment characterized by global transparency and interconnection, the Danish government's message, aimed at a domestic audience, was quickly spread to the international arena. This polarization of values resulted in an escalation and politicization of the crisis, where the Danish governments gradually eroded their ethical capital. By contrast, the Swedish government underlined both the need for religious respect as well as respect for the freedom of the press. Their framing made it possible to engage Muslim stakeholders in a dialogue. In order to strengthen their ethical capital toward Muslim stakeholders on the global level, the government even chose to coordinate their messages with key Swedish Muslim organizations.

To conclude, the chapter shows how, as the crisis proceeded, the Danish government lost all its ethical capital to act as crisis communicators due to a series of lost chances to establish dialogue and, in doing so, perceive Muslim actors as legitimate stakeholders. Eventually, the government understood that the message needed to be changed and that Muslim values and feelings had to be taken into account. However, the U-turn came too late. In the end, the government had to "borrow" ethical capital from other actors, in this case, the EU and Danish Imams, in order to solve the crisis. In contrast, the Swedish government gained ethical capital and credibility by initiating a dialogue with Muslim organizations. As an example of the success of this crisis communication strategy, the European Council for Fatwa and Research issued a counterfatwa against the taped death threats and called for dialogue and peaceful protests instead of instigating further escalation (Sjövall, 2007). The analysis of the two cases shows how ethical stakeholder management and message formulation contribute, not only to legitimate but also effective crisis management, in providing crisis managers with the ethical capital needed to resolve public diplomacy crises.

NOTES

1. These types of conflict spring from the spread of a global human rights regime.
2. The author would like to express her sincere thanks to Kristina Lindholm (2008) and Erik Edling (2009) for allowing her to draw on their case studies in this analysis.
3. At the time, this statement was controversial. France and Germany limited themselves to saying they opposed the invasion. Not even UN Secretary General Kofi Annan labeled the invasion and Washington as violating the UN charter. With his statement, Mr. Persson aligned Sweden with China in accusing President Bush of violating human rights and state sovereignty.
4. Sweden had 132,575 asylum applicants in 2003–2007 compared to Denmark's 14,579. The total population of Sweden is 9.3 million (Statistiska Centralbyrån), and Denmark's population is estimated at 5.5M (Danmarks Statistik). Worth noting is the recent growth in support for the Swedish Nationalist party (Sverigedemokraterna), which would make this party likely to take its first seat in parliament if a general election was to be held today (fall 2010).
5. At the annual meeting of the Conservative Party in 2005, Brian Mikkelsen said the following: "There are still many battles to fight. One of the most important ones is the confrontation we experience with immigrants from Muslim

countries and their refusal to accept Danish culture and European norms. In the midst of our country—our own country—parallel societies develop in which minorities practice their medieval norms and undemocratic ways of thinking. We cannot accept this. This is the new front for the cultural battle" (Bonde, 2007, p. 36). The reason why the Community of Islamic Faith turned to the Ministry of Culture in the first place was because Mikkelsen had held a speech at a meeting of the Conservative Party a couple of months earlier, during which he referred to an ongoing cultural struggle between Danish and Muslim values. In addition, the fact that the cartoons were published in the cultural section of *Jyllands-Posten* also played a role in the choice for Mikkelsen.

6. Turkey, Alger, Libya, Pakistan, Indonesia, Morocco, Bosnia Herzegovina, and the Palestine authorities.

7. Roundabout dogs were at the time a new type of pop art in Sweden; artists and civilians made their own interpretations of roundabout dogs and placed them in roundabouts all over the country. The objects were considered illegal and a matter of traffic safety by local authorities, who ordered the police to remove them from the roundabouts where they had been placed.

8. The newspapers *Dagens Nyheter, Expressen,* and *Aftonbladet.*

9. The fact that Egypt took the lead on the issue should be understood in light of the Egyptian parliamentary election, which was due to take place in December 2005. Egyptian President Mubarak's party (the National Democratic Party) was under strong pressure from Islamic political groups.

10. This group arranged meetings with the secretary general of the Arab League, Amr Moussa; the grand mufti of the Arabic Republic of Egypt, Ali Gomaa; and Muhammed Sayed Tantawi, leader of the influential Al-Azhar University in Egypt. This university is considered to be the leader in Arabic literature and Sunni Islam teaching.

11. The clause states that the EU Member States shall assist one another in a spirit of solidarity in the event of terrorist attacks, natural disasters, or human-made disasters.

12. From February 13 to 17, Solana met Ekmeleddin Ihsanoglu (the leader for the Islamic Conference), the Saudi Arabic Minister for Foreign Affairs, and the Secretary General of the Gulf Cooperation Council. On February 14, Solana was in Egypt and met President Hosni Mubarak and the leader for Al-Azhar University, the Egyptian Foreign Minister Ahmed, and the Secretary General for the Arab League. On February 15, Javier Solana was in Amman, Jordan, for a meeting with King Abdullah II and the Minister of Foreign Affairs. On February 16 and 17, Solana met with Mahmoud Abbas in Ramallah and the Minister of Foreign Affairs in Israel and then with Israeli Prime Minister Ehud Olmert as well as with the Minister of Defense (The Council of the European Union, 2006).

13. By the end of February 2006, the caricatures had been republished in at least 143 newspapers in 56 different countries, including a number of Arab and Muslim countries (eJour, cited in Olesen, 2007, p. 302).

REFERENCE

Acquier, A., Gand, S., & Szpirglas, M. (2008). From stakeholder to stakeholder management in crisis episodes: A case study in a public transportation company. *Journal of Contingencies and Crisis Management, 16*(2), 101–114.

Ammon, R. J. (2001). *Global television and the shaping of world politics: CNN, telediplomacy, and foreign policy.* Jefferson, NC: McFarland.

Alpaslan, C. M., Green, S. E., & Mitroff, I. (2009). Corporate governance in the context of crises: Towards a stakeholder theory of crisis management. *Journal of Contingencies and Crisis Management, 17*(1), 38–49.

Arab News. (2006, March 12) Retrieved March 17, 2009, from www.arabnews.com

Axelsson, C. (2003). "Kriget mot Irak splittrar riksdagen i synen på kriget Persson går längst i kritiken" Svenska Dagbladet 2003-03-22 Retrieved April 20, 2009 from http://www.svd.se/nyheter/inrikes/artikel_85072.svd

Beck, U., & Sznaider, N (2006). Unpacking cosmopolitanism for the social sciences: A research agenda. *The British Journal of Sociology, 57*(1), 1–23.

Benoit, W. (1997). Image repair discourse and crisis communication. *Public Relations Review, 23*(2), 177–189.

Bourdieu, P. (1972). *Outline of a theory of practice.* Cambridge, UK: Cambridge University Press.

Bourdieu, P. (1986). The forms of capital. In J. G. Richardson (Ed.), *Handbook of theory and research for the sociology of education.* New York: Greenwood.

Bonde Nørby, B. (2007). How 12 cartoons of the prophet Mohammed were brought to trigger an international conflict. *Nordicom Review, 28*(1), 33–48.

Bowen, M. G., & Power, F. C. (1993). The moral manager: Communicative ethics and the Exxon Valdez disaster. *Journal of Business Ethics, 3*(2), 97–115.

Brändström, A., & Kuipers, S. (2003). From normal incidents to political crises: Understanding the selective politicization of policy failures. *Government and Opposition, 38*(3), 279–305.

Brändström, A., Kuipers, S., & Daléus, P., (2008). The politics of tsunami responses: Comparing patterns of blame management in Scandinavia. In A. Boin, A. McConnell, & P. 't Hart (Eds.), *Governing after crisis: The politics of investigation, accountability and learning.* Cambridge, UK: Cambridge University Press.

Carlbom, M. (2007). "Reinfeldt mötte svenska muslimer." Dagens Nyheter. Publicerad 2007-09-04 21:26. Retrieved April 23, 2009 from http://www.dn.se/nyheter/sverige/reinfeldt-motte-svenska-muslimer

Castells, M. (2008). The new public sphere: Global civil society, communication networks, and global governance. *The Annals of the American Academy of Political and Social Science, 616*(1), 78–93.

Christensen, S. L., & Kohls, J. (2003). Ethical decision making in times of organizational crisis: A framework for analysis. *Business Society, 42*(3) 382–358.

Christians, C. G. (2005). Ethical theory in communication research. *Journalism Studies, 6*(1), 3–14.

Coombs, T. W. (1998). An analytical framework for crisis situations: Better responses from a better understanding of the situation. *Journal of Public Relations Research, 10*(3), 177–91.

Coombs, T. W., & Holladay, S. J. (2002). Helping crisis managers protect reputational assets: Initial tests of the situational crisis communication theory. *Management Communications Quarterly, 16*(2), 165–186.

Council of the European Union. (2006, February). *The Council of the European Union. The homepage of Javier Solana, agenda February 2006.* Retrieved January 16, 2008, from www.consilium.europa.eu/cms3_applications/applications/solana/archAgendaMonth.asp?cmsid=246&month=2&year=2006

Dagens Nyheter. (2007a). *Ingen svensk reaktion på Irankritik.* Publicerad 2007-08-28 19:47 http://www.dn.se/nyheter/sverige/ingen-svensk-reaktion-pa-irankritik Olsson

Dagens Nyheter. (2007b). *Global kortslutning.* 2009-01-01. Retrieved April 22 2009 from http://www.dn.se/opinion/huvudledare/global-kortslutning-1.752748

Danish Prime Minister's Office. (2006, January 1). *Anders Fogh Rasmussen's New Year's Address 2006.* Retrieved December 23, 2010, from http://www.stm.dk/_p_11198.html

De Vries, M. S. (2004). Framing crises: Response patterns to explosions in fireworks factories. *Administration and Society, 36*(5), 594–614.

Edling, E. (2009). *Prophet Muhammad as a roundabout dog: A study of stakeholders in political crisis communication.* Unpublished Master thesis. The Swedish National Defence College, Stockholm.

Falkheimer, J., & Heide, M. (2006). Multicultural crisis communication: Towards a social constructionist perspective. *Journal of Contingencies and Crisis Management, 4*(14), 180–189.

Freeman, R. E. (1984). *Strategic management: A stakeholder approach.* Boston: Pitman.

Gilboa, E. (2006). Public diplomacy: The missing component in Israel's foreign policy. *Israel Affairs, 12*(4), 715–747.

Gilboa, E. (2008). Searching for a theory of public diplomacy. *The Annals of the American Academy of Political and Social Science, 616*(1), 55–77.

Hale, J. E., Dulek, R. E., & Hale, D. P. (2005). Crisis response communication challenges: Building theory from qualitative data. *Journal of Business Communication, 42*(2), 112–134.

Hervik, P. (2008). Original spin and its side effects: Freedom of speech as Danish news management. In E. Eide, R. Kunelius, & A. Phillips (Eds.), *Transnational media events: The Mohammed cartoons and the imagined clash of civilizations.* Göteborg, Sweden: Nordicom.

Högfeldt, K., Sander, Å., & Larsson, G. (2008). *Muhammed-karikatyrer och rondellhundar: Reaktioner, bakgrund och sammanhang* (Report): Enheten för mångkulturell utveckling. Göteborgs stad, Sverige.

Holm, U. (2006). *The Danish ugly duckling and the Mohammed cartoons.* Copenhagen: Danish Institut for Internationale Studier.

Lindholm, K. (2008). *Politisk krishantering i Danmark: Krisen i samband med publiceringen av Muhammedkarikatyrerna 2005 och 2006* (Vol 37). Stockholm: Försvarshögskolan.

Lindholm, K., & Olsson, E-K (forthcoming 2011). Crisis communication as a multilevel game: The Muhammad cartoons from a crisis diplomacy perspective. *International Journal of Press and Politics.*

Melissen, J. (2005). The new public diplomacy: Between theory and practice. In J. Melissen (Ed.), *The new public diplomacy*. New York: Palgrave MacMillan.

Meyer, C. (1999). Political legitimacy and the invisibility of politics: Exploring the European Union's communication deficit. *Journal of Common Market Studies, 37*(4), 617–639.

Migrationsverket (2009). Asylsökande till Sverige. Migrationsverket. Retrieved April 20, 2009 from http://www.migrationsverket.se/swedish/statistik/asyl.html

Olesen, T. (2007). Contentious cartoons: Elite and media-driven mobilization. *Mobilization: An International Quarterly, 12*(1), 37–52.

Olsson, K.V., & Ingvarsson, P. (2007). "Konstnären Lars Vilks mordhotad" Aftonbladet 2007-08-31 Retrieved April 22, 2009 from http://www.aftonbladet.se/nyheter/article679129.ab

Pauchant, T. C., & Mitroff, I. I. (1992). *Transforming the crisis-prone organization*. San Francisco: Jossey-Bass.

Potter, E. (2003). Canada and the new public diplomacy. *International Journal, 58*(1), 43–64.

Rasmussen, A. (2006). New Year Speech 2006. Retrieved from http://www.stm.dk/_p_7521.html

Regeringskansliet (2007) "Uttalande av statsminister Fredrik Reinfeldt" Regeringskansliet 2007-09-04. Retrieved April 22, 2009 from http://www.regeringen.se/sb/d/9755/a/87185

Roux-Dufort, C. (2007). Is crisis management (only) a management of exceptions? *Journal of Contingencies and Crisis Management, 15*(2), 105–114.

Signitzer, B., & Coombs, T. (1992). Public relations and public diplomacy: Conceptual divergence. *Public Relations Review, 18*(2), 137–147.

Siomkos, G., & Shrivastava, P. (1993). Responding to product liability crises. *Long Range Planning, 26*(5), 72–79.

Sjövall, J. (2007). "Europeiska muslimer tar avstånd från hot" Sveriges Radio 2007-09-17. Retrieved April 20, 2009 from http://www.sr.se/cgi-bin/ekot/artikel.asp?artikel=1601130

Smith, D. (2006). The crisis of management: Managing ahead of the curve. In D. Smith & D. Elliott (Eds.), *Key readings in crisis management. Systems and structures for prevention and recovery*. London: Routledge.

Stephens, K. K., Malone, P. C., & Bailey, C. M. (2005). Communicating with stakeholders during a crisis: Evaluating message strategies. *Journal of Business Communication, 12*(4), 390–419

Stern, E. (2001). *Crisis decision making: A cognitive institutional approach*. Stockholm: Försvarshögskolan.

Sveriges Radio. (2007). "Reinfeldt besvarar kritiken om osynlighet" 2007-09-01 Retrieved April 23, 2009 from http://www.sr.se/cgibin/ekot/tema/artikel.asp?ProgramID=2974&artikel=1575864. Full interview available at http://www.sr.se/webbradio/?Type=broadcast&Id=750207&isBlock=1.

Thomsen, P. B. (2006). *Muhammedkrisen, hvad skete der, hvad har vi lært*. København: People's Press.

Thurfjell, K. (2007). "Nya protester mot profetbild" Svenska Dagbladet 2007-09-02. Retrieved April 23, 2009 from http://www.svd.se/nyheter/inrikes/artikel_258689.svd

Tuch, H. N. (1990). *Communicating with the world: U.S. public diplomacy overseas.* New York: St. Martin's Press.

Ulmer, R. R., & Sellnow, T. L. (2000). Consistent questions of ambiguity in organizational crisis communication: Jack in the box as a case study. *Journal of Business Ethics, 25*(2), 143–155.

Wang, J. (2006). Managing national reputation and internal relations in the global era: Public diplomacy revisited. *Public Relations Review, 32*(2), 91–96.

Zhang, J. (2006). Public diplomacy as symbolic interactionism: A case study of Asian tsunami relief campaign after 9/11. *Public Relations Review, 30*(2), 161–167.

CHAPTER 9

THE POLITICS-
ADMINISTRATION
DICHOTOMY AND THE
FAILURE OF SYMMETRICAL
RESPONSIBILITY DOCTRINES

Helena Wockelberg

THE POLITICS-ADMINISTRATION DICHOTOMY,
RESPONSIBILITY, AND CRISIS

Post hoc evaluations of how democratic institutions manage crises can be conducted to create meaning, to enable learning, or to fairly assign blame and praise. This chapter investigates two questions: (a) what responsibility doctrine are those actors involved in postcrisis evaluations advocating? (b) What ethical[1] issues are at the fore in postcrisis evaluations? The empirical focus of this chapter is the postcrisis evaluation of the Swedish government's response to the 2004 tsunami disaster. Values associated with democracy provide the normative backdrop for this analysis. Citizens' democratic right to make informed decisions at the ballot box and the idea that public decisions to some extent should be based on lessons learned will be discussed.

Ethics and Crisis Management, pages 163–182
Copyright © 2011 by Information Age Publishing
All rights of reproduction in any form reserved.

Regarding the question of what responsibility doctrine actors in post hoc crisis evaluations are advocating, we will, in this chapter, distinguish between two main perspectives on responsibility and then discuss which views on the relationship between politicians and bureaucrats these perspectives fall into. The first perspective is set on accomplishing a symmetrical match of mandate and responsibility. Such *symmetrical responsibility doctrines* prescribe that bureaucrats are to be held responsible for the use of discretionary power within their mandate. To be held responsible for actions within a mandate, said mandate must be supported by adequate resources.[2] Following the same logic, politicians are to be held responsible for the execution of power that follows from *their* own mandate, but their responsibility for the actions or failures of bureaucrats is limited to only bureaucratic actions a minister has had information about or had the power to influence (which is a very limited number in Sweden). The idea of a politics-administration dichotomy, at least in theory, fits nicely into this picture—one of the main points of separating politics from administration is to be able to clarify mandates and responsibilities.

Ideas on how to organize state accountability and responsibility have been central in the second wave of New Public Management (NPM). Importantly, the responsibility sought is of the symmetrical kind. In terms of actual public administration policy and reform, the concept of *agentification*, that is, the creation of autonomous state authorities that are protected against spontaneous political steering (Olsen, 2009; Peters & Pierre, 2001, p. 6), becomes an attempt to establish a real-world version of the politics-administrative dichotomy. In the NPM tool box, we also find *contractualism*, that is, formal contracts between governments and heads of autonomous state agencies. Such contracts are created to clarify mandates in order to delegate power to bureaucrats and to be able to measure performance *ex post* in order to attribute responsibility. While the alleged virtues of the politics-administrative dichotomy have been questioned from an accountability perspective, many attempts to implement NPM-related ideas have been made in modern democracies (Bull & Bremdal, 2009; Gregory & Grönnegard Christensen, 2004; Lagreid, 2000; Peters, 2010; Pollitt, 2003, 2006; Svara, 2001; Woodhouse, 1994).

The second perspective on responsibility is here labeled *asymmetrical* since it expects ministers to assume responsibility for actions and failures out of their immediate control. A real-world example of this idea is the classical version of the Westminster doctrine of ministerial responsibility. According to Kam (2000, p. 1f.), "classic interpretations of the doctrine state that ministers must accept the blame for all serious departmental errors."[3] In another version, asymmetrical responsibility means that bureaucrats are held responsible for the actions or failures of politicians. While we are not to expect the latter version to be formalized or explicitly supported by the actors involved, we know that blame games and the politicization of accountability procedures might nevertheless produce this kind of asymmetrical attribution of responsibility. We also know that politicians blaming bureaucrats in a seemingly unfair way might have negative effects on the relationship between politicians and bureaucrats ('t Hart & Wille, 2006). Bureaucrats in doubt over the validity of any *ex ante* contracts[4] might become overly careful, which in turn might hamper their effectiveness in crisis response. In this chapter, I will also discuss real-world examples of how politicians and top-level bureaucrats engage in an informal, asymmetrical contract where bureaucrats accept the role of scapegoat or fall guy in order to protect a minister or the government.

A number of values are commonly used to evaluate public sector crisis management in democracies. First, democratic governance brings with it various ideas of how governments should function in crises. Beckman (2003) suggests that democratic institutions must act in a way that is perceived as both *efficient* and *legitimate* by the public. Furthermore, looking to Dahl's criteria for the ideal type of democracy, we may argue that the fundamental democratic value of *equality* requires that citizens are able to act upon an *enlightened understanding* of their political context, of political leadership, and of society. Dahl's (2000) democracy also requires that the citizens have final control over the political agenda. These demands mean that post hoc evaluations of crisis must be conducted in ways that enable *transparency* and that generate unbiased and significant information concerning the performance of politicians and bureaucrats alike. Citizens who are lied to will not be able to make informed decisions at the ballot box. Withholding the truth from citizens also means that they lose their democratic agenda-setting privilege. The citizens should decide what the election is about (i.e., control the agenda) and in order to do so, they must have access to correct information concerning the performance of the government. Democratic decision making requires transparency and that information is *objective* and *impartial.* False or biased information is of little use to citizens evaluating their political leaders. From a democratic theory perspective, we should also consider that *the rule of law* may be perceived as important in postcrisis evaluations. While the exact relationship between rule of law and democracy is debated (Dahl, 2000; Cunningham, 2002, p. 31), democratic processes and values such as impartiality can be hard to sustain without rule of law.

Second, *transparency, objectivity,* and *impartiality* can also be discussed from a learning perspective. The pursuit of post hoc evaluations in democracies is not only motivated by the citizens' right to make informed decisions (at the ballot) but also by the idea that public office holders, bureaucrats, and their organizations should learn from experience. The idea is that democratic power should be executed on a rational basis. Hence, the ambition to learn[5] may be positively valued in democratic postcrisis evaluations.

Third, from the perspective of crisis management research, our expectations partially change on ethics in postevaluations. We might find that both during and after a crisis, effectiveness may be valued as more important than *the rule of law*. Indeed, there might not even exist a law to guide the management of certain unexpected situations. Or uncertainty in categorizing situations needing management, and hence which laws apply, might be genuine. Values such as *transparency, objectivity,* and *impartiality* might be threatened if evaluations turn into *blame games,* where the participants aim at hiding the truth to avoid responsibility (see, for example, Boin, McConnell, & 't Hart, 2008). Participants in post hoc evaluations might also try to reestablish or uphold the overall *legitimacy, stability,* and *effectiveness* of the state rather than try to find out what went wrong. Some scholars also argue that evaluations might be used primarily to generate meaning in a chaotic event, a strategy that can produce subjective results (Brown, 2003). Such symbolic action might hinder the ability to learn from experience. Others point to the possibility that evaluations are perceived by citizens as symbols of *fairness* and *objective, rational expertise,* and are hence useful in restoring these values after a crisis (Parker & Dekker, 2008, p. 260). Beyond the goal of *protecting* or *restoring* the political institutions and the state, the aim to respect and protect the integrity of individuals (e.g., victims of catastrophes or their next of kin) may sometimes be valued higher than *transparency*.

Concerning our first question, what type of responsibility doctrine the actors in the postcrisis evaluation are advocating, the Swedish case examined in this chapter is biased toward favoring a *symmetrical responsibility doctrine*. The Swedish executive has for hundreds of years (i.e., longer than democracy, parliamentarism, and indeed longer than NPM) featured formally autonomous agencies. The central government authorities are *administratively autonomous,* or *formally independent* in the implementation of law. Individual ministers have neither the power nor the ministerial responsibilities of their colleagues in Westminster-oriented executive models, like the British. Substantial delegation of matters concerning personnel, economy, and organization, combined with performance management, completes the picture. The formal independence of state agencies and the NPM-related delegation of authority of recent years have been guided by the values of *rule of law* and *efficiency,* respectively (Andersson, 2004; Pierre, 2001; Pollitt, 2006; Sundström, 2003; Wockelberg, 2003).

Moving to the second question posed in the introduction, what ethical issues are at the fore in postcrisis evaluations, Swedish-style democracy has traditionally been focused on reforming society in a rational, scientific way (Hermansson, 2003). This tradition highlights *learning* and hence, as argued above, can be said to require *transparency, objectivity,* and *impartiality.*

Within the Swedish context, these values are codified in law. The Swedish constitution (the Instrument of Government[6]) also emphasizes the *rule of law*. It is important to note that crises in Sweden are governed by the same laws that essentially govern everyday *normal* situations (Olsson, 2006).

We begin the empirical part of this chapter by taking a closer look at the analysis conducted by the independent inquiry into the Swedish government's response to the 2004 tsunami disaster—the Swedish Tsunami Commission (hereafter referred to as the Commission).[7] The Commission's report is viewed, within this chapter, as an authoritative interpretation of the Swedish responsibility doctrine in crises and as a qualified discussion on legitimacy from citizens' point of view. We then move on to the tsunami evaluation conducted by the standing parliamentary Committee on the Constitution[8] (hereafter referred to as the CoC), which focuses on legality. The CoC, in this chapter, is treated as an example of how ethical considerations are debated in a political environment. In order to move beyond the official arenas of postcrisis evaluation, I have also conducted focus group interviews with former and current director generals (DGs) of autonomous state agencies.

THE POSTCRISIS EVALUATION FOLLOWING THE DECEMBER 2004 TSUNAMI

Among the casualties of the 2004 tsunami disaster were over 500 Swedes, mainly tourists spending their Christmas holidays in Thailand. The tsunami disaster thereby constituted one of the most severe crises a Swedish government has ever managed (Hansén, 2005, p. 22). Crisis management was not smoothly executed, and a domestic blame game quickly ensued (Brändström, Kuipers, & Daléus, 2008; Grandien, Nord, & Strömbäck, 2005).

The Swedish Tsunami Commission: Crisis and the Limits of Formal Mandates

The Commission's report is here viewed as an authoritative interpretation of the Swedish responsibility doctrine and how it might apply after a major crisis. The Commission advocated a symmetrical view on responsibility and concluded that politicians are to blame if sufficient crisis management tools are not instituted. It is also possible to interpret an acknowledgement by the Commission that crises come with extraordinary demands, which include initiatives that might go beyond *à priori* established routines. The Commission concluded that the failures in the Swedish government's response to the tsunami disaster originated from a lack of organization and preparation, which in turn caused severe delays in and problems with collecting, analyzing, and sharing information. Furthermore, the Commission also found problems with the implementation of decisions that were made. These problems were identified in the Ministry of Foreign Affairs, the Government Offices as a whole, and in some state agencies (Katastrofkommissionen, 2005, pp. 104, 265ff.).

The Commission advocated a hierarchical responsibility doctrine in the postcrisis evaluation and stated that decision makers whose mandates are supported by adequate resources should assume responsibilities that equal their governmental powers, thereby advocating *symmetry* between authority and responsibility. The Commission also stated that in any situation where responsibilities are unclear, the higher level in the hierarchy assumes responsibility (Katastrofkommissionen, 2005, pp. 104, 166ff.). The most legitimate responsibility doctrine available was argued to be the promotion of individual responsibility within given mandates in a given organizational hierarchy (Katastrofkommissionen, 2005, p. 104, appendix 5). The Commission argued, for example, that Swedish Prime Minister (PM) Persson's ability to assume the responsibilities that followed from his mandate were dependent upon his knowledge of problems in the organization, of possible solutions, and his duration in office. Since the need for a national crisis management organization had long since been discussed by several experts, investigating committees, and Parliament, and since the PM had been in office for 8 years, ample time to implement changes, his responsibility for failures in the crisis management of the tsunami was undeniable (Katastrofkommissionen, 2005, pp. 104, 516f.). The Commission's analysis that the Government Offices[9] provided *inadequate after-hours service* illustrated that available resources must match the mandate in order for someone to be held responsible. Furthermore, the State Secretary of Foreign Affairs was found responsible for the shortcomings of the Swedish Rescue Service Agency since the agency had not been given relevant and necessary information from the Ministry of Foreign Affairs during the crisis (Katastrofkommissionen, 2005, pp. 104, 265ff.).

The Commission introduced two potentially competing standards: a match between mandates and responsibilities on the one hand, and the idea that following routine or protocol in a crisis was not sufficient response on the other. This was illustrated by the Commission's suggestion that the Swedish ambassador to Thailand followed protocol correctly, but that this was an insufficient response given the extremity of the circumstances. The ambassador *should* have acted outside protocol to ensure that the minister and the Ministry of Foreign Affairs were informed of the severity of the crisis and of the need for extra resources. We must, however, note that while the Commission stated how the ambassador should have acted, they did not detail how responsibility was to be apportioned.[10] The need for creativity and initiative *within* mandates was also underlined in a rare critique of an independent state agency by the Commission. The National Board of Health and Welfare was criticized by the Commission for not acting on its own accord and thereby failing to make the most of its mandate (Katastrof-kommissionen, 2005, pp. 104, 273ff.).

One possible answer to the question of what ethical considerations are at the forefront of consideration in postcrisis evaluations is that the Commission's focus on *legitimacy* underlines the value of *effectiveness*. The fundamental values at stake are the protection of *life* and the *security* of Swedish citizens. The Commission also asserted the virtue of showing *empathy* and *making extra efforts* in times of *potential* crisis. The Commission's views on its own function are explicitly described in terms of reestablishing citizens' faith in their governing institutions, as well as in terms of learning through transparent, objective, and impartial evaluation. In this process, the Commission is aware of the need to protect the integrity of individuals, the victims, and their next of kin.[11]

The Committee on the Constitution: Principles and Politics

The CoC[12] is the Swedish parliament's instrument for scrutinizing ministers and the government's activities from a constitutional perspective. *Rule of law*, or *legality*, is thus a value expected to be at the forefront of the CoC's analysis. At the same time, the committee consists of Members of Parliament (MPs) representing the political parties and thus provides an arena for politics. The analysis of the CoC illustrates two aspects of post hoc evaluations after a crisis: First, the CoC's *statement* is an example of how the Swedish parliament officially discusses the responsibility doctrine and how it applies to the tsunami crisis management. Second, the CoC's *hearings* are used to illustrate how scrutiny conducted in a political environment may challenge values such as impartiality, and thus might threaten rather than strengthen the legitimacy of post hoc evaluations.

When MPs file reports with the Committee concerning members of government, they appear aware of the Committee's mandate and the need for some type of legal basis for the complaints made[13] (Wockelberg & Ahlbäck Öberg, 2008). It is extremely rare that reports discuss civil servants in explicitly negative terms, and only rarely does a report discuss a specific state agency.[14] Scrutiny by the CoC can also take the form of a hearing and does not have to be based on a filed complaint. There are no formal rules for how or when CoC hearings are to be conducted. Civil servants, however, are rarely invited to these hearings.[15] The interrogative style often adopted in the hearings and, at times, the rough way the committee treats its *guests*[16] has been the focus of criticism. The CoC has also been accused of overstepping the boundaries of its constitutional mandate in regard to whom and what it investigates (Foyer, 1997, p. 320f.; Wockelberg & Ahlbäck Öberg, 2008).

In its examination of crisis management during the tsunami disaster, the CoC argued that since the Swedish legal landscape lacks special regulations for governing in crises, the government's general right and obligation to rule is crucial. Procedures and instructions guiding crisis management within the government offices at the time of the tsunami were, according to the CoC, too informal and too imprecise to free the government from the responsibility of executing active leadership during the crisis. The CoC tried to back its understanding of the limits of ministerial responsibilities by referring to earlier CoC statements. In these statements, the CoC asserted that an awareness of existing problems renders a minister responsible. The CoC is, however, less than clear concerning its views on whether lack of information and awareness can free a minister of responsibility (Konstitutionsutskottets betänkande KU8, 2005/2006, pp. 71ff.).

The CoC's conclusions about the government's responsibility for failures related to the planning, organization, and performance in crisis management were very similar to those of the Commission: given the constitutional right and obligation to rule, members of government must prepare for crises and take initiative during them. In the tsunami disaster, the PM and the Minister of Foreign Affairs were specifically criticized for their lack of initiative, that is, failing to seek information of their own accord. While a minister must be able to trust lower-level actors to provide him or her with information and to perform their duties, ministers must also make sure that the governmental organization is in fact working during a large-scale crisis. The CoC stated that the PM and the Minister of Foreign Affairs should have understood that the tsunami was a serious crisis and acted accordingly. Several members of government were criticized by the CoC for not sharing information and for not actively initiating formal decisions, such as establishing funding for agency activities and specifying agencies' mandates in the crisis, actions that could have increased the speed of state agencies' responses. According to the CoC, the lack of a clear decision-making procedure underlines the fact that responsibility lies with the politicians at the top. The CoC's critique touches on what I interpret as ministers' lack of awareness and imagination, and of being out of touch with the habits and lifestyles of Swedish citizens. The government had prepared for crises to some extent, but not for this type of crisis, something that should have been done. The CoC also briefly discussed the added value of documenting the management of crises while they are happening to promote transparency in postcrisis evaluations (Konstitutionsutskottets betänkande KU8, 2005/2006, pp. 191ff.).

During the CoC hearings, a variety of actors brought forward different perspectives on responsibility issues and ethical considerations. Did a clear idea of crisis management exist at the time of the tsunami disaster, and were relevant procedures known in the governmental organization? It is interesting to note that the PM, while accepting responsibility for deficiencies in the government offices, repeatedly advocated symmetrical responsibility (Konstitutionsutskottets betänkande KU8, 2005/2006, appendix 3, pp. 315, 320, 333f). Furthermore, several actors advocated the norm that it is better to do too much than too little to help Swedish citizens in potential danger. However, the practical limits of such an ambition were also brought forward (see Konstitutionsutskottets betänkande KU8, 2005/2006, appendix 3, pp. 40ff., 69ff.). The hearings were different than the Committee report, which was quite strict in its legal focus and tone. During the hearings, MPs on the CoC repeatedly posed detailed questions concerning who did what, when, and why. While such questions might clarify the responsibility of ministers, there are ample examples of questions that are not useful for the perspective of the CoC's mandate to scrutinize members of government. During the hearings, a discussion about the CoC's mandate ran parallel with questions concerning the government's performance. Some MPs, as well as some interviewees, protested when members of the CoC were perceived as straying too far from its mandate. The hearing with the PM's state secretary left the strongest impression that some Committee members were unable to resist the opportunity to criticize civil servants (which is an activity outside the CoC's mandate). This hearing contained several rhetorical questions with a critical edge implying, for example, that the state secretary was slower than others in processing information and reaching the correct conclusions, or that he was not being truthful. Not all questions posed to the state secretary contributed to the evaluation of his ability to serve the PM. Another feature of importance to our analysis of ethical considerations was the lack of common courtesy on behalf of some of the CoC MPs. The PM's state secretary was interrupted on several occasions, was pressed for details, and was repeatedly asked the same questions after he had previously answered clearly. To some extent, the same type of questioning was repeated in the interview with the State Secretary of Foreign Affairs and in the hearings conducted with members of the government. This method of investigation casts doubts on the MPs impartiality and objectivity, and gives the lasting impression that they are conducting a blame game rather than an objective inquiry. By contrast, the hearings conducted with civil servants of state agencies[17] were primarily aimed at gathering information concerning the actions of different parts of the government offices and particular individuals working there (Konstitutionsutskottets betänkande KU8, 2005/2006, appendix 3).

The ministers interviewed by the CoC were, on a manifested rhetorical level, humble and accepted responsibility for mistakes made. However, at the end of the hearing, Minister of Foreign Affairs Freivalds summarized her views on performance and responsibilities in a way that both spreads the responsibility for failure to civil servants and pointed to her own short-comings (Konstitutionsutskottets betänkande KU8, 2005/2006, appendix 3 pp. 156ff.). The PM argued that his organization, the Prime Minister's Office, acted *by the book* and that the situation was hard to foresee, under-stand, and manage. In his defense, the PM pointed out the fact that even the most capable people in the Ministry of Foreign Affairs failed to under-stand the situation. This might have been an implicit attempt to spread blame: if the experts failed, why should a mere politician succeed in draw-ing the right conclusions? At a manifested rhetorical level, however, the PM was clear in his defense of the civil service and, given the critique he had faced from the Commission earlier (see the Swedish Tsunami Com-mission: Crisis and the Limits of Formal Mandates above), this defense is perhaps not surprising. The PM admitted that he was responsible for regrettable failures but also argued that the tsunami crisis was of a kind that made *normal* expectations hard to fulfill. The PM underlined the need to look forward and to be constructive, that is, he chose a framework that is supported by the *ambition to learn.* (Konstitutionsutskottets betänkande KU8, 2005/2006, appendix 3, pp. 156ff.).

The responsibility doctrine discussed in the CoC's report—and support-ed by various actors in the hearings—was symmetrical. The hearings also illustrate how postcrisis evaluations in the parliamentary arena run the risk of undermining values such as *objectivity* and *impartiality* and the creation of *legitimacy.*

Expecting and Accepting Asymmetry: Responsibility According to Top-Level Civil Servants

Both the Commission and the CoC are public and official arenas; as such, they are of limited use in the search for informal or unofficial views on how responsibility is to be apportioned after a crisis, as well as for any hidden ideas concerning which values that are perceived as truly important by the actors involved. Focus group interviews with members of the Swed-ish bureaucratic elite[18] serve as an attempt to determine and capture such informal and hidden dimensions of post hoc analyses.

The postevaluation of the tsunami crisis management, in particular the symmetrical responsibility doctrine described by the Commission, did not cause excitement or astonishment among the bureaucratic elite. The only exception to this was the fact that the Commission was quite clear in its critique of the PM. Since few agencies were actually under scrutiny, the impression was that the discussion was not of general importance to the director general (DG) collective. The group discussions on the specific tsunami postcrisis evaluations inspired discussions, however, on both other real-world[19] and hypothetical crises.

The DGs' answers to the first question (concerning responsibility doctrines) are complex. The interviewees do believe that a version of the politics-administration dichotomy exists in Sweden. The tradition of independent state agencies and the NPM reforms support substantial delegation of power from political to administrative levels. The independent mandate of state agencies is respected by ministers and the government when agencies are implementing law in individual cases and in operative decision making. This politics-administration dichotomy comes with some ethical obligations: the DGs should speak truth to power, protest, and inform the government of significant problems. While the independence of agencies under normal circumstances is respected, or even exaggerated, by members of government, the interviewees mention examples of ministers not respecting agency independence in times of crises. These examples illustrate the claim that it is necessary and possible for DGs to alert ministers who are intruding on agency mandates. Other DGs argue that ministers' fears of intruding on agency independence limit possible government action and initiative in crises. A third opinion is that in crisis, the Swedish government offices and the agencies come together and are executively efficient as a whole. The lasting impression from the interviews is that the practical effects of a divided executive are limited. *Rule of law*, to some extent, supports agencies' independence toward the government, but the DGs consider themselves primarily as a tool of government and describe a *norm of loyalty* and *pragmatism* within the executive. This appears to have some important effects on their views of the values at stake in postcrisis evaluations.

A conclusion drawn from the interviews is that crises put extraordinary demands not only on management but also on post hoc evaluations and accountability procedures. In a large-scale crisis like the 2004 tsunami disaster, the expectations citizens have of the government may be enormous, perhaps unrealistic. These expectations, together with the fact that public decision making is a truly complex business, make casual reasoning on responsibility and the apportioning of responsibility complicated. The DGs describe informal rules where the views on responsibility are potentially asymmetrical, not in the classical Westminster way[20] but rather in the other version where bureaucrats accept responsibility for failures not linked to their mandate. The interviewees seem to stoically accept the possibility of being made a *scapegoat* or *fall guy* should a crisis (e.g., a policy or implementation fiasco) present itself in their policy area. From this perspective, the executive seems to operate as a cohesive rather than divided form of government. Some interviewees believe that the asymmetry that comes with scapegoating is actually facilitated by the form of a divided executive, and that this is a rational way of attributing responsibility. While ministers in other countries might end up with the full burden of responsibility, the Swedish system protects ministers from blame, which may be favorable. We may here interpret the DGs as valuing the possibility to avoid the instability that resigning ministers bring to the executive and the country as a whole.

Scapegoating requires planning: "You need to think of the possible need for firing a DG already as the crisis is unfolding. The PM and the DG should not be in a press conference together" (DG in focus group 1).[21] In one of the groups, the informal task of drawing negative attention away from the minister was openly discussed and confirmed. Another important skill for a DG is to allow politicians the right of deniability: to know when to inform them and when not to. This can be linked to the idea that responsibility within the Swedish context requires that the minister in question has actually been informed of the independent agency's activities or plans.

Some DGs bring forward an ethical foundation for the informal norm of asymmetrical responsibility and hence an answer to our second question. One important value is *effectiveness*, which requires *stability*. To succeed in preserving stability after a crisis, the main actors managing the crisis must act with the possibility of postevaluation in mind. Some interviewees believe that the long-sought-after creation of a crisis management organization *within* the PM's office that is now in place[22] will make the PM vulnerable in future postcrisis evaluations. Even though the "need for someone to resign" (DG in focus group 1) can be overarching in a large-scale national trauma caused by a crisis, this person should not be the PM. As one of the interviewees stated, "Sometimes you need to consider what is best for the country . . . you may need to release pressure . . . to cause a government crisis due to the PM resigning is not making things easier for the country. Then it is better to sacrifice the pawn" (DG in focus group 1). According to the interviewees, there are also known negative aspects to using scapegoating, such as the insecurity and reduced morale it might cause among the agency staff, as may be the case in the firing of director generals. Overly frequent changes in leadership will hamper the overall effectiveness and the ability of the agency to learn.

During the interviews, the DGs were confronted with values associated with learning, such as *transparency* and the value of *honesty*. One of the interviewees suggested that since the norm is the *reason of state*,[23] the DGs might "perhaps not tell lies, but rather not reveal everything" (DG in focus group 1). To learn from mistakes might be valued less than the need to keep the government machinery in operation. Some DGs, however, were inclined to argue that evaluations should aim at honesty and collecting as much relevant information as possible since "the citizens have the right to demand that" (DG in focus group 3). One interviewee concluded that while the state's interest in security might limit *transparency*, decisions to hide information should always come with the ambition to fix major problems and learn quietly. Crises may also come with the need to protect the integrity of individuals, which might be another possible limit to transparency, according to the interviewees.

As argued in the introduction, seemingly unfair treatment of bureaucrats by government politicians may cause future uncertainty and confusion over mandates: fairness is thus linked to future performance. The DGs are *not* inclined, however, to change their behavior in response to how responsibility is attributed to colleagues: the possibility of detecting logic is too small to enable rational calculations on the outcomes of accountability procedures. Discussing the *ultimate* negative outcome, that is, that a DG is fired, the interviewees underlined the need to realize and accept all factors that might determine the destiny of a DG: the government's political needs, the salience of an issue, how the media responds to a crises or failure, and whether there is a viable successor. At the same time, DGs discuss strange or remarkable cases in which DGs were fired by each other. The effect of seemingly unfair treatment of a DG might create overly careful and obedient bureaucrats, but according to the DGs, such effects are short-lived. One group described how the government's treatment of DGs had become tougher, causing a higher degree of uncertainty. One of the interviewees repeatedly brought forward the claim that "it is not about fairness!" (DG in focus group 1).

The asymmetrical views on responsibility described by the DGs are informal, but widely known and accepted, according to the interviewees. This informality, however, makes rules harder to grasp for organizational outsiders, that is, for DGs who lack hands-on experience working with the level of power they are now executing. When asked how DGs are made aware of the expectations, rules, and informal norms that form the relationship between politics and bureaucracy, the DGs reported that the veterans *knew* from experience,[24] while outsiders were left to find out for themselves.

CONCLUSIONS

This chapter has investigated two questions: (a) what type of responsibility doctrine the actors involved in postcrisis evaluations are advocating, and (b) what ethical issues are at the forefront in postcrisis evaluations? The second question has many answers, and we will only touch upon some of them in this concluding section. The first question came with an underlying hypothesis that the Swedish institutional setting, with its divided executive, would make actors more inclined to argue the virtues of a symmetrical responsibility doctrine. In the case example outlined in this chapter (the postevaluation of the 2004 tsunami disaster), the independent Commission and the CoC both advocated symmetrical responsibility within formal mandates. These ideas were confronted, however, with a potentially competing ethic demanding that politicians as well as bureaucrats act with initiative and creativity, even if it would mean that normal routines and procedures are abandoned.

The assumption that clear, formal mandates will enable symmetrical responsibility is wrong, as it neglects the fact that post hoc evaluations might be politicized or manipulated. This becomes clear and evident in the interviews with DGs of autonomous agencies. According to some DGs, it is actually the formal separation of politics and administration that enables efficient scapegoating. The DGs identify strongly with the political executive and with the role of serving the government. The ties with the government appear to be supported by a norm of promoting *effective government.* Interestingly, a lack of *clarity* and *symmetry* is both expected and accepted by the bureaucratic elite interviewed for this study. Their view on the divided executive is positive: they believe that it generally works well. They do not, however, expect to be able to foresee the outcome of a post hoc responsibility procedure or to fully understand why colleagues are fired. They bring forward normative arguments for the asymmetry that manifests itself in situations of scapegoating: to save the government is, under certain circumstances, the first priority. It is more preferable that a director general is fired than a minister or the PM resign. Postcrisis evaluations might seek to accomplish learning through *transparency* and *truth seeking*, but it may be the main priority of both politicians and bureaucrats to use such processes to maintain a stable government. When it comes to matters perceived as concerning the *reason of state*, or *national interest*, the Swedish executive might act and think as one rather than as a dual system. Finally, sometimes the need to respect the *integrity* and *privacy of individuals* will be given higher priority in the postcrisis evaluation process than *transparency.*

The analysis also illustrates how various actors in postcrisis evaluations might be inclined to stray from values such as *impartiality* and *objectiveness*, as was true for some of the MPs in the CoC's hearings. And as mentioned above, some of the DGs interviewed for this study proposed a set of ethical reasons for *transparency* avoidance. While we, as citizens in a democracy, might indeed support ambitions to protect the state, country, or integrity of individuals in postcrises evaluations, it is not as easy to accept the notion that members of the political and bureaucratic elite should decide by their personal discretion when *truth* is of lesser value than other objectives, for example the political destiny of the PM. While *transparency* may hamper both short- and long-term *effectiveness* in government, informed decision making cannot be executed in situations of severe information deficit. This holds not only for decision makers in public office and autonomous agencies, but also for citizens who use the ballot to apportion responsibility in modern democracies.

NOTES

1. Following the Concise Oxford Thesaurus, 2nd edition (2002), ethics is here treated as synonymous with moral code, standard of behavior, values, and principles.
2. For example, information and funding for the mandate.
3. Kam also points our attention to the fact that the Westminster doctrine changes over time, and that its temporary version "is somewhat less severe, requiring that ministers accept blame only for serious departmental errors of which the minister knew or should have known" (Kam, 2000, p. 1f.; see also Bovens, 1998, pp. 85ff.).
4. Contract is here not used literally; it is hence not a contract of the NPM-kind mentioned in the text above.
5. The actual ability of organizations to learn remains contested, however (Elliott & McGuiness, 2002; Seeger, Ulmer, Novak, & Sellnow, 2005; see also, for example, Stern, 1997).
6. Retrieved December 2, 2010, at the Swedish Parliament's Web site, www.riksdagen.se/templates/R_Page____6307.aspx
7. In Swedish, *Katastrofkommissionen*.
8. MPs in the Committee on the Constitution represent the political parties in proportion to party representation in the Swedish parliament (Riksdagen); hence, the Committee's conclusions may be debated and not supported by the opposition. In analyzing the CoC, we must distinguish between the ways individual MPs in the Committee, and the Committee (majority) respectively discuss the issues at stake.
9. "The Government Offices form a single, integrated public authority comprising the Prime Minister's Office, the government ministries and the Office for Administrative Affairs" ("The Government Offices including ministries." Retrieved November 9, 2010, from www.regeringen.se).
10. The Commission divided its concluding parts into two categories; each theme begins with a description/discussion, followed by a concluding section where responsibility is apportioned. The ambassador to Thailand is not discussed under the "responsibility" heading (see Katastrofkommissionen, 2005, pp. 104, 276ff.).
11. In Sweden, official documents are public and accessible: "To encourage the free exchange of opinion and availability of comprehensive information, every Swedish citizen shall be entitled to have free access to official documents" (Chapter 2, Article 1, Freedom of the Press Act. Retrieved December 2, 2010, from the Swedish Parliament's Web site www.riksdagen.se/templates/R_Page-Extended____6332.aspx). Documents sent to a public authority, for example, an inquiry like that of the Commission, are also covered by this principle. To

be able to collect testimony and personal stories from victims and their next of kin without harming their integrity, the Commission asked the government to initiate a legislative process, which led up to a law granting exceptions from the principle of public access, making it possible for the Commission to protect information concerning individuals' personal or economical circumstances (see Katastrofkommissionen, 2005, pp. 104, 142).

12. I am grateful to Peder Nielsen and the Committee on the Constitution for generously providing me with a dataset covering the CoC issues under scrutiny during the period of 1994–1995 to 2007–2008. This data does not contain scrutiny initiated by the Committee itself, i.e., special occasions such as the tsunami investigation. The data collected by the author however does. Also, since the Committee dataset does not discriminate between types of civil servants in government offices or state agencies respectively, I have conducted a complementary analysis of the public records to code individuals into different categories. Individuals are coded according to the post they had at the time of the event under investigation. Ambassadors are coded as civil servants in government offices and not as director generals of agencies, even though the latter strategy is perhaps more common in Sweden research. While ambassadors and director generals are in many ways similar occupations, they differ in (at least) one way of importance to my analysis: Embassies are formally a part of the Foreign Department and hence not independent state agencies.

13. Precise ideas on the (or rather some) legal grounds for the complaint in the reports exist in 42% of the complaints, while only 16% are totally lacking in legal references.

14. During the period 2002–2003 through 2006–2007, 144 reports concerning the conduct of government and individual ministers were made by MPs to the Committee on the Constitution. Of these, three are here coded as containing explicit negative remarks on specific state secretaries (a state secretary is a political appointee working close to a minister and an influential actor in planning and coordinating intra- as well as interdepartmental issues. In the Foreign Department, this function is called State Secretary of Foreign Affairs). In comparison, only three explicit negative remarks were made concerning specific director generals (i.e., heads of independent agencies, or "autonomous authorities," what British scholars might call chief executives; see for example, Woodhouse 1994; Hogwood, Judge, & McVicar, 2001). While the government offices and specific ministries were mentioned in negative terms in 40 reports, specific independent agencies were rarely criticized (explicit negative remarks of this kind are nine). Source: KU-anmälningar (Reports to the Committee on the Constitution), available at www.riksdagen.se/webbnav/index.aspx?nid=5599. Reports concerning the prohibited ministerial control of agencies are more frequent than effective. Of a total of 24 complaints concerning vertical ministerial control (i.e., the relationship between the government and a state agency) made to the Committee during the period of 1975–1976 through 2000–2001, 15 were not supported by the Committee majority or even by a minority of its members (Hammargren, 2002).

15. During the period of 1994–2008, 176 ministers were interviewed by the CoC, which is to be compared to 30 civil servants from the governmental

offices and 23 civil servants from state agencies, respectively. The number of state secretaries interviewed by the CoC in 1994–2008 was 13; the number of DGs interviewed was 13. Among lower-level civil servants interviewed, 25 were governmental department employees and only 14 worked in a state agency. Source: Utskottens betänkanden, utlåtanden och yttranden (Reports and statements of opinion), available at www.riksdagen.se/Webbnav/index.aspx?nid=3320. The difference between the categories is indeed substantial. The number of state secretaries usually is limited to one or two per minister, and the number of ministers in the postwar era is on average 19 (Bäck, Persson, Vernby, & Wockelberg, 2009). This stands in sharp contrast to the large if declining number of state agencies: the approximate total of 1,400 state agencies in 1990 had, by January 1, 2010, shrunk to 391, not counting the 100 or so embassies or other Swedish representation abroad (Statskontoret, 2010). The state agencies all have some type of top manager, i.e., the equivalent of a DG.

16. Indeed, the Committee invites guests, and the Committee have no sanctions on hand should a civil servant decline to participate.

17. The DG of the Swedish Emergency Management Agency and a middle-level manager at the Swedish Rescue Service Agency.

18. The interviews were conducted in Stockholm, August 2010. (The interviews constitute one empirical part of the research project *After Crisis: The Accountability of Swedish Top Level Civil Servants*, which is funded by the Swedish Civil Contingencies Agency.) Three groups (a total of 14 interviewees) were interviewed, two by the author and one by Associate Professor Shirin Ahlbäck Öberg, Uppsala University. The interviews lasted for 2 hours. Prior to the meetings, the participants were informed of the ideas on responsibility put forward by the Commission. The strategic sample includes DGs from small and large agencies as well as veterans and individuals who are newcomers, respectively. Some of the interviewees have served also as top-level civil servants within the government offices, as state secretaries or even as a minister. For literature on focus group interviews, please see Söderström (2011).

19. Such as the Estonia crisis in 1994, the foot-and-mouth disease crisis, 9/11, and the pandemic flu threat in 2009.

20. As discussed above (see The Politics-Administration Dichotomy, Responsibility and Crisis), the classical Westminster responsibility doctrine expects ministers to be held responsible for all major failures within their department, regardless of whether they were known to the minister or not. In its modern version, the Westminster doctrine requires that "ministers accept blame only for serious departmental errors of which the minister knew or should have known" (Kam, 2000, pp. 1f.).

21. All quotes have been translated from Swedish by the author.

22. This organization was established after the tsunami.

23. In Swedish, *statsnytta*n, i.e., what the Germans call *Staatsraison,* and what some political scientists in English would refer to as the national interest (but then they would mainly be thinking of a nation's interests in relation to other states).

24. The interview data hence supports Asplind's observation that DGs with experience from working within the governmental offices appear as more aware of the rules of the game than other DGs (see Asplind 2009, pp. 190f.).

REFERENCES

Andersson, C. (2004). *Tudelad trots allt. Dualismens överlevnad i den Svenska staten 1718–1987.* Stockholm studies in Politics 107. (Doctoral thesis). Stockholm: Department of Political Science, Stockholm University.

Asplind, J. (2009). *Generaldirektör: I rikets tjänst på politikens villkor.* Växjö, Sverige: Artéa Förlag.

Bäck, H., Persson, T., Vernby, K., & Wockelberg, H. (2009). In tranquil waters: Swedish cabinet ministers in the postwar era. In K. Dowding & P. Dumont (Eds.), *The selection of ministers in Europe: Hiring and firing.* London: Routledge.

Beckman, L. (2003). Hotet mot det öppna samhället och demokratin. In L. Beckman, S. Olsson, & H. Wockelberg (Eds.), *Demokratin och mordet på Anna Lind* (KBMs temaserie 2003, p. 6). Stockholm: Krisberedskapsmyndigheten.

Boin, A., McConnell, A., & 't Hart, P. (2008). *Governing after crisis. The politics of investigation, accountability and learning.* Cambridge, UK: Cambridge University Press.

Bovens, M. (1998). *The quest for responsibility. Accountability and citizenship in complex organizations.* Cambridge, MA: Cambridge University Press.

Brändström, A., Kuipers, S., & Daléus, P. (2008). The politics of tsunami responses: Comparing patterns of blame management in Scandinavia. In A. Boin, A. McConnell, & P. 't Hart (Eds.), *Governing after crisis. The politics of investigation, accountability and learning.* Cambridge, MA: Cambridge University Press.

Brown, A. D. (2003). Authoritative sensemaking in a public inquiry report. *Organization Studies, 25*(1), 95–112.

Bull, T., & Bremdal, P. (2009). *Parlamentarisk kontroll av regeringen: En forskningsöversikt.* Konstitutionella Kontrollfrågor: Rapporter från Riksdagen (2008/09, RFR14). Stockholm: Swedish Parliament.

Cunningham, F. (2002). *Theories of democracy. A critical introduction.* New York: Routledge.

Dahl, R. A. (2000). *On democracy.* New Haven, CT & London: Yale University Press/ Yale Nota Bene.

Elliott, D., & McGuiness, M. (2002). Public inquiry: Panacea or placebo? *Journal of Contingencies and Crisis Management, 10*(1), 14–25.

Foyer, L. (1997). Konstitutionsutskottet och offentligheten. In L. Leifland & N. Andrén (Eds.), *Brobyggare: En vänbok till Nils Andrén.* Stockholm: Nerenius & Santérus Förlag.

Grandien, C., Nord, L., & Strömbäck, J. (2005). *Efter flodvågskatastrofen: Svenska folkets åsikter om och förtroende för myndigheter, medier och politiker* (KBMs temaserie 2005, p. 4). Stockholm: Krisberedskapsmyndigheten.

Gregory, R., & Grönnegard Christensen, J. (2004). Similar ends, differing means: Contractualism and civil service reform in Denmark and New Zealand. *Gover-*

nance: An International Journal of Policy, Administration, and Institutions, 17(1), 59–82.

Hammargren, L. (2002). *Offensiven Från Meniga riksdagsledamöter: En analys av KUs Granskningar av Ministerstyre 1975–2001.* (Student paper). Department of Government, Uppsala University.

Hansén, D. (2005). Den Svenska hanteringen av tsunamikatastrofen: Fokus på regeringskansliet. In *Sverige och tsunamin: Expertrapporter från 2005 års Katastrofkommission* (p. 104). Stockholm: Fritzes.

Hermansson, J. (2003). *Politik på upplysningens grund: Om den demokratiska reformismens möjligheter och Problem.* Malmö, Sverige: Liber.

Hogwood, B. W., Judge, D., & McVicar, M. (2001). Agencies, ministers and civil servants in Britain. In B. G. Peters & J. Pierre (Eds.), *Politicians, bureaucrats and administrative reform.* London: Routledge.

Kam, C. (2000). Not just parliamentary "cowboys and indians": Ministerial responsibility and bureaucratic drift. *Governance: An International Journal of Policy, Administration, and Institutions, 13*(3), 365–392.

Katastrofkommissionen. (2005): *Sverige och tsunamin, huvudbetänkande från 2005 års katastrofkommission* (p. 104). Stockholm: Fritzes.

Konstitutionsutskottets betänkande KU8. (2005/2006). *Regeringens krisberedskap och krishantering i samband med flodvågskatastrofen 2004.* Retrieved December 2, 2010, from www.riksdagen.se/Webbnav/index.aspx?nid=3322&dok_id=GT01KU8

Lagreid, P. (2000). Top civil servants under contract. *Public Administration, 78*(4), 879–896.

Olsen, J. P. (2009). Democratic government, institutional autonomy and the dynamics of change. *West European Politics, 32*(3), 439–465.

Olsson, S. (2006). *Så fungerar författningen vid kriser. En studie av hur statsmakterna hanterat morden på Olof Palme och Anna Lind* (KBMs rapportserie 2006, p. 3). Stockholm: Krisberedskapsmyndigheten.

Parker, C., & Dekker, S. (2008). September 11 and post crisis investigation: Exploring the role and impact of the 9/11 Commission. In A. Boin, A. McConnell, & P. 't Hart (Eds.), *Governing after crisis: The politics of investigation, accountability and learning.* Cambridge, MA: Cambridge University Press.

Peters, B. G. (2010). *The politics of bureaucracy. An introduction to comparative public administration* (6th ed.). London: Routledge.

Peters, B. G., & Pierre, J. (2001) Civil servants and politicians: The changing balance. In B. G. Peters & J. Pierre (Eds.), *Politicians, bureaucrats and administrative reform.* London: Routledge.

Pierre, J. (2001). Parallel paths? Administrative reform, public policy and politico-bureaucratic relationships in Sweden. In B. G. Peters & J. Pierre (Eds.), *Politicians, bureaucrats and administrative reform.* London: Routledge.

Pollitt, C. (2003). *The essential public manager.* Maidenhead, UK: Open University Press.

Pollitt, C. (2006). Performance management in practice: A comparative study of executive agencies. *Journal of Public Administration Research and Theory, 16*(1), 25–44.

Seeger, M. W., Ulmer, R. R., Novak, J. M., & Sellnow, T. (2005). Post-crisis discourse and organizational change, failure and renewal. *Journal of Organizational Change Management, 18*(1), 78–95.

Söderström, J. (2011). Focus groups in post-conflict settings. In K. Höglund & M. Öberg (Eds.), *Understanding peace research.* New York: Routledge.

Statskontoret. (2010). *Färre men större. Statliga myndigheter åren 2007–2010.* Retrieved December 2, 2010 from www.statskontoret.se/upload/Publikationer/Om%20offentlig%20sektor/Om-offentlig-sektor-6.pdf

Stern, E. (1997). Crisis and learning: A conceptual balance sheet. *Journal of Contingencies and Crisis Management, 5*(2), 69–86.

Sundström, G. (2003). *Stat på villovägar. Resultatstyrningens framväxt i ett historisk-institutionellt perspektiv.* (Doctoral thesis). Stockholm studies in Politics 96. Stockholm: Department of Political Science, Stockholm University.

Svara, J. H. (2001). The myth of the dichotomy: Complementarity of politics and administration in the past and future of public administration. *Public Administration Review, 61*(2), 176–182.

't Hart, P., & Wille, A. (2006). Ministers and top officials in the Dutch core executive: Living together, growing apart? *Public Administration, 84*(1), 121–146.

Wockelberg, H. (2003). *Den Svenska förvaltningsmodellen: Parlamentarisk debatt om förvaltningens roll i styrelseskicket.* (Doctoral thesis). Uppsala, Sverige: Acta Universitatis Upsaliensis Uppsala: Skrifter utgivna av Statsvetenskapliga föreningen i Uppsala, 155.

Wockelberg, H., & Ahlbäck Öberg, S. (2008). Ansvarsfullt ansvarsutkrävande: Om bruk och missbruk av KU. In S. Gustavsson, J. Hermansson, & B. Holmström (Eds.), *Statsvetare ifrågasätter. Uppsalamiljön vid tiden för professorsskiftet den 31 Mars 2008* (Skrifter utgivna av Statsvetenskapliga föreningen i Uppsala, 170), Uppsala, Sverige: Acta Universitatis Upsaliensis.

Woodhouse, D. (1994). *Ministers and parliament. Accountability in theory and practice.* Oxford, UK: Clarendon Press.

CHAPTER 10

THE PURPOSE, FUNCTIONS, AND ETHICAL DIMENSIONS OF POSTCRISIS INVESTIGATIONS

The Case of the 9/11 Commission

Charles F. Parker

INVESTIGATING THE 9/11 ATTACKS

In the wake of the terrorist attacks of September 11, 2001, it might seem obvious that an official public inquiry would be set up to establish exactly what happened, identify the problems that left the United States vulnerable to attack, and suggest remedies to repair the documented deficiencies. However, the National Commission on the Terrorist Attacks Upon the United States, popularly termed the 9/11 Commission, almost did not happen and most certainly would not have been created without the public efforts of the families of the victims. Once established, it was, in the words of its chairman, "set-up to fail" (Kean & Hamilton, 2006, p. 14; Kean, quoted in May, 2005, p. 30) with a shoestring budget and an impossibly short dead-

Ethics and Crisis Management, pages 183–198
Copyright © 2011 by Information Age Publishing
183

line among the many obstacles it faced. Nonetheless, the 9/11 Commission avoided the fate of oblivion typical of most commissions and reform efforts, and produced a widely hailed final report that enjoyed broad public support and spurred the reform of the entire U.S. intelligence community.

Every aspect of the 9/11 Commission, its origins, goals, the way it carried out its mission, the influence of the families of the victims, the decision to hold public hearings, its decision to focus on unity and making recommendations for reform rather than establishing individual responsibility, and even the monitoring activities the commissioners undertook after their mandate had formally ended, were infused with multiple ethical implications and choices, and involved navigating between dueling decision rationales. For this reason, the 9/11 Commission offers an important opportunity to probe how ethical considerations can impact the role, functioning, and consequences of postcrisis inquiries. Moreover, it provides a chance to explore how postcrisis inquires can create arenas of opportunity in which blame-game politics, political power struggles, and reform efforts play out, often with profound consequences for the future.

THREE RATIONALES FOR OFFICIAL POSTCRISIS INVESTIGATIONS

The establishment of postcrisis inquiries is a recurring pattern in Western democracies, and launching an official investigation potentially serves a number of core functions. What motivates the creation of official postcrisis investigations and what functions do they perform? At the top of the list is the need for fact finding and lesson drawing (Elliot & McGuinness, 2002). Politicians and government officials often emphasize this rationale, and one of the primary roles for official postcrisis commissions is to draw lessons from the crisis events they are charged with investigating. Public statements, founding legislation, and commission mission statements invariably make explicit the goal of learning. A postcrisis inquiry provides a means for discovering what happened and learning from it.

Second, a postcrisis commission ostensibly creates a fair and rational procedure for establishing what happened, assigning responsibility, and gaining wisdom. A neutral, dispassionate interpretive authority, in the form of a commission, made up of objective experts and wise laypersons, provides a ritualized and recognized course of action to accomplish these goals (Boin, 't Hart, Stern, & Sundelius, 2005, pp. 86, 109–110). The essence of symbolic policymaking lies in shaping a certain image and reassuring the public in order to restore or maintain confidence in public authorities and institutions (Dye, 1987; Edelman, 1985, 1988; Lasswell, 1935).

A third, and darker, interpretation of what motivates the establishment of postcrisis inquiries is pure political self-interest. This view stresses how commissions can be used to postpone difficult decisions, build momentum for action on urgent issues, serve as mechanisms to deflect blame, or to pin blame on responsible officials and current power holders (Boin et al., 2005, pp. 99–105; Lipsky & Olsen, 1977; cf. Platt, 1971). In fact, due to the complexity of the postcrisis process, there is a tendency of investigatory bodies to become *garbage cans* full of contentious issues with a variety of different participants with different perspectives, interests, and expectations vying for influence (March & Olsen, 1983, p. 286). Thus, in addition to functioning as fact-finding/learning vehicles and interpretive authorities for symbolic meaning making, postcrisis inquiries also are *realpolitik* arenas of opportunity in which a variety of political players and societal stakeholders attempt to pursue their own agendas in the postcrisis political process.

To better understand the origins, workings, and consequences of official postcrisis investigations in general and the 9/11 Commission in particular, it is helpful to view them through the prisms of all three rationales: fact finding/learning, symbolic meaning making, and political self-interest and competition (Parker & Dekker, 2008). In what follows, this chapter will examine the 9/11 Commission's creation, its functioning, and its outcomes with the aid of each perspective. Throughout, special attention will be paid to the ethical dynamics and implications at play, as these are important if one is to understand the genesis, role, and impact of the commission. For example, ethical issues were at the heart of many of the controversies related to the commission. Ethics are also key to making sense of the favorable reception that greeted the 9/11 Commission's report and its recommendations. The perception that the commission had carried out its investigation in a fair and ethical manner was crucial for its legitimacy and credibility.

THE CREATION OF THE 9/11 COMMISSION

How did the 9/11 Commission come about? An examination of the public statements and the legislative language that established the commission might lead one to conclude that the 9/11 Commission was simply a rational response. It constituted a fair and ethical mechanism for learning vital lessons from the tragic events of that day. The 9/11 Commission's explicit purpose, to provide a comprehensive account of what went wrong in order to avoid future terrorist attacks, closely mirrors what the fact finding/learning imperative perspective would predict.[1] However, while this rationale helps make sense of the specifics of the inquiry's mandate and the conduct of the commission in carrying out its business, uncritically accepting such a straightforward explanation for the creation of the commission oversimplifies and obscures a far more complex reality. In fact, at the outset, the Bush administration and Republican leaders in Congress were acutely aware of the political dangers posed by an independent inquiry and opposed the creation of an independent commission; they only reluctantly established one in the face of public pressure generated by the families of the victims of the 9/11 attacks (Whitney, 2004, p. xxii).

Although U.S. Senator Robert Torricelli called for a board of inquiry a little more than 2 weeks after the attacks, patterned after the post–Pearl Harbor board of inquiry into what he termed a "stunning failure" of U.S. intelligence (CNN, 2001), there was little momentum behind his proposal initially. On February 14, 2002, Senator Bob Graham (D-FL) and Congressman Porter Goss (R-FL) announced a joint inquiry by the Senate and House Select Committees on Intelligence. Graham and Goss said their 9/11 inquiry would focus specifically on the role of the intelligence agencies. The Bush administration made it clear that it believed that this investigation would suffice.

However, the limited focus of this inquiry did not satisfy the families of the victims of 9/11. They mounted a vocal campaign for a broader investigation conducted by an independent commission, which would include the role of all relevant agencies, the Congress, and the executive branch. The Bush administration, however, did not share this view. It argued that the Congressional joint inquiry into the attacks was more than adequate and that an independent blue ribbon commission was an unnecessary distraction that would divert attention from the war on terror (Falkenrath, 2004/05, p. 170; Whitney, 2004, p. xxi).

Consistent public pressure and an effective lobbying campaign persuaded enough House Republicans to join Democrats and produce a majority vote on July 25, 2002, to set up an independent commission. Still, the White House continued to resist. The families would not give up, and the need for a thorough review gained momentum as the joint inquiry's investigation produced disturbing revelations about missed warning signals and coordination failures by government agencies. On September 20, 2002, the Bush administration finally agreed to create a bipartisan independent investigation. It took another 2 months of tough negotiations before the White House reached an agreement with Congress on the specifics of the inquiry. On November 27, 2002, just 14 months after the attacks on the Twin Towers and the Pentagon, President Bush signed into law an act that established the 9/11 Commission.[2]

Why did Bush reverse his administration's course and agree to the creation of a commission, then repeatedly express support in public for the commission, and eventually publicly endorse its conclusions and recommendations? A complex ethical, symbolic, and political calculus makes these decisions comprehensible. Viewed solely from the perspective of political self-interest, the White House's behavior might be seen as a tactical response to a political setback. However, the White House also realized that the commission could and did serve a number of useful symbolic purposes for them as well. Rather than being blamed for blocking the creation of an independent commission and appearing as an impediment in the process of finding out what went wrong on September 11, 2001, President Bush could take credit for the commission. Once it was created, the White House went out of its way to publicly endorse the commission's work. Bush called for the commission to learn important lessons from 9/11 and hailed its work as "important for future administrations" (White House, 2002). Doing so allowed Bush to make the case that he had made the moral judgment that "we must uncover every detail and learn every lesson of September the 11th" (White House, 2002).

While the evidence suggests that Bush's motives were far from pure, his repeated remarks lauding the commission can be seen as more than political posturing. As March and Olsen (1983) observed, "Virtuous words sustain the meaning and importance of virtue, even among sinners" (p. 290). In this sense, Bush's statements and support of the 9/11 Commission reflect and symbolize fundamental societal beliefs about the possibility of learning, improving government performance, and gaining mastery over the forces that affect our lives and future. Ethics, or at least the desire to appear to have acted ethically, is central for understanding how the 9/11 Commission came into being, despite much initial opposition.

ETHICS AND THE 9/11 COMMISSION'S ROCKY START

Ideally, an official postcrisis inquiry represents a fair and neutral means for determining what happened, establishing responsibility, managing value conflicts, and making recommendations for the future. If the process is to be perceived as ethical and fair, the members of the inquiry and its staff must be viewed as qualified to carry out the investigation, independent, and free of any conflicts of interest or disqualifying partisan political agendas (March & Olsen, 1983, p. 290; Seidman, 1980, pp. 10–11). A failure to build trust and any evidence of dishonesty or unfairness could result in the postcrisis commission's work being dismissed as a whitewash or a witch hunt. In the case of the 9/11 Commission, it was crucial that it not be seen as a White House-owned panel or as a runaway investigation with a political agenda. The need for transparency and a freedom from conflicts of interest would be central to whether it succeeded or its efforts would be greeted with cynicism.

Not surprisingly, concerns about conflicts of interest and ethics were at the heart of several controversies surrounding the 9/11 Commission.

There were concerns over whether Henry Kissinger should lead the investigation (Dao, 2002); whether Phillip Zelikow, with his ties to Condoleezza Rice, President Bush's national security adviser, and his participation in the Security Council transition for the incoming George W. Bush administration, should serve as the commission's executive director (Shenon, 2008); and whether Commissioner Jamie Gorelick, the former Deputy Attorney General who served during the Clinton administration, should step down and "testify on her alleged role in building the 'wall' between intelligence and law enforcement in the mid-1990s" (Fessenden, 2005, p. 110).[3]

Ethical issues concerning conflicts of interest can call into question the first rationale of these bodies, namely whether an official inquiry can be trusted with its fact-finding mission to provide a full accounting of what happened. This in turn jeopardizes the second rationale of postcrisis inquiries: symbolic meaning making by an interpretive authority that is perceived as fair and just. Finally, the third perspective sheds light on how ethical issues can be part of the battle for influence in the postcrisis process and struggle for influence and political advantage. Henry Kissinger's short-lived tenure as the chairman of the 9/11 Commission is illustrative of how these dynamics can play out.

Congressional and administration negotiators agreed that a 10-member commission would be equally divided, with 5 Republican appointees and 5 Democratic appointees. The president would name the chairman, and the Democratic congressional leadership would pick the vice-chairman. President Bush's selection of Henry Kissinger, the Republican former Secretary of State and foreign policy heavyweight, to head the commission created a firestorm of controversy. At the root of the controversy was whether Kissinger, who ran an international consulting firm, Kissinger Associates, known to advise foreign governments and multinational corporations, would have to divulge his client list. According to the Senate Ethics Committee, since the commission was created by an act of Congress, all commissioners would have to follow congressional rules concerning the disclosures of possible conflicts of interest. This would require Kissinger to make public any client that had paid him more than $5,000 in the last 2 years. The White House disagreed and said that as an Executive Branch appointee, he was not subject to the same rules of disclosure as those appointed by Congress (Schmitt, 2002). The attempts to keep Kissinger's client list a secret alarmed critics concerned about a whitewash and raised questions about whether Kissinger would be able to aggressively investigate events that might in some way involve or prove embarrassing to his clients (Dao, 2002; Firestone, 2002).

A *New York Times* editorial (2002), entitled "The Kissinger Dodge," called for Kissinger to make his clients public or step aside. The same editorial also reported that this struggle was causing a "growing sense among some victim families that the commission is being orchestrated to see that the panel never rises above a partisan divide" ("Kissinger Dodge," 2002).

In an attempt to assuage concerns over his role as the chairman of the commission, Kissinger met with a group of family activists at his consulting offices. The meeting went poorly. According to some family members who attended the meeting, Kissinger did not respond well to questions concerning his client list, potential conflicts of interest, and to a direct question of whether he had any Saudi clients or if any of his clients were named bin Laden (Shenon, 2008, pp. 10–15). The next day, December 13, 2002, Kissinger resigned as chairman. George Mitchell, the Democratic choice for vice-chairman, unwilling to cut ties with his law firm's interests, had resigned just 2 days before.

The 9/11 Commission was off to a troubled start. The mission of making the commission work would fall to Kissinger and Mitchell's replacements, Chairman Thomas H. Kean, President of Drew University and a former Republican Governor of New Jersey (1982–1990), and Vice-Chairman Lee Hamilton, former Democratic congressman from Indiana.

MAKING IT WORK: THE CONDUCT AND FUNCTIONING OF THE 9/11 COMMISSION

According to its chairmen, Kean and Hamilton, the 9/11 Commission had been "set up to fail" (Kean & Hamilton, 2006, p. 14). In Kean's view, "If you want something to fail you take a controversial topic and appoint five people from each party. You make sure they are appointed by the most partisan people from each party—the leaders of the party. And, just to make sure, let's ask the commission to finish the report during the most partisan period of time—the presidential election season" (Kean, quoted in May, 2005, p. 30).

As Kean and Hamilton (2006) observe in their memoir of the commission, their endeavor faced many dangerous pitfalls that could result in failure: the commission could "splinter down partisan lines; lose its credibility by leaking classified information; be denied the necessary access to do its job; or alienate the 9/11 families that had fought on behalf of its creation" (p. 15).

In attempt to avoid the many problems that could lead to failure, the commission pursued a course that took into account all three of the rationales that animate and affect official postcrisis investigations. First, Kean and Hamilton enthusiastically embraced the commission's fact-finding and lesson-drawing mandate, pursued a strategy for achieving it, and made a public effort to communicate what their goals were and how they were going to achieve them. Their chief goal was to have the commission's findings and recommendations accepted. "To succeed," Kean decided, "*The 9/11*

Commission Report had to be a historical document, not simply a government report with a list of conclusions. We had to be clear where those facts were coming from. We could not simply recommend a policy change because it was a good idea: every single recommendation that we made had to spring from the story of 9/11" (Kean & Hamilton, 2006, p. 6).[4]

Senior advisor Ernest May (2005), a Harvard historian, writes that Kean, Hamilton, and executive director Philip Zelikow made a conscious and novel decision to produce a "professional-quality narrative history" (p. 31) to tell the story of 9/11 rather than producing a standard government report more typical of this *genre*, reports that have a tendency to focus on "findings" (p. 31) and "array the evidence accordingly" (p. 31). Instead, as Kean put it, what the panel wanted was "a report that our grandchildren can take off the shelf in fifty years and say, 'This is what happened' " (Kean, quoted in May, 2005, p. 31).

Secondly, Kean and Hamilton were acutely aware of the importance of the symbolic requirements of their mission. The essence of symbolic accountability procedures lies in shaping an image of probity and convincing the public that it should have confidence in the investigation's process and outcome (Dye, 1987; Edelman, 1985, 1988; Lasswell, 1935; March & Olsen, 1983; Peay, 1996). For example, Pearl Harbor inquiries like the Roberts Commission had failed, in part, because they were widely seen as partisan attempts to pin blame on particular individuals. Instead of clarifying matters, the work of the Warren Commission that looked into the Kennedy assassination, due to the secrecy surrounding it, led to distrust and fueled a raft of conspiracy theories. The chairmen of the 9/11 Commission knew that if their investigation was to succeed, and avoid the fate common to failed commissions of the past, it would need to appear neutral, conduct an open and transparent investigation, abstain from partisan politics, and generate public and media interest in its work (Kean & Hamilton, 2006, pp. 22–30).

To this end, the commission decided to hold open public hearings as a strategy for building credibility with the public and the media, and to build support for its findings (9/11 Commission, 2004, p. xv). The 19 days of public hearings with testimony from 160 witnesses resulted in substantial media attention and contributed to the perception that the commission was living up to its pledge to be as transparent as possible. These hearings opened up a window into the inner workings of the government, and revelations from the public testimony of key officials helped shape public opinion. The commissioners were available to the media while the commission was still deliberating, a practice that raised the panel's public profile. Another novel innovation for an inquiry of this kind was the decision to publish staff reports prior to the hearings. A total of 17 staff statements, covering subjects such as aviation security, counterterrorism, threat warnings and responses, the performance of the intelligence community, and homeland defense were made public in advance of the final report.[5] This provided the commission a mechanism for previewing its findings and keeping the public and media engaged and invested in its work.

In the end, the commission fulfilled its fact-finding mission by producing a history of September 11 that provided a gold mine of material and information. In addition to the 17 staff statements, the commission produced two monographs, as well as its 567-page final report. The final report devoted 11 of its 13 chapters to the history of 9/11, supported by 116 pages of meticulously documented footnotes, and concluded with two chapters of recommendations. In carrying out its work, the commission examined more than 2.5 million documents and interviewed more than 1,200 individuals in ten countries (9/11 Commission, 2004, p. xv).

Finally, Kean and Hamilton and the other commissioners were savvy political operators. They knew that the 9/11 Commission would be the locus of potential clashes for power and influence, and that a potential agent for change, like the commission, might attract opposition from threatened status quo interests, and that these individuals and groups would fight for their own protection (Kean & Hamilton, 2006, pp. 57–79). If the 9/11 Commission was to succeed, it could not appear toothless; it would have to pick some battles and win. However, it would have to pick its fights wisely, for both practical and symbolic reasons. While it was important that the commission be seen as independent, if it appeared unreasonably adversarial, it risked having its credibility and fairness called into question, and it might be forced to fight unnecessary and protracted legal disputes.

Although President Bush had pledged to cooperate with and support the investigation, the administration battled with the commission on a variety of fronts (Drew, 2004; Kean & Hamilton, 2006; May, 2005; Shenon, 2008). The administration and Congressional Republicans initially tried to deny the commission sufficient time or financial resources to carry out its work. The White House also forced the commission to fight time-consuming skirmishes over access to sensitive documents, such as the President's Daily Briefs (PDBs); attempted to assert executive privilege to prevent presidential advisers, such as Condoleezza Rice, from giving sworn public testimony; and tried to limit the commission's access to President Bush to a single one-hour meeting with the two chairmen and not with the full commission. The commission encountered resistance from other quarters as well, such as the Federal Aviation Administration and the North American Air Defense Command.

By being "both conciliatory and confrontational" (Kean & Hamilton, 2006, p. 37), the commission skillfully utilized the resources at their disposal, the threat of their subpoena power, issuing subpoenas when needed, deploying the families of the victims, and making appeals to the public and the media, in the pursuit of the commission's goal of gaining access to the government documents and people that would allow them to say, "we have asked for everything that has to do with the 9/11 story, and seen everything we asked for" (Kean & Hamilton 2006, p. 25). Although they did not win every battle, and compromised on a number of issues, they were remarkably successful.

The commission managed to get an additional $11 million of funding added to their shockingly inadequate original budget of $3 million. They won a 2-month extension until July 26, 2004, on their reporting date, and a 1-month extension on the life of the commission, despite the initial opposition from the administration and the even more reluctant House Speaker Dennis Hastert (R-IL). Condoleezza Rice ended up publicly testifying before the commission. The PDB, "Bin Laden Determined To Strike in US," given to Bush on August 6, 2001, was made public and eventually declassified (9/11 Commission, 2004, pp. 261–262).

On other issues, full access to the PDBs, interviews with top executive office officials, and the conditions of an interview with President Bush and Vice-President Cheney, the commission compromised. For example, they agreed to a complicated arrangement with the White House that allowed executive director, Philip Zelikow (R), Commissioner Jamie Gorelick (D), and Kean and Hamilton to review the full run of PDBs (9/11 Commission, 2004, p. 533; May, 2005, p. 32). Concerning the interview with the president and vice-president, the White House offered a meeting with the full commission and ended up imposing no time limit, but rejected the request for separate meetings and did not allow the meeting to be recorded or transcribed, although Zelikow was allowed to attend as a note taker.

One conflict that the 9/11 Commission failed to win or, in the eyes of some, sufficiently fight to win, an issue with a number of profound moral implications, was its dispute with the CIA over access to al-Qaeda detainees. CIA Director George Tenet refused to let the commission directly question key detainees involved in the September 11 plot, including most significantly, the plot's mastermind Khalid Sheikh Mohammed. The CIA also prevented the commission from naming any detainees in the final report other than the ones whose custody had already been officially acknowledged. Parts of the final report relied "heavily on information obtained from captured al-Qaeda members," (9/11 Commission, 2004, p. 146), although the commission acknowledged that assessing the truth of this material was "challenging" (9/11 Commission, 2004, p. 146).[6]

Another ethical problem with this material concerns the interrogation methods, including coercive techniques such as *waterboarding*, which were reportedly used to obtain it (Drew, 2004, p. 6). Information that might have been elicited with coercive methods brings with it legal and moral questions as well as concerns about the reliability of the information. Senior advisor Ernest May faults the commission on the detainee issue, writing, "I think the commission could have successfully challenged the CIA on both access to the detainees and release of the names, but it chose not to fight these battles" (May, 2005, p. 35).

ASSESSING THE 9/11 COMMISSION'S IMPACT: THE COSTS AND BENEFITS OF ITS CHOICES

In contrast to the typical fate of most postcrisis commissions and reform efforts, which generally do not garnish much interest and usually fail to produce major change or dramatic reform (March & Olsen, 1983; Olsen & Peters, 1996; Zegart 2005), the 9/11 Commission's final report had an enormous public impact and turned out to be a major impetus for the reform and transformation of the U.S. intelligence community (Parker & Dekker, 2008).

The final report was released on July 22, 2004, directly in the midst of a heated presidential campaign and both candidates, Democratic challenger John Kerry and Republican George W. Bush, praised the report, publicly endorsed the report's recommendations, and entered into a political bidding war over the reforms they intended to enact. Congress responded to the report by taking the unusual step of holding hearings on its recommendations during its August recess. In early August, President Bush responded to the report by quickly issuing a number of executive orders, which, among other things, created a Director of National Intelligence and a National Counterterrorism Center.

The report also spurred legislation for a major overhaul of the U.S. intelligence community (Falkenrath, 2004/05, p. 188; Posner, 2005, p. 57; Zegart, 2005, p. 109). Despite furious opposition from the Pentagon and its supporters, Congress passed a historic bill to remake the U.S. intelligence system and implement many of the 9/11 Commission's key recommendations into law. In December 2004, President George W. Bush, who had won reelection, signed into law what he called "the most dramatic reform of our nation's intelligence capabilities since President Harry S. Truman signed the National Security Act of 1947" (White House, 2004)— the Intelligence Reform and Terrorism Prevention Act. How did the 9/11 Commission achieve its success, and what were some of the ethical implications of the trade-offs, compromises, and decisions the panel made in the pursuit of its goals?

A major reason for the 9/11 Commission's success was the fact that five Republicans and five Democrats unanimously endorsed the final report (May & Zelikow, 2005, p. 208). The 9/11 commissioners and chairmen felt that if their final report was to have any impact, it had to be unanimous (Kean & Hamilton, 2006, p. 291). Unanimity was crucial for two of the commission's main goals: a compressive account that would be widely perceived as legitimate and the acceptance of its recommendations. A contested and divided final report could easily be dismissed as a flawed partisan product and would have virtually no chance of having its recommendations implemented.

However, this bipartisan result did come with some ethical trade-offs and costs. Unanimity probably could not have been achieved without soft-peddling the interpretation of some sensitive topics and avoiding the assessment of individual culpability (Drew, 2004; May, 2005; May & Zelikow, 2005; Posner, 2004). In effect, individual accountability was exchanged for unanimity and political punch. The 9/11 Commission deliberately chose not to make judgments regarding individual responsibility. As stated in the preface of the final report, "our aim has not been to assign individual blame. Our aim has been to provide the fullest possible account of the events surrounding 9/11 and to identify lessons learned" (9/11 Commission, 2004, p. xvi). Thus, rather than singling specific individuals out for blame, the commission zeroed in on institutional, structural, and procedural failures, particularly in the FBI and CIA. Thus, when it came to individual sanctioning or consequences, there were none to be had. No one lost their job over mistakes or failures related to 9/11.

This caused some to criticize the report for perpetuating a "no fault" (Falkenrath, 2005, p. 211) view of governance that sent future officials and those who train them "exactly the wrong message" (Falkenrath, 2005, p. 211). In the view of one critic, "the starting point in any after-the-fact governmental analysis should always be the concept of personal responsibility" (Falkenrath, 2005, p. 211).

Producing a report that all the commissioners could endorse also entailed a number of other costs, which resulted in some weaknesses in the final product. For example, according to May (2005, p. 34), the report in places "pairs contradictory evidence without helping the reader evaluate them"; was at times too "indulgent" in its treatment of Clinton, Bush, and some of their top advisers; and unnecessarily balanced its harsh criticism of institutions, such as the CIA and FBI, with some "words of praise" that were not always "deserved." May does acknowledge that the decision not to apportion blame directly and to write the report as a straightforward just-the-facts narrative did have some redeeming benefits as well. It made it easier to present unflattering material because "any point potentially reflecting unfavorably on one administration could be balanced with a point reflecting unfavorably on the other" (May, 2005, p. 33). This resulted in a report that includes a wealth of information and facts that allows citizens and scholars to connect the dots themselves concerning the formation and execution of counterterrorism policy across several presidential administrations (Parker & Stern, 2005; cf. Perrow, 2005; Posner, 2005). Moreover, had the commission attempted to pin blame and make value judgments on exactly which officials were most responsible, it is highly unlikely that all 10 commissioners would have signed off and endorsed the final report.

CONCLUSION

As this chapter has shown, it is clear that in the pursuit of its goals, the 9/11 Commission's members and leadership made choices and reached compromises that required them to make moral judgments that entailed ethical trade-offs and had concrete costs. Ultimately, however, the 9/11 Commission's conduct, the way it carried out its investigation, and its ability to produce a unanimous final report allowed it to capture the public's imagination and gave it status as a trusted interpretive authority, all of which contributed to its unusual political impact (Parker & Dekker, 2008).

For example, in its goal to bring the country together and gain widespread public support for its account of what happened, the 9/11 Commission clearly succeeded. A survey conducted in July 2004, just prior to the release of the final report, showed that by more than a two-to-one margin (61% to 24%), the American people—Democrats (62%) and Republicans (61%) alike—approved of the job that the commission had done.[7] The commission was also widely commended by the media, academics, and policy experts for producing a historical document that was comprehensive and credible (Drew, 2004; Perrow, 2005, p. 99; Posner, 2004). Publications such as the *Economist, Time, The New Republic,* and *The New Yorker,* among others, praised the report as a masterpiece.

After the 9/11 Commission formally disbanded, the commissioners took the unusual step of coming together to form the 9/11 Public Discourse Project. The project aimed to "educate the public on the issue of terrorism and what can be done to make the country safer" (9/11 Public Discourse Project, 2004) and played an important role in the push for enacting major security and intelligence reform legislation. Through the project, the 9/11 Commission lived on as a symbolic public watchdog and advocate for the implementation of the commission's recommendations. In the estimation of Kean and Hamilton (2006), the efforts of the 9/11 families and the staff of the Public Discourse Project was "critical" (p. 329) to the successful passage of the intelligence reform bill.

In the final assessment, the 9/11 Commission had an extraordinarily successful public and policy impact, in large part because it effectively navigated among the three rationales, fact finding/learning, symbolic meaning making, and political self-interest and competition, that motivate the creation and affect the functioning of official postcrisis inquires; because it was widely perceived as carrying out its work ethically, fairly, and responsibly; and because it produced findings and recommendations that triggered debate and political momentum for action. These are important lessons for those interested in why some official postcrisis investigations fail and why some succeed. A common outcome for postcrisis inquiry reports is to be ignored and then forgotten—to gather dust on a shelf. The 9/11 Commission escaped this fate by avoiding the major ethical and substantive missteps that could have destroyed it and instead produced a final report that achieved the symbolic and political clout that helped enable the passage of a major reform package.

NOTES

1. The commission's official remit was sweeping. It had to "examine and report upon the fact and causes relating to the terrorist attacks of September 11, 2001" and "report to the President and Congress on its findings, conclusions, and recommendations for corrective measures that can be taken to prevent acts of terrorism" (Intelligence Authorization Act for Fiscal Year 2003, Public Law 107-306, title VI, 107th Cong., 2d sess., November 27, 2002, p. 2408).
2. Intelligence Authorization Act for Fiscal Year 2003, Public Law 107-306, title VI, 107th Cong., 2d sess., November 27, 2002.
3. Attorney General John Ashcroft attempted to deflect attention from his performance prior to 9/11 by attacking Gorelick during his public testimony before the commission (John Ashcroft testimony, Tenth Public Hearing, Tuesday, April 13, 2004). The commission's final report debunked his charges (9/11 Commission, 2004, p. 539).
4. It should be noted that, in the view of some critics, the commission did not always succeed in adequately grounding its recommendations with the final report's empirical findings (Falkenrath, 2004/05; Posner, 2005, p. 12).
5. The staff statements are available at www.9-11commission.gov/staff_statements/index.htm#statements
6. To cope with this problem, the commission says it "evaluated their statements carefully" and "attempted to corroborate them with documents and statements of others" (9/11 Commission, 2004, p.146).
7. The Pew Research Center. Survey report at http://people-press.org/reports/display.php3?ReportID=219

REFERENCES

9/11 Commission (National Commission on Terrorist Attacks Upon the United States). (2004). *The 9/11 Commission Report.* New York: Norton.
9/11 Public Discourse Project. (2004) *About the project.* Retrieved December 14, 2010, from http://www.9-11pdp.org/about/index.htm
Boin, A., 't Hart, P., Stern, E., & Sundelius, B. (2005). *The politics of crisis management: Public leadership under pressure.* Cambridge, UK: Cambridge University Press.

CNN. (2001, September 26). *Torricelli wants probe into 'stunning' intelligence failure.* Retrieved December 14, 2010, from http://articles.cnn.com/2001-09-26/us/inv.intelligence.board_1_robert-torricelli-inquiry-intelligence?_s=PM:US.

Dao, J. (2002, November 28). Making a return to the political stage—Henry Alfred Kissinger. *New York Times.* Retrieved May 6, 2011 from http://www.nytimes.com/2002/11/28/us/threats-responses-appointee-man-making-return-political-stage-henry-alfred.html

Drew, E. (2004). Pinning the blame. *The New York Review of Books, 51*(14), 6–12.

Dye, T. R. (1987). *Understanding public policy.* Englewood Cliffs, NJ: Prentice-Hall.

Edelman, M. (1985). Political language and political reality. *Political Studies, 18*(1), 10–19.

Edelman, M. (1988). *Constructing the political spectacle.* Chicago: University of Chicago Press.

Elliott, D., & McGuinness, M. (2002). Public inquiry: Panacea or placebo. *Journal of Contingencies and Crisis Management, 10*(1), 14–25.

Falkenrath, R. A. (2004/05, Winter). The 9/11 Commission report. *International Security, 29*(3), 170–190.

Falkenrath, R. A. (2005). Sins of commission? Falkenrath and his critics: The author replies. *International Security, 29*(4), 209–211.

Fessenden, H. (2005). The limits of intelligence reform. *Foreign Affairs, 84*(6), 106–120.

Firestone, D. (2002, December 14). Kissinger pulls out as chief of inquiry into 9/11 attacks. *New York Times.* Retrieved May 6, 2011 from http://www.nytimes.com/2002/12/14/us/threats-responses-investigation-kissinger-pulls-chief-inquiry-into-9-11-attacks.html

Kean, T. H., & Hamilton, L. H. (2006). *Without precedent: The inside story of the 9/11 Commission.* New York: Knopf.

Kissinger Dodge. (2002, December 13) Editorial. *The New York Times.* Retrieved May 6, 2011 from http://www.nytimes.com/2002/12/13/opinion/the-kissinger-dodge.html

Lasswell, H. D. (1935). *World politics and personal insecurity.* New York: Whittlesey House.

Lipsky, M., & Olsen, D. J. (1977). *Commission politics: The processing of racial crisis in America.* New Brunswick, NJ: Transaction.

March, J. G., & Olsen, J. P. (1983). Organizing political life: What administrative reorganization tells us about government. *The American Political Science Review, 77*(2), 281–296.

May, E. R. (2005, May). When government writes history: A memoir of the 9/11 commission. *The New Republic,* 30–35.

May, E. R., & Zelikow, P. D. (2005). Sins of commission? Falkenrath and his critics. *International Security, 29*(4), 208–209.

Olsen, J. P., & Peters, B. G. (Eds.). (1996). *Lessons from experience: Experiential learning in administrative reforms in eight democracies.* Oslo, Norway: Scandinavian University Press.

Parker, C. F., & Dekker, S. (2008). September 11 and post crisis investigation: Exploring the role and impact of the 9/11 commission. In A. Boin, A. McConnell, &

P. 't Hart (Eds.), *Governing after crisis: The politics of investigation, accountability and learning.* Cambridge, MA: Cambridge University Press.

Parker, C. F., & Stern, E. K. (2005). Bolt from the blue or avoidable failure? Revisiting September 11 and the origins of strategic surprise. *Foreign Policy Analysis, 1*(3), 301–331.

Peay, J. (1996). *Inquiries after homicide.* London: Duckworth.

Perrow, C. (2005). Organizational or executive failures? *Contemporary Sociology, 34*(2), 99–107.

Platt, A. (1971). The politics of riot commissions, 1917–1970: An overview. In A. Platt, (Ed.), *The politics of riot commissions, 1917–1970: A collection of official reports and critical essays.* New York: Macmillan.

Posner, R. A. (2004). *The 9/11 report: A dissent.* The New York Times Book Review. Retrieved May 6, 2011 from http://www.nytimes.com/2004/08/29/books/the-9-11-report-a-dissent.html

Posner, R. A. (2005). *Preventing surprise attacks: Intelligence reform in the wake of 9/11.* Lanham, MD: Rowman & Littlefield.

Schmitt, E. (2002, December 12). Clash between democrats and white house on need for Kissinger disclosure. *The New York Times.* Retrieved May 6, 2011 from http://www.nytimes.com/2002/12/12/us/threats-responses-appointees-clash-between-democrats-white-house-need-for.html

Seidman, H. (1980). *Politics, position and power: The dynamics of federal organization* (3rd ed.). New York: Oxford University Press.

Shenon, P. (2008). *The commission: The uncensored history of the 9/11 investigation.* New York: Twelve.

White House. (2002, November 27). President signs 911 Commission bill. *Office of the Press Secretary.* Retrieved December 14, 2010, from http://georgewbush-whitehouse.archives.gov/news/releases/2002/11/20021127-1.html

White House. (2004, December 17). President signs Intelligence Reform and Terrorism Prevention Act. *Office of the Press Secretary.* Retrieved December 14, 2010, from http://georgewbush-whitehouse.archives.gov/news/releases/2004/12/20041217-1.html

Whitney, C. R. (2004). Introduction. In S. Strasser (Ed.), *The 9/11 investigations.* New York: Public Affairs.

Zegart, A. B. (2005). September 11 and the adaptation failure of the U.S. intelligence agencies. *International Security, 29*(4), 78–111.

CHAPTER 11

UNCERTAINTY, ACCOUNTABILITY, AND THE CONDUCT OF POSTCRISIS INQUIRIES

Daniel Nohrstedt

INTRODUCTION

One defining characteristic of crises is that they are events that call for urgent public action. In the midst of crisis events, decision makers at different levels have to make decisive calls about courses of actions during difficult conditions of value complexity, short response time, threat, and uncertainty. In contemporary democratic society, those actions are increasingly being subject to public scrutiny and review by permanent investigative bodies, ad hoc commissions, or other public inquiries. Such postcrisis evaluations are generally appointed to provide an objective assessment or to construe the officially certified version of the course of events and the decisions taken by public organizations in response to those events (Boin, McConnell, & 't Hart, 2008). Broadly speaking, policy evaluation involves making claims about the ethics and morality of public performance (Schwandt, 1989). Evaluation of crisis events is thus a normative enterprise (Vedung, 1997),

Ethics and Crisis Management, pages 199–215
Copyright © 2011 by Information Age Publishing
199

which involves defining *in retrospect* what actions were appropriate and the right thing to do, given both situational and institutional constraints.

Prior research on postcrisis inquiries sheds light on the different functions inquiries have in practice (Boudes & Laroche, 2009; Elliott & McGuinness, 2002; Gephardt, 1993; Parker & Dekker, 2008; Seeger, Ulmer, Novak, & Sellnow, 2005). First, inquiries have a framing role by defining expectations; that is, the rules, norms, and values decision makers are supposed to follow. Expectations are the benchmarks against which crisis performance is judged. Second, inquiries are arenas that allocate responsibility by analysing the degree of fit between expectations and (in)actions. Third, inquiries ideally fill the role of learning devices by which mismatches between expectations and crisis performance generate recommendations or suggestions for systemic improvement. It can be hypothesized that these functions are causally related. Expectations guiding the inquiry are likely to affect the logic according to which moral behavior is assessed (accountability), which in turn will shape the outcome of the inquiry in terms of policy recommendations. From this perspective, it is critical to study more closely the terms of inquiry, including the formal rules and informal norms that evaluators expect crisis decision makers to follow. A related rationale is the general expectation that the efforts of decision makers to cope with crisis problems will be subject to fair or reasonable treatment (Bowen & Power, 1993). Accordingly, crisis decision-making and efforts to cope with crisis problems should ideally be judged in relation to the expectations imposed by formal rules and informal norms (Perrow, 1984; Senge, 1990).

Against this background, the objective of this chapter is to explore how public inquiries balance the tension between crafting clear standards to assess crisis performance, while acknowledging the uncertainty characterizing crisis management. The analysis starts by elaborating a simple analytical model that seeks to clarify the linkage between expectations, accountability, and outcomes of public inquiries. Managerial problems identified by the Pitt review during the 2007 flood disaster in the United Kingdom are used to explore the validity of the model.

ETHICAL FUNCTIONS OF CRISIS INQUIRIES

Regarding the practice of moral judgment, crisis evaluations generally take on several specific ethical functions. First, they directly or indirectly identify core societal values that should or must be protected when a crisis hits (see Chapter 1, this volume). If provided with a relatively open mandate, investigators can have substantial freedom to frame the scope of the problem they have been set to review. A postcrisis evaluation can thereby become a venue where the nature and scale of events are defined. Framing the scope of a crisis or emergency is partly about assessing material costs resulting from an event or series of events (for example, estimating the amount of property destroyed or the number of people killed or injured in a natural disaster) but also, in part, about identifying potentially disastrous risks and threats that did not actually materialize. These costs, risks, and threats reveal what societal values are at stake during a crisis or emergency. These values tend to be broadly defined societal values such as security, safety, economic development, democratic legitimacy, environmental protection, and so on.

A second function filled by crisis evaluations is to set standards for what actions (and inactions) are considered to be morally acceptable behavior. Postcrisis inquiries seek to define the boundaries that separate good and bad practice, appropriate and inappropriate behavior, and effective and ineffective responses to crisis problems. (This is not always the case, however, as the mandate and/or resources allocated to evaluations might be restricted for political or other reasons.) Such judgments are generally based on informed causal reasoning about the relationship between decision problems, organizational and institutional resources, and choice. Did individuals and organizations do what was expected from them during difficult external conditions, or should they have been able to perform better? Were flaws in the crisis response due to poor structural conditions, or were they rather the result of bad personal judgment? Part of this judgment also involves assessing the relationship between governmental plans and emergent norms instigated by the needs of a population affected by a crisis or disaster (Schneider, 1992). As mentioned above, these standards are derived from a mix of socially imposed rules and norms expressed in legislation, bureaucratic mandates, and public expectations.

Third, in the long run, crisis evaluations might contribute to institutionalize moral standards into formal rules or codes of conduct. When taking a holistic approach, evaluations assess behavior, given a set of organizational and institutional constraints. This is part of an effort to make realistic or fair judgments about crisis response actions proportionate to preexisting resources (e.g., personnel, equipment) and rules (e.g., laws, guidelines, and crisis plans). When evaluations offer recommendations for improvement, they often prescribe changes in structural conditions that aim to ensure better preparedness capacities for future crises and emergencies (Elliott & McGuinness, 2002; Parker & Dekker, 2008).

Rules, Norms, and Regulatory Uncertainty

Postcrisis inquiries commonly set out by taking into consideration the institutions, organizations, and legal frameworks set up to prepare for and mitigate the effects of threatening and harmful events (Gephart, 1993,

p. 1475). Consequently, actions, decisions, and outcomes are appraised *relative* to the structural conditions and constraints imposed by bureaucratic organizations and the formal rules imposed by generic crisis management institutions. Formal rules, however, are not the only precondition considered in public inquiries. Another element guiding postcrisis evaluation, yet less discernible in practice, involves attempts to identify socially imposed expectations in terms of norms (Schneider, 1992). Hence, one core objective of postcrisis inquiries is to judge how well public agencies and other organizations coped, given a set of predefined formal and informal constraints. As Bovens (1998) states, "there can be no accusation without norms and values" (pp. 28–29).

Even if the private sector is increasingly involved in the response to crises and disasters, crisis management is first and foremost a public activity. The task facing postcrisis inquiries to appraise crisis management therefore involve the application of moral principles (defining what is right and wrong in conduct) to the behavior of officials (individuals and collectives) in public organizations (Thompson, 1985). From a perspective of administrative ethics, it follows that agents that become involved in crisis response operations will face a plethora of expectations, obligations, and objectives. Officials are expected to act in ways that are consistent with laws and regulations, and organizational rules and goals, at the same time as they live up to standards set by the general public and the news media. Thus, expectations come from many different sources and often conflict with the realities that crisis managers confront (Boin & 't Hart, 2003). During the process of judging the ability of crisis managers to cope with these tensions, crisis inquiries must define or clarify what principles are used as benchmarks to judge performance (Cameron, 2004; Chapter 1, this volume). For the purpose of simplification, one can make a rough distinction between formal rules and informal norms.

Building on the work of Schneider (1992, pp. 136–137), formal rules can be viewed as having four common bureaucratic properties that are all relevant parts of generic crisis and emergency response systems. These properties include (a) clearly defined objectives; (b) a formal structure tying together different organizations; (c) a division of labor; and (d) policies and procedures guiding organizational activities. The formal rules are phenomenologically distinct from *informal norms* established within the population at large, but especially within groups affected by a disaster. Informal norms can be said to refer to symbols and ideas expressing appropriate standards of behavior.

A well-known limitation plaguing efforts to assess public crisis performance retrospectively is the blurred boundary between success and failure (Bovens & 't Hart, 1996; Hogwood & Gunn, 1984). Formal rules and informal norms that are supposed to provide firm guidance in times of crises oftentimes turn out to be imprecise, unclear, and in some cases even unknown. This kind of regulatory uncertainty is a recurrent feature of crisis events, which are typically characterized by lack of information regarding the nature of the situation, the viability of alternative courses of action, and the terms of choice (Boin, 't Hart, Stern, & Sundelius, 2005, pp. 3–4). Clearly defined written objectives in terms of desirable ends are sometimes lacking, except for the rather evident goal of stabilizing the situation and facilitating recovery. In addition, the rule of law might not always be an indisputable value; in some cases, efforts to cope with a crisis event might be characterized as failure in retrospect, even if decision makers acted in accordance with preexisting rules and norms. Conversely, in other cases, violation of rules and norms can be defined in terms of success if the outcome was a happy one (McConnell, 2003). The occurrence of regulatory uncertainty arguably brings the matter of retrospective moral judgment to a head (Bowen & Power, 1993). Above all, it places evaluators in the delicate position of determining post hoc if poor crisis performance was due to systemic flaws or poor personal/collective judgment. This assessment, in turn, influences allocation of responsibility and, longer term, the crafting of proposals for structural improvement.

A Model of Expectations, Accountability Logics, and Outcomes

The conditions guiding postcrisis inquiries can be combined into a two-dimensional model that isolates different precrisis conditions. Expectations involve combinations of (a) formal rules (including the laws and rules that public organizations have to obey in the midst of crisis) and (b) informal norms (public expectations and general codes of conduct that are not regulated by statutes). These are the principles that guide crisis actors and become viable criteria for assessing performance. Tangibility refers to the extent to which rules and norms provide clear guidance in a crisis situation. Figure 11.1 summarizes these dimensions, which in practice constitute distinctions with blurred boundaries.

In this model, preconditions are assumed to affect the type of accountability logic an inquiry adopts, which, in turn, is likely to influence the outcomes of the inquiry process. Accountability logics basically refer to ways of allocating responsibility for poor performance after a crisis. The model postulates that the object of blame will either be crisis decision makers (individuals, single organizations, or networks of organizations) or the institutional system (specific statues or combinations of different rules and norms) (Bovens, 1998; Brändström & Kuipers, 2003).

Tangibility

	Clear	**Unclear**
Rules	Reinforcement	Adaptation
Norms	Legitimizing	Sense-making

Expectations

Figure 11.1 The relationship between expectations, tangibility, and outcomes.

In the upper left corner of Figure 11.1, the formal rules guiding the crisis response are clearly defined. Actors are obligated to stay informed of these rules and, therefore, they can be held accountable when violating the rules. This type of situation is unlikely to be followed by calls for institutional change. In this scenario, investigators can be expected to emphasize the viability of preexisting rules (what I refer to as reinforcement) and attribute poor performance to decision makers. The same logic applies to the situation in the lower left corner, where action is guided by clearly defined norms, which are not being questioned but rather legitimized in the retrospective process. A different scenario is predicted if the formal rules are perceived to be unclear (upper right corner). Unclear formal rules are likely to generate different expectations on decision makers, and failure to abide by the rules is likely to be attributed to flaws in system design rather than crisis decision makers' faulty judgment or inability to perform. The identification of diffuse rules usually results in adjustment where evaluators either highlight specific uncertainties or propose specific solutions for clarification. Similarly, decision makers faced with unclear norms are not likely to be held responsible for poor crisis performance, which in these cases, is more likely to be attributed to vague expectations. In this scenario, evaluators are likely to engage in sense making by providing insight into the gap between public expectations and crisis performance (Boudes & Laroche, 2009).

Observations that deviate from the ideal-typical categories in this model (see Figure 11.1) are perhaps the most interesting cases from the perspective of administrative ethics. A particularly intriguing scenario involves situations where actors are being held accountable for poor performance in the absence of clearly defined rules and norms. What makes this scenario intriguing from an ethical perspective is that performance judgments in these situations deviate from the consequentialist postulate that moral behavior is conditioned by the level of uncertainty managers face (Bowen & Power, 1993, p. 104). The postulate suggests that actors cannot be blamed for mishaps if they acted in a context of uncertain rules and norms. This outcome, however, stands in stark contrast to the perception that public officials are specialized, knowledgeable, and well-trained individuals who, based on professional experience and merit, should be able to use personal judgment to cope autonomously with uncertainty and the chaotic conditions that characterize crisis environments (see Bovens, 1998, pp. 35–36).

APPRAISING THE ETHICS OF FLOOD RESPONSE: THE PITT REVIEW

A case-analysis of the review of the 2007 floods in the United Kingdom (Pitt, 2008) conducted by Sir Michael Pitt provides an empirical base to assess the relationship between expectations, accountability logics, and outcomes in postcrisis inquiries. This case is a suitable starting point to explore the practical application of the ethical functions of postcrisis inquiries. First, the magnitude of the 2007 floods and the impact of the disaster on different parts of British society are a useful illustration of the complexity and the cross-sectoral nature of contemporary natural disaster events. The 2007 floods, which destroyed some 55,000 properties and killed 13 people, represented the largest loss of essential services in the U.K. since World War II, leaving about half a million people without water or electricity. According to the review, the floods ranked as the most costly flood in the world in 2007 and were the most serious inland floods in England and Wales since 1947 (Pitt, 2008, pp. 3, 15). Second, even if the floods had regional impacts, where some areas were more badly affected than others, the crisis response engaged multiple actors at different levels, from local emergency responders to the central government crisis machinery. Third, the floods turned attention to the multifaceted nature of U.K. disaster preparedness and mitigation policy. As acknowledged by review, floods raise the need for coordinated action in multiple overlapping policy fields, including weather forecasting, building and planning, flood defense, risk legislation, insurance, emergency response, water supply systems, critical infrastructure, community resilience, and other related areas. Taken together, the extreme nature of the 2007 floods, the large number of people and property affected, and the complex crisis response make this case particularly interesting to study through the prism of moral judgment.

Another characteristic that makes the Pitt review useful for the purpose of this analysis is that the results of the review had substantial impact on U.K. flood management policy. The recommendations presented by the review on June 25, 2008, were unanimously accepted by the government (DEFRA, 2009), and many of them were eventually implemented in the 2010 Flood and Water Management Act. These long-term impacts underscore the importance of studying, in some depth, the expectations guiding performance assessment in this case. The analysis therefore begins by identifying a set of managerial challenges that, in different ways, illustrate the relationship between expectations, accountability logics, and outcomes. These challenges are a selection of deficiencies in the emergency response. An obvious caveat is that the challenges discussed here do not provide full coverage of the multiplicity of problems facing British society in the summer of 2007. Neither do these examples shed light on what went right during the response operations.

Weather Warnings

The review concluded that the weather warnings issued by the Met Office (the U.K.'s National Weather Service) were "generally detailed as accurate within the limits of current technology" (Pitt, 2008, p. 327). Similarly, flood warnings posted by the Environment Agency "generally worked well" (p. 328). However, the review noted that the current system, which focused on coastal and river flood warning, was insufficient in this case since most of the emergencies in 2007 were caused by groundwater and surface water flooding (see below). Many people that were affected by the floods were therefore unaware of the situation even as it unfolded (p. 328). Another problem identified by the review was that many people did not actually understand the system of flood codes (prescribing different levels of severity and contingency measures), which proved too complicated and not tailored to different types of people and places. The work conducted by the review regarding the suitability of the early warning systems in place was not based on a counterfactual analysis involving an assessment of the costs of not having an efficient system in place at the time of the floods. Instead, the point of departure was analyses of how the general public perceived the different warnings posted. Consequently, with respect to accountability, the review did not point to a single actor that was being held responsible for not communicating comprehensible public weather warnings. Instead, based on the finding that many people found the current system to be confusing, the review called on the Environmental Agency to "urgently complete the production of a sliding scale of options for greater personalization of public warning information" (p. 334). Along similar lines, the review endorsed the initiative by the Met Office to improve alerts for severe and extreme weather (p. 328).

Responding to Surface Water Flooding

Surface water flooding, which occurs when natural or man-made drainage systems are incapable of dealing with large volumes of rainfall, was one of the major sources contributing to the magnitude of the 2007 floods. One of the examples was Hull, where a large part of the city was flooded as the pipe drainage system could not cope with the heavy rainfall. The review reported that responsibility for responding to surface water flooding was split between several public agencies at local and national levels, and that no single authority took the lead in coordinating the emergency response. A related problem was that investment decisions related to drainage systems, road networks, and other infrastructure were made in isolation, resulting in inefficiency and an increased aggregate risk of flooding (Pitt, 2008, p. 84). The review therefore noted that the division of responsibility among the different actors was unclear. As a consequence, no single actor was blamed for the poor local response to surface water flooding; rather, the lack of coordination was attributed to the lack of existing guidelines. The review therefore recommended that "local authorities should lead on the management of local flood risk, with the support of the relevant organizations" (p. 85). Furthermore, it suggested that other relevant organizations should have a duty to share information and cooperate with local authorities, and that development of local surface water management plans should be the basis for cooperation (p. 90).

Acquisition of Emergency Supplies

Experiences with the 2007 floods revealed a lack of emergency supply preparedness. Ad hoc solutions were adopted in order to meet the urgent needs of people affected by the floods. For example, private sector companies stepped in to fill the gap by providing emergency supplies through their established distribution networks. Due to the urgent demand for consumables, central government departments and the central crisis machinery became directly involved in the logistical challenge of distributing supplies on an ad hoc basis (Pitt, 2008, p. 175). Acquisition of emergency supplies, in the view of the review, was a matter of coordination, which called for development of clear guidance to local authorities. While the review pointed to some success stories, it concluded that "there are few structured arrangements for mutual aid" (p. 179). Further, it notes that in some instances, agencies were called in to help, but their personnel were not properly integrated into the response effort. Responsibility for the problems that were related to emergency supply logistics was hereby not attributed to any specific actor. Yet the review underscored that all organizations that are members of Local Resilience Forums (networks of community emergency response organizations) have a collective responsibility to ensure that all organizations develop a more thorough understanding of not only local capabilities but also of capabilities offered through regional and national mutual aid agreements (p. 179).

Flood Rescue

According to the review, many members of the general public were caught offguard when the floods struck. People were generally aware that heavy rains were expected but did not think they would be personally affected, and many were caught by surprise. Emergency responders rescued some 7,000 people from the flood waters (Pitt, 2008, p. ix), and the review praised the collaborative effort of many different organizations that were involved in flood rescue missions. Still, the review observed several deficiencies in the response, which in aggregate, "placed both the public and responders at unnecessary risk" (p. 181). Ultimately, the review concluded that there were no clear guidelines specifying the division of responsibility for carrying out and coordinating flood rescues, which ultimately was due to the fact that there was no organization in place within the system to take on a lead role in flooding events. On this basis, the review concluded by urging the government to establish a statutory duty that would specify the FRAs (Fire and Rescue Authorities) leading role. However, even if many of the problems characterizing flood rescue operations were attributed to the lack of statutory regulation, the review also criticized the Local Resilience Forums (multi-agency partnerships of representatives for Category 1 responders) for not realizing the full potential of mobilizing capabilities at local, regional, and national levels (p. 183).

Mitigating Critical Infrastructure Impacts

The 2007 floods had a substantial negative impact on different parts of British infrastructure, causing costly disruptions to essential services. Electricity and drinking water supply systems as well as motorway and rail networks were affected. In addition to these disruptions, the review highlighted some *near misses*, involving, for example, electricity substations in Walham and around Sheffield, and the great potential for dam breach at the Ulley Reservoir near Rotherdam, that further exposed the vulnerability to infrastructure losses (Pitt, 2008, pp. 237–238). Analyzing the causes and effects of these disruptions, the review concluded that "fundamental gaps and weaknesses in a number of areas" (p. 239) would complicate efforts to reduce vulnerabilities and ensuring an effective crisis response. With respect to the allocation of responsibility, the review pointed to the central government arguing that the approach to mitigating the effects of natural hazards on essential service "has largely been uncoordinated and reactive" (p. 239). The problems, according to the review, originated in the government's lack of understanding of just how vulnerable society is in regard to floods and the lack of a clear centrally defined standard to drive response actions. The review also expressed its support for post-flood actions initiatives, taken by the government, to develop a systematic program to reduce the disruptions caused by natural hazards.

Information Sharing

Information sharing is a fundamental precondition for the coordination of efforts to cope with complex emergencies. In the case of the 2007 floods, the review pointed to several serious flaws related to information sharing and interagency cooperation, something which ultimately hampered an effective crisis response. As suggested by the review, the underlying explanation for these shortcomings was twofold. First, information was incomplete. It is noted, for instance, that the information that local emergency planners needed to enable adequate emergency planning "was at best inconsistent, and at times completely unavailable" (Pitt, 2008, p. 285). The second reason identified by the review was regulatory uncertainty. The review acknowledged that Category 2 responders (actors performing functions that are vital to the life of the community or that are part of the local community infrastructure), according to the Civil Contingencies Act (CCA), had the primary responsibility for emergency response planning at the local level. At the same time, the review noted that the CCA obligation of Category 2 responders to "cooperate and share" (p. 288) was open to interpretation. Furthermore, the review observed that this obligation conflicts with various legal impediments to transparency and hence, that many Category 2 respondents faced "a myriad of conflicting requirements, and that this is leading to uncertainty about what they can and cannot share" (p. 288). While recognizing that the CCA does not provide clear enough guidance, the review placed some of the blame on Category 2 responders for not sharing information with Category 1 responders (organizations at the core of the response to most emergencies) and other responders in accordance with the CCA (pp. 287–288). Based on these observations, the review called on the government to craft clearer regulatory guidance at the national level in order to "strengthen and enforce the duty on Category 2 responders to share information" (p. 293).

Coordinating Recovery

Public efforts to facilitate recovery from the 2007 floods had mixed results, according to the review. On the one hand, the review concluded that recovery arrangements were successful, especially when there was clear leadership, and the roles and distribution of responsibility were well understood by the actors involved. Key to the success was the establishment of a central Flood Recovery team, within the Communities and Local Government (CLG), which provided centralized guidance and coordination of the recovery effort. On the other hand, the review also found inconsistencies in the recovery arrangements, which reduced effectiveness in the recovery phase and hampered fair treatment across communities (Pitt, 2008, p. 369). In brief, the review identified four factors that complicated the effort to organize an even more effective recovery. First, there were some inconsistencies between local recovery plans that hampered recovery efforts between adjacent areas. Second, preestablished structures to guide representatives of government offices working on recovery at a regional level were lacking, which complicated the task of relaying information from local emergency responders to the central government. Third, even if local authorities had a coordinating role regulated by law, some local authorities lacked well-rehearsed plans for disaster recovery. Fourth, due to the absence of national guidance, many Recovery Coordinating Groups (RCG), which provide a multi-agency decision-making structure for recovery, were not activated at an early stage. Responsibility for these deficiencies was not assigned to any specific actors but rather was attributed to a lack of clear and centralized policy direction. For example, even if local authorities had the formal responsibility to activate RCGs, these authorities were not blamed when it turned out that many RCGs had not been properly activated. Rather, the review concluded that "delays in setting up RCGs usually arose from the absence of clear national guidance" (p. 373). As an underlying explanation for these problems, the review noted that matters related to emergency recovery had not been prioritized by the central government. Consequently, the review called for a review of current guidelines and for an effort to clarify roles and responsibilities among the actors involved in the recovery phase of disasters (p. 374).

Concluding Case Summary

This rather condensed selection of observations from the Pitt review shed light on the linkage between expectations, accountability logics, and outcomes. As suggested by this evidence, most of the case observations fit in the upper right corner of Figure 11.1, where performance deficiencies are largely explained by regulatory uncertainty. As predicted, this accountability logic is followed by adaptation, that is, policy recommendations aiming at clarifying regulation, standard operating procedures, and other guidelines directing crisis response operations. Managerial problems identified by the Pitt review are in different ways causally related to the absence of clearly defined structures, guidelines, rules, or regulations. The predominant explanation for inefficiency in this case, in other words, is regulatory uncertainty. What is also consistent with the model (see Figure 11.1) is that the review does not hold any specific organization(s) directly accountable for managerial mishaps or the inability to respond effectively to the flood disaster. One exception is Category 2 responders who, despite some level of statutory uncertainty, were criticized by the review for not doing enough to communicate with Category 1 responders, thereby hampering the effectiveness of the response. Similarly, with respect to problems related to emergency supplies, the review argued that Local Resilience Forums could have done more to enhance familiarity with the available emergency supply capabilities. What is interesting about these two examples is that responsibility was still not attributed to specific individual organizations but rather to amorphous networks of actors; Category 2 responders is a fairly wide constellation involving multiple local community actors. Similarly, Local Resilience Forums are constituted by multi-agency partnerships composed of Category 1 responders.

These observations also accentuate the problem of identifying viable criteria to guide the appraisal of moral judgment within the context of crisis management (Chapter 1, this volume). In this case, *effectiveness* is a frequently cited benchmark for assessing performance. The Pitt review essentially defines effectiveness according to how the general public and emergency response organizations judged the crisis response in retrospect. In the Pitt review, the ability to satisfy the public's needs is an explicit performance indicator: "we start with the needs of those individuals and communities who have suffered flooding or are at risk" (Pitt, 2008, p. x). The commitment to serve the needs of the public is consistent with the conduct of moral judgment more generally, which involve judgment of actors' ability to serve public interests and contribute to the common good (Thompson, 1985). However, this case also shows that in practice, performance is not exclusively evaluated on the basis of the ability to meet the needs of an affected population. Performing managerial tasks such as interagency communication and collaboration well also matters and might qualify as a value in its own right, without being explicitly tied to a certain goal or end. Crisis performance is then not assessed only on outcome-focused performance indicators (see Dunn, 2008). A lesson to be drawn from the Pitt review is that in practice, public crisis performance is also judged on *process measures*, which solely allude to the value of the means chosen to deal with crisis problems and how well those means are applied (see Carter, Klein, & Day, 1995).

Regarding accountability, the Pitt review defined responsibility in a way that called on specific organizations to correct regulatory problems, rather than blaming actors for mishaps or the inability to satisfy public needs. Thus, the review repeatedly held central government bodies responsible for performance deficits since these bodies are formally obliged to keep the crisis response machinery up-to-date. This is illustrated by the fact that the review concludes by calling upon various national-level organizations to take the lead in realizing the suggested structural reforms (Pitt, 2008, ch. 13). This definition of accountability has implications for how we deal with the ethical dimensions of crisis performance assessment. In essence, the task of defining single actions or inactions as ethical or unethical is overshadowed by the more fundamental challenge of designing institutional solutions that facilitate community resilience and improve crisis management performance.

CONCLUSION

As learning devices, postcrisis inquiries have the potential to contribute to the long-term development and improvement of society's capacity to respond to crises and disasters (Elliott & McGuinness, 2002; Parker & Dekker, 2008). One step toward this goal is to retrospectively appraise crisis performance, which involves a *post hoc* assessment of judgments related to serving the public interest under conditions of crisis and emergency. Postcrisis inquiries fill three interrelated ethical functions by identifying underlying societal values, standards separating right from wrong conduct, and areas where regulatory change is needed. Due to regulatory uncertainty, these functions are circumscribed in practice, generating murky expectations that complicate the assessment of moral judgments within the context of crisis management. As hypothesized in this chapter, and as the Pitt review confirms, regulatory uncertainty generates unclear expectations and a tendency to attribute fallible crisis performance to systemic flaws. Regulatory uncertainty also affects accountability since the lack of clearly defined structural guidance increases the tolerance or acceptance of poor crisis performance.

Meanwhile, it should be stressed that the absence of clear regulatory guidance is not the sole cause explaining why relatively few organizations were being held responsible for managerial mishaps during the 2007 floods. A complementary explanation is the well-known problem of many hands, complex decision and action situations where it is difficult to discern who did what (Bovens, 2007; Thompson, 1980), which has become a more common feature of contemporary crisis management. Scholars report that crisis management is increasingly taking place within complex multi-organizational, transjurisdictional and polycentric networks such as the emergency response networks involved during the 2007 floods in the U.K. Long gone is the myth of the centralized crisis response, where leaders take charge and provide direction in times of destabilization and turbulence (Boin & 't Hart, 2003, p. 547). The consequences for the pursuit of administrative ethics are profound, since clarification of roles and mandates guides the evaluation schemes used to assess ethical performance (see Chapter 1, this volume; Gatewood & Caroll, 1991). More generally, the gradual transformation to network governance has been accompanied by calls to reformulate the basic concepts of liberal democracy including standards for assessing bureaucratic performance (Sørensen, 2002; Mathur & Skelcher, 2007). Crisis and disaster management is no exception in this regard, which gives us reason to rethink the principles and methods used to assess ethical behavior within this context as well as the conditions for crisis-induced learning (Brower, Choi, Jeong, & Dilling, 2009; Moynihan, 2008; Wise, 2006).

REFERENCES

Boin, A., McConnell, A., & 't Hart, P. (2008). *Governing after crisis: The politics of investigation, accountability and learning.* Cambridge, MA: Cambridge University Press.

Boin, A., & 't Hart, P. (2003). Public leadership in times of crisis: Mission impossible? *Public Administration Review, 63*(5), 544–553.

Boin, A., 't Hart, P., Stern, E., & Sundelius, B. (2005). *The politics of crisis management: Public leadership under pressure.* Cambridge, MA: Cambridge University Press.

Boudes, T., & Laroche, H. (2009). Taking off the heat: Narrative sensemaking in postcrisis inquiry reports. *Organization Studies, 30*(4), 377–396.

Bovens, M. (1998). *The quest for responsibility.* Cambridge, MA: Cambridge University Press.

Bovens, M. (2007). Analyzing and assessing accountability: A conceptual framework. *European Law Journal, 14*(4), 447–468.

Bovens, M., & 't Hart, P. (1996). *Understanding policy fiascoes.* New Brunswick, NJ: Transaction Publishers.

Bowen, M. G., & Power, F. C. (1993). The moral manager: Communicative ethics and the Exxon Valdez disaster. *Business Ethics Quarterly, 3*(2), 97–115.

Brändström, A., & Kuipers, S. (2003). From 'normal accidents' to political crises: Understanding the selective politicization of policy failures. *Government and Opposition, 38*(3), 279–305.

Brower, R. S., Choi, S. O., Jeong, H-S., & Dilling, J. (2009). Forms of inter-organizational learning in emergency management networks. *Journal of Homeland Security and Emergency Management, 6*(1), 1–16.

Cameron, W. (2004). Public accountability: Effectiveness, equity, ethics. *Australian Journal of Public Administration, 63*(4), 59–67.

Carter, N., Klein, R., & Day, P. (1992). *How organizations measure success.* New York: Routledge.

DEFRA (Department for Environment, Food and Rural Affairs). (2009). *The govern-ment's response to Sir Michael Pitt's review of the 2007 summer floods: Progress report.* London: DEFRA.

Dunn, W. N. (2008). *Public policy analysis: An introduction* (4th ed.). Upper Saddle River, NJ: Pearson-Prentice Hall.

Elliott, D., & McGuinness, M. (2002). Public inquiry: Panacea or placebo? *Journal of Contingencies and Crisis Management, 10*(1), 14–25

Gatewood, R. D., & Caroll, A. B. (1991). Assessment of ethical performance of or-ganization members: A conceptual framework. *Academy of Management Review, 16*(4), 667–690.

Gephart, R. P. (1993). The textual approach: Risk and blame in disaster sensemak-ing. *Academy of Management Journal, 36*(6), 1465–1514.

Hogwood, B. W., & Gunn, L. A. (1984). *Policy analysis for the real world.* Oxford, UK: Oxford University Press.

Mathur, N., & Skelcher, C. (2007). Evaluating democratic performance: Methodolo-gies for assessing the relationship between network governance and citizens. *Public Administration Review, 67*(2), 228–237.

McConnell, A. (2003). Overview: Crisis management, influences, responses and evaluation. *Parliamentary Affairs, 56*(3), 363–409.

Moynihan, D. (2008). Learning under uncertainty: Networks and crisis manage-ment. *Public Administration Review 68*(2), 350–365.

Parker, C., & Dekker, S. (2008). September 11 and postcrisis investigation: Explor-ing the role and impact of the 9/11 commission. In A. Boin, A. McConnell, & P. 't Hart (Eds.), *Governing after crisis: The politics of investigation, accountability and learning.* Cambridge, MA: Cambridge University Press.

Perrow, C. (1984). *Normal accidents: Living with high-risk technologies.* New York: Basic Books.

Pitt, M. (2008). *The Pitt review: Learning lessons from the 2007 floods.* London: DE-FRA.

Schneider, S. K. (1992). Governmental response to disasters: The conflict between bureaucratic procedures and emergent norms. *Public Administration Review, 52*(2), 135–145.

Schwandt, T. A. (1989). Recapturing moral discourse in evaluation. *Educational Re-searcher, 18*(8), 11–16.

Seeger, M. W., Ulmer, R. R., Novak, J. M., & Sellnow, T. (2005). Postcrisis discourse and organizational change, failure and renewal. *Journal of Organizational Change Management, 18*(1), 78–95.

Senge, P. M. (1990). *The fifth discipline: The art and practice of the learning organization.* New York: Doubleday.

Sørensen, E. (2002). Democratic theory and network governance. *Administrative Theory & Praxis, 24*(4), 693–720.

Thompson, D. F. (1980). Moral responsibility of public officials: The problem of many hands. *American Political Science Review, 74*(4), 905–916.

Thompson, D. F. (1985). The possibility of administrative ethics. *Public Administra-tion Review, 45*(5), 555–561.

Vedung, E. (1997). *Public policy and program evaluation.* New Brunswick, NJ: Transaction Publishers.

Wise, C. R. (2006). Organizing for homeland security after Katrina: Is adaptive management what's missing? *Public Administration Review, 66*(3), 302–318.

CHAPTER 12

CONCLUSIONS

Lina Svedin

FUNDAMENTAL CHALLENGES
IN ETHICAL CRISIS MANAGEMENT

As one of the chapters in this book outlines, there is a growing body of research that

> explains why it is hard to recognize and understand impending crises in time; why it is hard to collect and analyze the information needed to make sense of an evolving crisis; why it can be excruciatingly difficult to make the right calls under immense pressure; why it is nearly impossible to coordinate a dense network of response organizations; why it is surprisingly hard to mobilize resources, and why it always is a challenge to effectively communicate with an angst-ridden public. (Chapter 5, Introduction)

In light of this, is it tempting, both as a researcher and stakeholder, to agree with those decision makers that say they were simply doing the best they could, that no one thought it would happen there, that crises are unique situations that require centralization of decision making to a small group of trusted public servants, and so on. However, in this book, we have tried to do what, up to this point, has seemed too difficult: to push the discussion further and start a debate about ethics and crisis management. We have

---

Ethics and Crisis Management, pages 217–246
Copyright © 2011 by Information Age Publishing
217

done so in an effort to be helpful to decision makers on the ground and to the public that suffer the consequences of crises handled badly. Moreover, we have done this because we feel that ethics is important, *especially* in crises. The foundations of legitimate governing bodies depend on it, and the public's trust in these institutions is forged or squandered at these critical moments when public organizations are put to the test. The sections below outline key findings and conclusions about the inherent ethical challenges decision makers and organizations face when managing crises.

VALUE CONFLICTS AND TRAGIC CHOICES

How do you deal with value conflict, with dilemmas that are the result of ambiguous or inconsistent policy or with crisis situations where it is impossible to move toward one goal without simultaneously moving away from others?

Value conflicts and tragic choices between two undesirable outcomes often face humanitarian intervention organizations as examined by Zijlstra, Zwitter, and Heyse in Chapter 4. One such conflict is whether or not to provide medical attention to girls that have been subjected to female circumcision and risk providing support for or aiding in this kind of circumcision procedure. Some humanitarian organizations prohibit providing care after female genital circumcision, even if this is done from a purely medical point of view in order to prevent disease and death as a consequence of the practice. A human rights perspective thus sometimes leads humanitarian organizations to withhold care from people in need in order to avoid breaching of human rights. This kind of value judgment presents a picture of humanitarian organizations that provide aid on their own terms, pressing for their own Western beliefs and values in the country they are working in, and not solely providing aid based on need.

In Chapter 4, the fact that humanitarian organizations followed soon after the military intervention to provide aid in Iraq and Afghanistan led to local recipients to view these humanitarian organizations as partial or dependent allies of the invading states. During the humanitarian work in these countries, the distinction between humanitarian organizations providing relief and the coalition forces performing military actions became increasingly blurred. The ethical dilemma of providing aid in any military conflict zone is, how do you avoid becoming part of the conflict? Practical dilemmas that this generates involve how to mitigate the effects of war when you need military protection from one of the warring parties in order to do your aid work.

In light of an increasing tendency to decentralize decision making in crisis response structures, Boin and Nieuwenburg (Chapter 5), look at the unintended consequences[1] of pushing policy dilemmas, particularly tragic choices, down the chain of command. They argue that the *policy twilight zone* that is created, through this downward shift that makes first responders policy leaders, has unforeseen and undesirable consequences. In this chapter, staff at a hospital in New Orleans during Hurricane Katrina faced the tragic choice of which patients should get a share of the hospital's very limited resources. Added to the tragic choice was a sense of crisis-induced *Aporia* regarding who should make the decision and what could be done for those patients that were not getting any resources. Under increasingly horrible conditions in the hospital and limited evacuations, the staff faced what seemed to them two impossible options; to quicken the weakest patient's death or to abandon them in the hospital. One doctor found seven patients (judged closest to death) left on an abandoned floor of the hospital and proceeded to give them a lethal injection, which a colleague of hers had instructed her how to administer, and after this, she moved on to euthanize a substantial number of the category 3 patients[2] who were waiting on the evacuation floor of the hospital. She was assisted in the euthanization process by another doctor and the administrator in charge of the hospital's ethics committee. In the aftermath of the hurricane, the doctor and two nurses were arrested for murder, but the Grand Jury, consisting of fellow Louisianans, refused to indict them. Boin and Nieuwenburg's assertion is that, even in light of the staff's remarkable lack of ethical consciousness, the larger ethical dilemma that the case presents is that first responders in this disaster had to face the *Aporia* of nigh impossible policy decisions because the hospital management had neglected to make these decisions ahead of time.

Crisis Management as a Mission Impossible

Sometimes crisis management is perceived as a *mission impossible* for policymakers, and for good reasons. Crises present major decision making, information processing and action-related challenges under great time pressure and with considerable values at stake. Arguably, the surge in concern with administrative ethics had done little more than add rules and codes that state that crisis managers should follow the law, and if the law is unclear, do the right thing. However, as Daléus and Hansén point out, "the right thing to do, in situations where laws and regulations provide poor guidelines, arguably looks very different depending on where in the administrative complex one sits, to whom one is primarily accountable, and if the task environment is stable or not" (Chapter 2, Introduction). There are, however, organizations that show us that crisis management does not, in fact, have to be a mission impossible. These same organizations operate almost exclusively in the chaos of crises and seek their mission and purpose there.

Humanitarian organizations, examined in Chapter 4, are in a sense *professional* crisis managers. What we are learning about in Zijlstra, Zwitter, and Heyse's chapter is not how humanitarian organizations manage crises per se, but rather how they approach and operate in disaster environments, and what ethical challenges their work brings about. Humanitarian organizations are charged with a mission to alleviate human suffering, often in war zones, in disasters, and in perceived humanitarian crises. These kinds of situations are rife with uncertainty, hostility, fear, and human needs. They often have multiple adversaries on the ground, which makes it both hard and imperative for humanitarian aid organizations to try and stay neutral in the local conflicts. Sometimes the international community is both hostile and judgmental of the parties on the ground (pursuing them as war criminals), placing humanitarian organizations in the dilemma of whether or not to provide aid.

For most organizations, however, crises pose gigantic information, decision, and action problems. Even organizations tasked with actively monitoring and preventing crises are often plagued with the fear that they are failing in their mission. In Chapter 11, Parker examined the questions asked by virtually everyone after the devastating terror attacks in New York and the Pentagon, but particularly the 9/11 Commission: How could we have missed this? In this case, like many other intelligence and crisis prevention organizations, the challenge comes in determining and separating signals from noise, and in *connecting the dots* in terms of what real-life consequences those signals might result in. Did the lack of coordination between the intelligence services in the United States represent an ethical transgression? Was the system set up in a way that made it impossible for these organizations to do an adequate job? Was the administration negligent in its assessment of the threat as it came into office, and did it stall the implementation of the plans developed under the previous administration for unjustifiable political reasons?

Interestingly enough, it was this same challenge of *connecting the dots* and the failure to muster an appropriate and sufficient response to these impending consequences that plagued the Swedish bureaucracy and political decision makers in the wake of the 2004 tsunami disaster. In Chapter 2, Daléus and Hansén show how the Swedish bureaucracy was paralyzed by fear and indecision, worrying about overstepping boundaries of authority and assuming responsibilities that the organization would later have to pay for. Wockelberg's review in Chapter 9 of the post-tsunami hearings also makes it painfully clear that Swedish political decision makers, out of touch with the habits of their own citizens, could not foresee what impending consequences a tsunami hitting Southeast Asia over Christmas could bring. Now, is it ethically defensible to be this out of touch with the citizens you represent and then to diffuse the blame among both politicians and bureaucrats in a way that will make accountability and change less likely?

Once the organizations that set out to prevent crises have clearly fall-en down on their job, and policymakers and bureaucrats find themselves having to manage crises, what kinds of ethical dilemmas do they face? In Chapter 3, Bynander follows how both United States and the U.K. decision makers reasoned around the decision of going to war in Iraq as part of the policy response to the 9/11 crisis. The main ethical dilemma, Bynander argues, rested in the failure to balance the values relevant to the main are-nas of scrutiny (arenas with domestic stakeholders, with international al-lies, international community representatives like the UN), in a way that hindered a sustainable justification strategy (for the policy option chosen). As Bynander points out, international relations operate in shades of grey, while domestic politics tend to strive for clarity. The latter choosing to focus on one story and one societal value at a time.[3] The clash between these two ways of dealing with values and value conflicts in crises came back to haunt and hurt U.S. and U.K. administrations as they announced the decision to go to war with Iraq. Despite having used different reasoning paths to the decision to go to war, both governments ended up with a justification strategy for the war that was unsustainable. The ethical failure, Bynander argues, came with the inability to balance their desire (and perceived need) to stand up to a tyrant with the need for an international legal basis for the war. Each of the stories of reason the U.S. and U.K. policymakers presented to their domestic and international audiences unraveled individually (as domestic investigators started examining them one by one and, real-world events unfolded contrary to the administrations' predictions), which meant that the justification for going to war was no longer sustainable. The state-centric value of standing up to challengers on the international arena came out as grossly overprivileged (and dishonestly so) to audiences in arenas that support other values.

The decision to go to war with Iraq suggests that crisis management is not a *mission impossible*, rather it is a honed skill that decision makers and bureaucrats exercise with discretion in several different arenas and involv-ing the conflicting values of several stakeholder groups simultaneously. Ethical crisis management, this case illustrates, is the result of a deliberate stand to practice the skill or approach of balancing values. Furthermore, decision makers' actions in this case suggest that they are aware of the value of an ethical approach to crises, but that they will try to maximize the credit they can get from being perceived as ethical or in the right, while simul-taneously getting what they want (which might or might not be ethical). What Chapter 3 teaches us, in the lessons-learned-the-hard way category, is that acting unethically (by not balancing values in individual decisions) and being deceitful about it (creating the illusion of balancing, or lying) will create twice the negative feedback if it is uncovered.

In Chapter 7, Kuipers, Kochanska, and Brändström show us how disregard of ethics in crisis management within the larger War on Terror policy led to a crisis in ethics management for policymakers in the United States and U.K. What this case shows is that, like in the decision to go to war with Iraq, ethical crisis management is the result of deliberate choices and stands. In not deciding for an ethical approach to managing the War on Terror, but rather choosing controversial and ethically questionable strategies as a part of the counterterrorism strategy in Iraq, the United States and the U.K. set themselves up for ethical criticism. Furthermore, how each state handled this criticism, when accused of torturing POWs in Iraq, led to significantly different outcomes in terms of how long the crisis lasted and how severe the consequences were for top-level policymakers. In the choice between a deliberate stand for or against an ethical management of crises, an actor's credibility and deemed trustworthiness seems circumscribed by historical precedents (prior incidents of similar types of (un)ethical behavior) and the response the actor displays in relation to allegations of unethical behavior.

In the U.K. case of alleged torture, the proportionality of the response by the British government, scapegoating only a few military soldiers and then showing a successive assumption of blame by six Ministers of Defence for years after the incidents, seems to have helped U.K. policymakers maintain credibility. The U.K. policymakers were also not burdened by a history of brutality against POWs, and the full scope of the British abuse in Iraq surfaced only 7 years after the initial need to defend the ethics of its War on Terror policy in 2009. The U.S. response to the allegations of torture was, however, marred by a history of prisoner abuse, ongoing simultaneous instances of reported abuse in other prisons outside Iraq, and the Bush administration's staunch simultaneous defense of its controversial strategies for countering terrorism, as well as its claim that it did not torture prisoners despite mounting evidence to the contrary. Once the abuses had been confirmed, U.S. policymakers inadvertently implicated the whole chain of command in the unethical conduct by shifting blame progressively to higher and higher levels. Eventually, the only way to stop the blame from spreading to the president was to let Secretary of Defense Rumsfeld take the blame, again and again, as new allegations surfaced.

What this case tells us, among other things, is that the impact of a crisis where unethical conduct is the disputed core of the crisis can be tremendous in terms of its duration, the number of levels of decision makers it affects, as well as citizens' and international stakeholders' perception of the country and its role in the international community. The case also indicates that managing an ethics crisis requires considerable skill and a great amount of luck in order to play out favorably for the managing actors. Having an ethical track record, or at least not having unethical behavior as your documented history or the repeated pattern you are currently displaying, helps maintain policymaker's credibility and grants them the benefit of the doubt in the public mind when they face allegations of unethical behavior. The importance of appropriate and proportional responses to allegations and uncovered unethical behavior also seems important. That the policymakers managing the crisis resonate, in action and focus, with the ethical outrage or reprehension that the public is displaying seems important for containing the public debate. Displaying contradictory behavior and words, such as denying wrongdoing while staunchly defending policies and actions that are controversial instead signals that policymakers are not in agreement with or in line with the outraged public raising the allegations. As such, it is no wonder that U.S. policymakers lost credibility with the public. Add to this mounting evidence of abuse in several separate locations, and failed attempts to point fingers at lower levels of government eventually necessitated top-level officials to assume some responsibility for the abuse, but they then had to do so in a reactive way and from a point where the administration had already expended all its moral capital.

Dealing with Others' Bad Choices and Behaviors

Not all ethical challenges in crises are, as in the cases above, necessarily caused by your own actions. Some ethical dilemmas in crises are the direct cause of other people's behavior and poor choices. How do you deal with a crisis in an ethical manner when other actors, that you have limited control over, place you in a situation where you need to make a choice and face a moral decision?

In the situation that humanitarian organizations face in the field, many times the actors involved in the conflict or disaster have had, or still have, an active part in making the situation worse and potentially deadly for many people the organizations are trying to help. As Zijlstra, Zwitter, and Heyse point out in Chapter 4, among the people seeking help are injured or starving soldiers from warring parties and accused war criminals who, as soon as you help them, have every intention of going out and continuing the conflict and the atrocities that are taking place. What is the ethical way to manage humanitarian aid in disasters where you might be helping war criminals and prolonging conflicts by providing aid to warring parties? In this type of crisis, humanitarian organizations also often face the additional problem (should they choose not to provide aid to parties being responsible for unethical behavior) of not clearly knowing or being able to discern who is a war criminal or a warring party from the general suffering population.

In the economic crises examined in Chapter 6, Svedin shows how the government that faced managing the crises (but in one, chose not to get directly involved) had actively contributed to brining about the conditions under which other parties could take advantage of the system and, in the process, cause great harm to the public. Nevertheless, it was other people's behavior over which the U.S. government, including the watchdog regulatory agencies in the sectors, had limited control. In both cases, the government faced the challenge of not even being clear about, or understanding, the sophisticated deception schemes that led the actors to be able to take advantage of the system in place. Like in the humanitarian aid situation, the government in these two economic crises would have had a hard time discerning who was deserving of aid and who was not. In the Enron case, the company that brought about the economic disaster had been celebrated as the best-run company in America, and its accounting practices were considered the cutting edge of what was known about business and asset management. Similarly, in the 2008 financial crisis, the largest and most successful investment banks were the ones at the heart of the crisis, and the government was indirectly involved in the largest mortgage holders in the U.S.—Fannie Mae and Freddie Mac—that had created a huge part of the problem.

In the economic crisis cases, Svedin argues that the United States had created its own ethical crisis dilemmas by promoting a culture that favored values, such as *innovation, risk-taking, deregulation, massive wealth accumulation,* and *consumption* on credit not related to an ability to pay accumulated debt. The government was then being surprised when the smartest actors in these markets felt justified in using their knowledge to accumulate their own wealth through risky innovations and under poor regulatory supervision. The greatest ethical violation, Svedin asserts, might have occurred in the 2008 Wall Street financial crisis, when the government suspended the very rules it had itself set in place (because it can and because it felt it needed to) in order to avoid the full consequences of the rules it had put in place. It thereby not only rewarded other people's bad behavior and poor judgment, but set a precedent that the government will bail companies out of the consequences of their bad behavior if the companies are big enough. It also signaled at a metalevel that it is okay to not take responsibility for ones own choices if you do not like the consequences. This signal, Svedin argues, makes economic crises of this variety more likely in the future.

In Chapter 5, the hospital staff faced *Aporiatic* situations that were largely or even exclusively the result of other people's arguably poor choices and behavior. The fact that the hospital had proved resistant to hurricane winds before led large masses of people to gather at the hospital rather than evacuating, despite the fact that the hospital was located in a low-lying area, ultimately aggravating the evacuation situation once the hospital was flooded. The failure of several government bodies before and during the hurricane contributed to the levees breaking, which caused the hospital to flood and lose power, and contributed to the lack of rescue helicopters.

The hospital and people's individual choices and behavior had seriously immobilized patients on floor 7 rather than on the ground floor: a 350-pound woman that needed to be carried on a floor with no working elevator, an emergency plan that did not prioritize patients in the case of an evacuation, no plan for evacuations in flooding situations, and staff working around the clock without recognizing the risk of poor judgment. In a sense, that the management of the crisis ended poorly (both in terms of the logistics of management and from an ethical point of view) is hardly surprising, even if killing patients without their consent or knowledge should not be a *necessary* result of that situation.

Accountability and Public Trust in Governing Institutions

The ethical management of crises has a lot of bearing on people's trust in their governing institutions. That good management is often assumed to be ethical management is seen in a number of cases in this volume. Furthermore, the public disappointment, rage, and distrust that emerges when the management by actors in crises is revealed as unethical or is perceived as unethical can be palpable.

In Chapter 4, the authors showed several examples where humanitarian organizations have entered a disaster zone and, by the virtue of the cultural values they bring with them, have betrayed the recipient populations' trust in governing institutions. The backlash against the Western cultural ideas and standards that humanitarian interventions often come with cause the victims of the disaster to ask if these organizations are really there to help them, or if they are there to teach them how to live and do things "right" culturally.

In Chapter 2, Daléus and Hansén display the expectation that Swedish citizens had of their governing institutions; that someone was looking out for them even on Christmas Day, and that the state would function even after hours. When the response to the South Asia tsunami did not kick in and, in the aftermath of the crisis, it became apparent that those left in charge would not even consider waking their minister, or any other minister for that matter, citizens were appalled and understandably shaken in their trust of government. Furthermore, the apparent lack of alarm and concern that several ministers showed by choosing not to follow the news after they heard about the tsunami, to discuss it with their deputy during the daily briefing, or to cancel their plans to attend the opera, stunned their citizens.

In Chapter 7, Kuipers, Kochanska, and Brändström convey the sense of disbelief that many U.S. and U.K. citizens felt in the face of overwhelming evidence that Iraqi prisoners had indeed been tortured at the hands of

British and American soldiers while in captivity. The conclusion on most people's minds seemed to be that this was the fault of a few bad apples. Surely it had to be, because our government—we—do not torture prisoners, right? The contrast between the rhetorical message of the governments and the graphic and disturbing pictures nurtured a doubt about the ethical conduct and the honesty of the governments' professed strategies. The memos signed by George W. Bush justified torturing al-Qaeda members as one way to reach the objectives of the War on Terror. Meanwhile, the president insisted repeatedly that "the U.S. does not torture, and that's important for people around the world to realize" (Chapter 7, Abu Ghraib as a structural problem). The U.S. government's efforts and, to a lesser degree, the British government's efforts, to explain what had obviously taken place only served to solidify the public's distrust of government and instilled a deep sense of shame and fear among many who had previously supported the war effort in Iraq.

ETHICS OF CRISIS MANAGEMENT: LESSONS LEARNED THE HARD WAY

A defining characteristic of crises is, indisputably, "that they are events that call for urgent public action" (Chapter 11, Introduction). What is important, and frequently disputed from an ethical point of view, is that "in contemporary democratic society, those actions are increasingly being subject to public scrutiny and review by...investigative bodies" (Chapter 11, Introduction). In broad terms, "policy evaluation involves making claims about the ethics and morality of public performance. Evaluation of crisis events is thus a *normative enterprise,* which involves defining *in retrospect* what actions were appropriate and *the right thing to do* given both situational and institutional constraints" (Chapter 11, Introduction). This volume has presented many hard-learned lessons about ethical behavior and decision making in crises. Some of these lessons are about whether it is legitimate or justifiable to go into and manage a crisis in the first place. Other lessons are about the need to specify the criteria that justified a particular choice, policy, or strategy for managing the crisis. In cases where the ethical conduct and decisions of crisis managers are in question come difficult questions about whether to assume responsibility or to avoid it. A lot of the ways in which these dilemmas play out and get their resolution is through crisis communication. Several chapters in this volume shed light on why unethical behavior in crises so seldom leads to an effective truth-finding dialogue and why ethical breaches in crises tend instead to lead to highly politicized blame games where the actual course of events is obscured and masked rather than exposed.

Intervening or Not Intervening

Sometimes crisis managers are forced to choose between intervening or not intervening. The ethical challenge here comes with examining the motives for going in, for example in Iraq (Chapter 3), and trying to manage the crisis through military means, intelligence gathering, or aid (see Chapters 3, 4, & 7). There is a compelling pressure on decision makers to do something, almost anything, in order to show that someone is in charge, that there is still some level of control, that leaders are leading, that politicians care about their citizens, and so on. It is incredibly hard for anyone, but particularly for aid organizations (see Chapter 4), to watch a train wreck in slow motion and to not get up and do something—take action.

Examining your motives for getting into the management of a crisis involves thinking about your responsibilities and capabilities, something that was uniquely illustrated in both the Enron and the 2008 Wall Street financial crises (see Chapter 6). It also means thinking about what values your presence and your actions in this case signify and how those values will be perceived by others, as almost all the chapters in this book show. In some of these cases, it is likely that whoever is contemplating going in should in fact not get involved, because getting involved in managing the crisis is unethical. Such would be the case, for instance, when aid organizations insist on providing aid in a way that undermines the local culture and local values. Another case would be intervening in a financial crisis in a way that rewards those who created the crisis through their unethical behavior, spreads the cost of the crisis to people who had little to nothing to do with the crisis, and when the way of intervening violates systemic rules of the game set in place by the entity violating the rules.

A more complex case is presented when humanitarian interventions have been justified by political leaders as proceeding on humanitarian grounds (see Chapter 4). The Bush and Blair administrations both used humanitarian arguments to support their international justification for intervening militarily in Iraq and Afghanistan (Chapter 3). The poorly structured arguments, involving "a responsibility to act when a nation's people are subjected to a regime such as Saddam's," provided only a thin justification for an intervention on humanitarian grounds, and the military intervention had low legitimacy with the international community and countries that are usually the recipients of humanitarian aid. Zijlstra, Zwitter, and Heyse (Chapter 4) point out that this kind of thinly justified and low-legitimacy intervention is seen as cultural imperialism in a way that taints other humanitarian efforts.

Decision-Making Criteria

How do crisis managers go about making decisions in situations where the rationales for actions conflict? Against what criteria do we judge the legitimacy of crisis decisions? These criteria should be "explicitly stated values that underlie recommendations for actions" (Dunn, 2008, p. 221). In policy analysis, the six common criteria are *effectiveness, efficiency, adequacy, equity, responsiveness,* and *appropriateness* (Chapter 1, On decision criteria). The chapters in this volume present several ways in which decision makers wrestle with these often competing criteria, and ultimately make decisions to act or not to act.

On what basis do you make decisions? And what if you have to extend that decision beyond the specific instance or person you are making that decision about? In Chapter 5, decision makers onsite at the Memorial Medical Center faced an impossible situation; the many patients and staff at the hospital, together with the deteriorating conditions at the hospital, seemed to call for a prioritization of which patients and staff would be evacuated in what order. The lack of a preestablished evacuation priority plan left staff under great duress to try and reconcile the incompatible values and goals of evacuating those who were strong enough to endure the evacuation, those in most need, and those who wanted to live. The criteria for making the decision of who should be evacuated and in what order started out utilitarian, but became increasingly blurred as staff became more fatigued, and poorly deliberated decisions started down paths where only worse decisions were to follow. In this situation, a reliance on professional standards and norms for ethical guidance proved questionable as doctors and nurses aided each other in euthanizing severely ill patients without informing them. The lack of guidance from higher levels in the decision-making hierarchy, such as from the hospital's management body, let those needing to make decisions on the ground drown in the discretion at their disposal.

In Chapter 7, decision makers in the United States and the U.K. alternatively defended atrocities and tried to avoid blame for unethical decisions and behavior in the public eye. In the cases of Abu Ghraib and Baha Mousa, high-level decision makers ran up against internationally established rules of war and human rights that both countries allegedly subscribed to. The situation raised questions like, are all prisoners of war the same, or are there ethically defensible categories of enemies that justify torture? If torture in not justified, how should the government explain what happened in a way that restores legitimacy to the overarching policy in place guiding the War on Terror? Elaborate blame-deflection strategies were put in place by both British and American top-level decision makers, and the result, the view of the legitimacy of the decisions and the government's behavior by the public, was very different.

A recurring, or endemic, decision dilemma for humanitarian aid organizations is whether to provide aid to those in need or only those who are
perceived as deserving (excluding those who abuse human rights or participate in war crimes) (Chapter 4). Often these kinds of value judgments turn
out to be ineffective in terms of really helping those they aim to help or
promote, and might inadvertently undermine community cooperation and
coping mechanisms in place. The value judgment that comes with thinking
about individuals deserving of aid brings a focus on individuals rather than
respecting existing social hierarchies or communities as collectives, something that also inadvertently can undermine humanitarian organizations
achieving their policy goals (to provide aid or promote human rights). This
judgment and focus pits individuals against communities and families, and
it communicates that something was culturally wrong with how the recipient communities were living before the aid organization entered the scene.
Humanitarian organizations are often dependent upon local ruling parties
giving organizations access to recipient communities, on military intervention by the international community, or on military protection from an
intervening state. The decision criteria in the delivery of services by humanitarian organizations in crisis situations is deeply value laden, and the
competition of these values makes the everyday operation of these organizations challenging.

Recognizing that the bureaucratic scene for ethical choice and decision
making is marked by contradictory ideals and realities, Daléus and Hansén
(Chapter 2) examine to what degree bureaucratic actors' criteria for ethical
evaluation correspond to that of postcrisis evaluations. The chapter shows
how lower-level bureaucrats judged and acted on the situation differently
than midlevel bureaucrats. Lower level bureaucrats were focused on the consequences of their actions; they were repeatedly trying to make things happen and get results. Their superiors—the midlevel bureaucrats—were concerned with the nature of the actions and were reluctant to disturb high-level
superiors without significant cause. Out of the seven decisions examined in
the chapter, the postcrisis evaluation deemed only two of them highly legitimate. Both of these decisions and actions were carried out by lower-ranking
civil servants. The five decisions judged illegal or illegitimate involved action
by higher-level civil servants and top-level political decision makers.

In this case, some situations required bending or breaking rules and
standard operating procedures in order to achieve goals and get positive
results. The government, Daléus and Hansén note in Chapter 2, was not
criticized for these decisions and actions but was rather seen by the postcrisis evaluators as "having acted naturally in response to an unprecedented
disaster" (Chapter 2, Conclusions). The process that led to decisions about
financing actions was criticized and deemed illegitimate because it did not
display an appropriate amount of political will. The tension between politi-

cal logic and administrative expediency in this case was palpable, as was the anxiety within bureaucracy that resulted from having to confront these two competing rationales (to act or not to act, to alert or not alert the boss who is sleeping).

As illustrated in Chapters 3 and 6, in any one decision, you need to balance the values presented to you by different arenas or stakeholder groups in order for your actions, policy, or strategy, to be sustainably justifiable. In Chapter 3, and the deliberation over whether or not to go to war with Iraq, decision makers failed to balance the values presented by the international community, allied states, the intelligence services, and the public. In Chapter 6, and the cases of the Enron collapse and the 2008 Wall Street crisis, the government failed to balance the values and interests of corporate leaders, bankers, shareholders, and homeowners with the values of taxpaying citizens and future generations that faced the long-term consequences of these decisions.

Policy and Strategy Evaluative Criteria

For sound policy to be adopted, one or more criterion for evaluating competing options must be identified. There is no obvious right or wrong in what specific criteria decision makers choose, but they need to evaluate the policy options according to these criteria and, in that process, weigh the pros and cons of each option. Then they need to make a decision, knowing that they have chosen some drawback because they want to achieve or benefit from some advantages. Choosing a policy direction is an act of ethical judgment.

Chapter 4, on humanitarian interventions, addresses the ethical dilemmas that emerge when trying to specify what policy values should guide intervention strategies. The wider question of policy values for humanitarian organizations working in disasters and humanitarian crises include on which value basis they should deliver their aid. The value of human rights and humanitarianism loom large in the international community, and specific organizations choose to specifically advocate for human rights and deny aid to both perpetrators and victims of human rights abuses. Some humanitarian organizations go so far as to request military intervention by states in the international system in order to alleviate the suffering of populations facing human rights abuses or to stop a humanitarian disaster. So, for human rights organizations, the work of humanitarian aid often comes down to the question of whether they should deliver aid to people in need or if they should promote respect for human rights. Some organizations see greater value in providing aid regardless of who the recipients are or if they abuse human rights. Others choose their recipients based on human rights considerations, and still others will not provide aid to or in situations characterized by human rights abuses.

The process of deliberating over and the setting of criteria, including the justification of prioritizing one criteria over other possible policy criteria, is the focus of postcrisis evaluations and commission inquiries. People want to know if decision makers thought of all the possible consequences of their decisions and strategies, and how they chose to allocate the good and bad effects of the policies they adopted (see Chapters 3, 6, & 7). Did they know? Did they consider how all different stakeholder groups would be affected (see Chapters 2, 9, & 10)? And if they knew some people were going to be hurt by or suffer large consequences from the decisions or strategies they adopted, how did they justify this to themselves, and did anyone disagree (see Chapters 7 & 9)?

People want to know on what grounds decisions were made, who made the decision, and whether or not the negative impact of the decision was due to ignorance, incompetence, or the consequence of malicious or callous intent (see Chapters 2, 6, 7, & 8). These are the kinds of judgments about crisis managers' performance that the public wants to make and, I would argue, needs to make for accountability mechanisms in crises to have a chance of working. The result of this kind of judgment is either a continued or an eroded trust in government, represented by specific crisis managers. Postcrisis evaluative processes aim to help clarify the facts that will make this kind of judgment possible. Another aim is to examine whether there are any grounds for formal disciplinary or legal action against individual decision makers or the government as a whole (see Chapters 2, 9, 10 & 11).[4]

Looking at the responsibility doctrines that actors claim in postcrisis evaluation situations, Wockelberg (Chapter 9) finds a conflict between what she describes as the legally mandated symmetrical responsibility doctrine and an informal but widely accepted asymmetrical responsibility doctrine. The two accountability mechanisms used to evaluate the Swedish government's response to the 2004 tsunami disaster highlighted a number of values that should have guided the government's response to the crisis. Symmetrical responsibility within mandates; that is, that "bureaucrats are to be held responsible for the use of discretionary power within their mandate" and that "politicians are to be held responsible for the execution of power that follows from their mandate, but their responsibility for actions or failure of bureaucrats is limited," (Chapter 9, The Politics-Administration Dichotomy, Responsibility, and Crisis) to bureaucratic action a minister has information on or the power to influence. However, they also asserted that *initiative* (actively seeking information and taking actions that are within your mandate) and *creativity* (realizing when a situation requires you to act outside of your mandate in order to avoid predicted harm or helping providing protection for citizens) can and should be demanded of politicians and bureaucrats in these situations, even if it means procedures and normal routines have to be set aside. The values that the postcrisis evaluations espouse, on the one hand *rule of law* and a *clear separation of politics and administration,* and *effectiveness* and *flexibility* on the other hand, conflict.

Furthermore, the chapter shows that while there is much support of the symmetrical responsibility doctrine by the evaluation committees and the political decision makers involved in the crisis, top-level bureaucrats bear witness to a strong informal asymmetrical responsibility doctrine, where the executive arm of the government (the ministers and top-level civil servants of formally autonomous agencies) acts as one and with the understanding that political priorities (maintaining a stable government and respecting the integrity and privacy of individuals) often demand that bureaucrats take the fall for top-level politicians or the whole government, even when the actions and decisions in question fall outside of their agency mandate. Seeing themselves as sacrificial lambs on the altar of public opinion or media scrutiny, the top-level bureaucrats argued that *transparency* and *fairness* need to be subordinate to keeping *the business of governing* going and doing so *effectively,* possibly while government organizations *learn* from major crises quietly and on the sly.

Chapter 11 examines how postcrisis inquiries balance the tension between setting clear standards for assessing crisis performance and recognizing the uncertainty that characterizes crisis management. Looking at specific performance shortcomings identified by the Pitt Review, Nohrstedt states that the review consistently found that failures were the consequence of *regulatory uncertainty,* that is, formal rules and informal norms failing to provide clear, precise, or known guidance for crisis managers. Taking the uncertainty of these formal and informal guidelines into consideration, the review also reliably (continuously and in accordance with Nohrstedt's model) allocated responsibility to the system level rather than to individual organizations or decision makers. In its efforts to be a vehicle for learning and response improvement, the review pointed to specific organizations and encouraged them to take the lead in correcting regulatory problems the review had identified. This approach to accountability in the postcrisis setting, Nohrstedt suggests, has important implications. "The task of defining single actions or inactions as ethical or unethical is overshadowed by the more fundamental challenge of designing institutional solutions that facilitate community resilience and improves crisis management performance" (Chapter 11, Concluding case summary).

Furthermore, a complementary explanation for why relatively few individual organizations were held accountable by the Pitt Review involves the *problem of many hands*— that in complex decisions and actions it is hard to discern who did what—and that this is an increasingly common situation in contemporary crisis management. As organizations charged with managing crises increasingly work in complex multiorganizational, transjurisdictional, and polycentric networks, assessing any one organization or decision maker's performance (on any criteria) will also become increasingly difficult. The prevalence of network governance in Western democracies might cause us to "rethink the principles and methods used to assess ethical behaviour in [crises] . . . as well as the conditions for crisis-induced learning" (Chapter 11, Conclusion).

The 9/11 Commission, as a postcrisis inquiry, had to make a number of decisions and choices of an ethical nature in order to maximize the likelihood that their mission would be successful and that their report and findings would have an impact (Chapter 10). In an attempt to avoid the many problems that could lead to failure, the commission decided to pursue a course of action—a strategy—that took into account all three of the rationales that underline and affect postcrisis investigations. With the primary goal established, to have the commission's findings and recommendations accepted, the two commission chairmen set out to balance the three competing rationales for postcrisis inquiries. In order to succeed, one chairman stated that the 9/11 Commission Report had to be a historical document, not just a list of conclusions. It had to be clear where the facts that supported the conclusions came from so that it would be equally clear that the commission was not simply recommending policy changes for the sake of signifying reform (Chapter 10, Making it Work). The commission also made an active and novel choice to produce a narrative history of professional quality instead of a report that would have been more in the genre of a traditional government report. Furthermore, the commission chose to hold public hearings to build credibility, which the commission chairmen came from an appearance of neutrality, an open and transparent investigation, an abstinence from partisan politics, with the media and the public. Parker also states that the commission utilized its resources skillfully by being both conciliatory and confrontational in its approach to policymakers that were proving to be unwilling participants (Chapter 10, Making it Work).

The cost of the commission's pursuit of its primary goal was a perceived necessity for unanimous endorsement by its Republican and Democratic commissioners. In order to achieve this kind of unanimous support, the report treaded softly on some sensitive issues and avoided assessing individual culpability. The commission zeroed in on institutional, structural, and procedural failures, particularly in the FBI and CIA, instead of individual accountability and sanctioning. As a result, no one lost their job over mistakes made or failures related to 9/11 (Chapter 10, Assessing the 9/11 Commission's Impact).

For sound policy to be adopted, one or more criterion for evaluating competing options must be identified. Chapter 7 presents two painful cases where it seems decision makers deliberated and chose the policy option of torturing and ultimately killing prisoners of war in favor of winning the War on Terror. When these decisions were uncovered and evaluated by the public and the international community, they found the decisions unethical at best, crimes against humanity at worst. The strategies each country adopted for explaining how the unethical actions happened, for dealing with the unethical behavior, along with historical precedents and timing, produced very different perceptions of the government's role in torture in the two cases. The British transgression was ultimately seen as a technical one-time error, whereas the American behavior came to be viewed as a structural problem and a systemic failure of ethics and accountability.

Assuming or Avoiding Responsibility

How do you deal with something that you were okay with but the public, now that it has found out, does not agree was ethical, like in the case of the tortured POWs? How do you handle a situation where your view of the division of responsibility is not shared by postcrisis evaluators?

Wockelberg's chapter showed a discrepancy between the judgments made and actions taken (not taken) by decision makers in the crisis, and the assessment of those same judgments and actions (inaction) in the postcrisis evaluations.[5] One commission argued that "decision makers whose mandates are supported by adequate resources should assume responsibilities that equal their powers" and that in situations "where responsibilities are unclear, the higher level in the hierarchy is in fact responsible" (Chapter 9, The Swedish Tsunami Commission). The commission argued that the Swedish prime minister's "ability to assume the responsibilities that followed from his mandate depended on his knowledge of the problems in the organization, of possible solutions, and his duration in office" (Chapter 9, The Swedish Tsunami Commission). The commission felt that all these conditions left the prime minister undeniably responsible for the failures in the government's crisis management efforts related to the tsunami. Furthermore, the commission also criticized an agency for a lack of initiative and for the failure to act of its own accord and thereby failing to make the most of its mandate.

The commission's focus on legitimacy underlined the value of effectiveness in government operations. It stated that the *protection of life and safety of citizens* was at stake and that there is virtue in showing *empathy* and *making extra efforts* already in times of *potential* crisis" (Chapter 9, The Swedish Tsunami Commission). In his defense, facing the commissions' critique, the Swedish prime minister rhetorically defended the actions of bureaucrats and assumed responsibility for the crisis management failures. However, he also simultaneously deflected culpability from himself by stating that is was not reasonable to assume that he would understand the severity of the situation when bureaucratic experts had not; that the situation had been extraordinary, rendering normal procedures insufficient or inapplicable; and that the focus should be on learning and looking to the future. The foreign minister, who also bore the brunt of the commission's criticism, defended her actions by identifying her own shortcoming but also spread the blame to the bureaucratic organization left in charge of urgent situations (but had inadequate resources).

The main ethical failure, Bynander argues in Chapter 3, was made in the failure to balance the values relevant to the main arenas of scrutiny in a way that hindered a sustainable justification strategy. They failed to balance their own desire (and perceived need) to stand up to a tyrant with the legitimate need for an international legal basis for the war. As each of the reasons the United States and U.K. had provided unraveled, individually the justification for going to war was no longer sustainable. What really turned the domestic audience off and embarrassed stakeholders that had supported the policy were the apparent intelligence failures that led to a faulty assessment of one of the key reasons for going to war: weapons of mass destruction. When it became apparent that the administration's desire for a certain type of intelligence might have steered the intelligence community to produce the faulty information, the state-centric value of standing up to challengers in the international arena came to look grossly overprivileged, and dishonestly so, to audiences that felt they had been deceived into not voicing discontent or into giving their support. The failure to balance values in the decision making, in this case, also signifies a larger pattern of avoiding responsibility. By finding a way to justify the means (going to war), the administration was trying to avoid having to take responsibility for the other value driving their decision making: the desire to stand up to a rogue state and challenger of the international system.

Ethical Communication in Crises

In Chapter 10, Parker examines the unlikely case of a postcrisis evaluation that was set up to fail but ended up producing a widely hailed final report that enjoyed broad public support and spurred the reform of the entire U.S. intelligence community. Ethical issues, Parker shows, were at the heart of the controversies surrounding the 9/11 Commission, but ethics were also the key to the favorable reception that the commission's report and its recommendations received. The perception that the commission had carried out its investigation in a fair and ethical manner was crucial for its legitimacy and credibility. Ethical behavior and decisions, in other words, laid the groundwork for successful communication regarding what happened in the crisis and what important lessons the administration needed to draw from it.

How the message is received depends not only on the message itself, but how you choose to communicate it. As Olson shows in the Mohammad cartoons case (Chapter 8), the way you communicate, as well as when and how you engage stakeholders affected by the crisis (both as receivers of communication, reference point, or information shaping, and as a feedback loop on your messaging) are critical to the perceived legitimacy of the response and the ability to diffuse the crisis.

Not talking honestly about the other values driving the decision to go to war with Iraq (Chapter 3), in the end, became the undoing of the policy as it became apparent that the stated reasons for going to war had little to no support. It became apparent to the audiences that, rather than the stated reasons for going to war with Iraq (that were quickly unraveling), the value of teaching Iraq a lesson or standing up to a tyrant probably carried more weight and drove the policy. The dishonesty in the communication about the justification for the decision to go to war, and war as a strategy to combat terrorism, was fundamental to undermining public support of the Bush administration, the wars in Afghanistan and Iraq (see Chapters 3, 5 & 7), and to public perceptions of the origins of American versus the British cases of torture (Chapter 7).

It also seems in Chapter 2, looking at bureaucrats' response to uncertainty, that fear of saying too much or taking initiative would lead to getting stuck with the costs of necessary actions, or being reprimanded for being hysterical or out of order, prevented a great deal of internal and interdepartmental communication that could have led to a more timely and effective response. Boin and Nieuwenburg argue in Chapter 5 that the lack of guidance in how to interpret or implement policy that is vaguely formulated is in and of itself unethical. The way that higher-level policymakers left lower-level bureaucrats (see Chapters 2 & 5) to figure out and implement policy in a situation that was clearly stressful and where value conflicts abounded was in this sense immoral and tragic. These chapters illustrate how informal communication and a lack of communication and cross-hierarchical deliberation of important value decisions can leave street-level bureaucrats and first responders in *Aproatic* paralysis or lead them to bad decisions.

THE THEORY AND PRACTICE OF ETHICS IN CRISIS MANAGEMENT: MOVING FORWARD

Looking over our findings regarding the ethical challenges inherent in crises and crisis management, as well as the lessons that different cases present, we should think about how to move forward in terms of doing this business of ethics more skillfully and legitimately. The preceding sections lead us to a number of conclusions and points from which to build a more ethical management of crises. One important conclusion is that

> people at different hierarchical levels in a public bureaucracy experience ethical rationales differently.

The difference in weight and tangibility of bureaucratic rationales emphasizing values such as *effectiveness* and *efficiency*, strongly felt at the bottom of hierarchies, versus the political rational emphasizing, for instance, *compromise, symbolism, rule of law* felt more strongly at mid and top levels of hierarchies is significant. If bureaucratic organizations are to manage crisis situations ethically and effectively, we need to build crisis response mechanisms and plans that acknowledge the values that this organizational form is built upon (such as impartiality and respect for rules and authority) and that provide street-level bureaucrats and first responders with the decision support structures they need (a map of values and priorities they should follow) to make appropriate choices on the ground. Midlevel managers, we have seen, can be caught in the middle of contradictory or competing rationales and values, being squeezed from both ends of the hierarchy. Because of their key function in communication and information analysis going up and down bureaucratic chains, the predicament of middle managers is important to look into more closely.

A second conclusion that stands out and that is likely to have an impact on how we plan for and respond to crisis is the fact that

> crises that occur primarily on the international (as opposed to a domestic) arena have dynamics that present unique ethical challenges for crisis decision makers.

International relations operate in shades of grey; whereas domestic politics tend to concentrate on one story, and one societal value, at a time. This arena difference, combined with the large amount of discretion[6] that governments hold in foreign policy and national security matters and the potential for large information asymmetries can really backfire on crisis managers. The two largest concerns here are that the domestic audience that the government depends on for its legitimacy and authority will evaluate the government's decisions and actions on one criteria or value at a time rather than the complex web of values and action alternatives that the government took into consideration when it made the decision or took the action. This is more likely to be the case with regard to decisions and actions that the government is not forthcoming about, but then become public anyway, or the public has limited information access to (basically, any type of national security situations and negotiations with foreign powers).

The second related aspect is that because of the nature of the arena, a disconnect develops over time between how crisis managers and the public view a crisis and how it should be handled over time. Limited information access for the public means that there really is not an open discussion about the policy or strategy that decision makers are taking that would really provide them with feedback on what the public thinks of the approach they are taking to the crisis, and to the extent that governments act on their discretion in this area, they are likely to take farther steps out of line with public opinion before the conflict becomes evident than they would in any other policy area. We can say that ethical transgressions and illegitimate crisis management are more likely to occur in foreign policy or international crises than in domestic crises, because of this risk of isolation (limited feedback to decision makers on what the public thinks of what they are doing) and increased ability to act (without prior approval of other democratic bodies that could stop or delay ethically questionable actions).

In situations that present legal or moral grey zones for decision makers, it would be wise to set up and institutionalize mechanisms that support and enhance the ability to do moral reasoning and expose biases into the crisis management effort. The dangers of group decision making under extreme pressure are well-known, and several mechanisms and processes have been identified that make unintentional bias, dysfunctional discussions, and premature decisions less likely (see for instance Allison, 1971; 't Hart, Stern, & Sundelius, 1997; Morris, 2004; Vertzberger, 1990, 1998). Several of the chapters in this book testify to the importance of applying these kinds of safeguards to improve crisis decision making and to avoid a growing gap between what decision makers consider necessary and the public considers ethically defensible.

Dilemmas of Discretion

In some sense, the great advantage to creating bureaucracies is that they provide "an institutional method for applying general rules to specific cases, thereby making the actions of government fair and predictable" (Wilson, quoted in Chapter 2, Ethical Expectations on Bureaucratic Behavior). It would seem that a Weberian bureaucracy, with its "hierarchical organization, extensive use of rules, impersonality of procedure, and the employment of specialists on a career basis" (Downs, quoted in Chapter 2, Ethical Expectations on Bureaucratic Behavior), would avert many ethical dilemmas that would otherwise fall on individual bureaucrats. In these admittedly ideal situations, a bureaucrat's personal views or other individual qualities should not be part of the equation. Bureaucracy as an organizational form can therefore be seen as an answer—if not the answer—to some of the inherent ethical challenges of public decision making regarding resource allocation and is-sue priorities.[7]

It turns out, however, that a bureaucratic organizational structure is a poor fit for crises in other ways because they often work slowly, are large, full of red tape, and generally attract people who might have a public ser-vice ethic but are not *doers* the way that people from the private sector are, as one chapter stated in this volume (Chapter 2, The Swedish Bureaucracy During the 2004 Tsunami Disaster). It is furthermore, as discussed in the section above, very plausible that different hierarchical levels in a public bureaucracy experience different ethical rationales in crises. *Abiding by the law* and *obeying superiors* pertain to the ethical rationality of the bureaucratic floor. At the top, there is a *political rationality* that guides action in ethi-cally tricky situations, which does not necessarily heed Weberian ideals of *fairness* and *predictability*. As long as the politics-administration dichotomy is preserved, ethical challenges inherent in the nature of bureaucracy are unlikely to manifest, even in times of crises. But then again, we know the politics-administration dichotomy frequently breaks down both in practice and in theory.

The typology presented in Chapter 2 (see Table 2.3) helps illustrate that illegitimate processes might still provide legitimate outcomes. By contrast, the processes that were *by the book* were criticized and deemed illegitimate, because they did not show sufficient amounts of political will. Furthermore, strictly abiding by the law might in fact be viewed as rigid and unimagina-tive. This illustrates the third conclusion that

> the legal grey zones (identified in Chapter 2) many bureaucrats find them-selves in provides room to maneuver but also make bureaucrats vulnerable to public criticism.

Furthermore, while it might be perfectly sensible to decentralize deci-sion making in crises, shifting authority down the chain of command to those on the ground, it creates an often overlooked problem. This kind of shift of authority downward comes with agonizing dilemmas, which fall into the lap of first responders instead of with top-level decision makers who have the training, the mandate, and the experience in making these kinds of decisions. When decision dilemmas sink to the bottom and street-level bureaucrats (by necessity) become policy leaders, a policy twilight zone is created, with potential negative consequences.

Discretion is both necessary and inevitable in the process of policy imple-mentation, particularly in crisis situations. As street-level bureaucrats be-come the receptors of inherent or emerging dilemmas, they look for norms and values that can guide the decisions they have to make. Discretion works best when it is accompanied by some mental road map or technology that can assist street-level policymakers in the decision-making process. Simply trusting street-level bureaucrats to *do the right thing* will not help them avoid negative consequences or poor decisions. What it does mean is a *lack* of central guidance on how street-level bureaucrats should apply their increased discretion that comes with decentralized decision making. If policymakers and street-level officials must cope with dilemmas because these cannot be solved at a higher level, these decision makers should at least be entitled to guidance as to how abstract policy intentions should be applied to concrete situations. We cannot simply trust professional norms and values to guide decision makers in these situations. This leads us to the fourth conclusion of this book:

> When guidance is forsaken in the name of trust, the street-level bureaucrats will spend their energy on averting drowning in discretion.

This situation in and of itself is unethical. What is needed in this type of structure, with decentralized decision making, is a clear philosophy or value judgment that reconciles and translates existing incompatible policy aims so that street-level bureaucrats know which way to prioritize and can make the most of their implementation discretion. It is clear that political-administrative elites are ultimately responsible for this part of the policymaking process.[8]

Crisis Decision Making with 20–20 Hindsight

There has been a lot of mention of crisis management being a virtual *mission impossible* for policymakers. When it comes to decision making, Chapter 2 highlighted that "the impossibility of crisis management, in this sense, is that the verdict of posterity is uncertain in the heat of events." In other words, it is hard for decision makers in crises to know whether the reasoning they go through and the decisions and strategies they choose will stand the test of time and whether other people (in a position to judge them) would agree with them that this was the right thing to do.

It is possible that bureaucrats, if given a free mandate to act, will be more responsive and behave proactively rather than reactively (argued in Chapter 2). However, such discretionary power in the hands of civil servants undermines the Weberian notion of how ideal bureaucracies function, and the implementation of decisions might shift from being predictive to arbitrary. This underlines the idea introduced in Chapter 1, that the ethical dilemmas of bureaucracies in crises are truly inherent. Hierarchies, organizational loyalty, and a foreseen shadow of accountability are elements that affected how both civil servants and politicians acted in Chapter 2.

The fact that decision makers and bureaucrats in several cases predicted, and subsequently adjusted, their decisions and messaging to foreseen post-crisis hearings and evaluations tells us that there is potential for change in this area. The kind of endeavor this volume represents could in fact have an impact on and possibly improve crisis performance if crisis managers and the public become more aware of the ethical nature of crisis management and the importance of its consequences.

Another chapter made the larger point that some kinds of decision-dilemmas should never have occurred in the first place (Chapter 5). It is *unethical* to let people, who are coping with an intense, scary, and life-threatening disaster make decisions about who gets to live and who gets to die, who should be evacuated and who should be left behind. As several chapters illustrate, a fifth conclusion can be drawn from this book;

> The time to have the necessary discussion about what to do in ethical dilemmas "is not when the wheels are coming off." (Fink, quoted in Chapter 5)

In the Chapter 5 case, this kind of discussion had not happened before the crisis, and the first responders were left by the hospital's management to make the hardest decisions. This represents a moral failure by the higher level of authority with devastating consequences for first responders and those who were placed in their care.

It is clear from the chapters presented in this volume that decision criteria and evaluative criteria for policies and strategies are seldom explicitly stated. This is confirmed by the need by postcrisis commissions to go on substantial fact-finding missions to establish first, what happened (situations, actions, and behaviors) and second, who made what decisions and on what bases they think or argue they did what they did. One postcrisis inquiry's comment (Chapter 9) that it is essential to document decisions and information flows also in crises speaks to this point and to the de facto evasion of accountability mechanisms that decision makers weary of postcrisis evaluations of their performance display in several of the cases presented here (see Chapters 2, 3, 7, 9, & 11). This leads us to the sixth conclusion drawn from this volume:

> The failure to explicitly state decision and policy evaluative criteria has a number of troubling consequences from an ethical perspective.

First, it makes public crisis management undemocratic. In these circumstances, it is next to impossible for the public to perform its part in the democratic process; to *evaluate, judge,* and *sanction* good and poor performances by public crisis managers. Second, in the cases where decision makers truly have not made explicit to themselves, and those they made decisions with, what the underlying and possibly conflicting values inherent in decision and policy options were, it leads to poor decisions and strategies. In fact, several cases presented in this book show how this kind of failure to explicitly state and balance competing values leads to decisions that have to be revisited, strategies that are not sustainably justifiable, and a loss in public trust in governing institutions. Third, it is clearly difficult for anyone—postcrisis inquiries, the media, the public, or researchers—to judge whether or not the processes and structures in place to manage crises promote or hinder ethical management of crises when these criteria are not made explicit. Consequently, learning from crises and improving public performance (except perhaps from the most outrageous cases that blow up in decision makers' faces) based on what happened in past crises clearly becomes difficult. Several chapters in this book show how decision makers' own accounts of the reasoning they went through in the lead-up to a decision are clearly unreliable sources of postcrisis information for psychological (see Chapters 3 & 5) and self-serving strategic reasons (see Chapters 2, 3, 7, & 9).

Deliberation

If centralization is not a great option in many crisis management efforts, and if the empowerment of bureaucrats results in undesirable behavior or decisional paralysis, then what is the solution? Boin and Nieuwenburg present the idea that the solution might lie in a balanced combination of both centralization and empowerment. They make a case for cross-hierarchical deliberation[9] as a means of providing guidance to the use of street-level discretion. They argue that street-level discretion is both inevitable and potentially beneficial to policy outcomes, but that responsible politicians and policymakers should be actively involved in policy setting.

By participating in an interaction process where the participants do collective reasoning around ethical dilemmas and value conflicts, sources of *Aproia* can be identified, and actionable guidelines can be designed to negotiate these dilemmas. Through a process of collective practical reasoning, potential dilemmas are identified and actionable guidelines are designed to negotiate these dilemmas. Often, deliberation consists of weighing considerations for or against a certain course of action. Since *Aporia* involves a deliberative deadlock, deliberation between responsible politicians and bureaucrats before there is a crisis and a need to act on an ethical dilemma is the way to prevent crisis induced *Aporia* (Chapter 5).

Policy ends and values frequently are stated in such abstract or general terms that they obscure possible conflicts between these ends and values, only to become tangible when an actual decision has to be made by street-level bureaucrats in crises. Deliberation not only serves to get means-end reasoning going, but it also makes it possible to detect paths to institutional *Aporia.* Just as specification of ends requires a discussion of feasible means, cross-hierarchical deliberation requires that the experience of street-level bureaucrats is fed into the process.

Creating venues for deliberation across hierarchical levels, in order to detect and avoid *Aporia,* is a good alternative to shifting authority in crises through either centralization or decentralization. The creation of this kind of venue also treats discretion as a real power to exercise practical reasoning at all levels of public organizations as a basis for decisions. Moreover, it draws on the experiential knowledge of those that discretion is meant to help. However, it is important to realize that deliberation takes time and should therefore take place before crises occur. During crises, communication is strained and deliberation often becomes impossible.[10]

Postcrisis Inquiries as an Ethical Tool

Based on the chapters in this volume that examine or relate to postcrisis inquiries, we can draw a seventh and final conclusion in this volume:

> How postcrisis inquiries are set up, in terms of their procedure and focus, significantly shape their impact;

that is, make it more or less likely that organizations will accept their findings and make changes. In four of the chapters (Chapters 7, 9, 10, & 11), we see that a focus on public hearings (rather than internal investigations and one-man investigative reports like the U.S. Army's own investigations and the Taguba report) and identifying *systemic* rather than *individual* failures seem to increase the legitimacy of the postcrisis inquiry process and can lead to significant reforms.

For example, the 9/11 Commission managed to avoid the fate of oblivion that has killed many commissions and reform efforts in the United States. The commission produced an acclaimed report that enjoyed great public support and spurred a reform of the entire U.S. intelligence system. Parker argues in Chapter 10 that every aspect of the 9/11 Commission was infused with multiple ethical implications and choices that ultimately paved the way for its relative success. Some of these implications and choices related to the commission's origins and goals: the way it carried out its mission, the influence of the families of the victims, the decision to hold public hearings, its decision to focus on unity and making recommendations for reform rather than establishing individual responsibility, and the monitoring activities the commissioners undertook after their mandate had formally ended. Thinking carefully about these design choices seems worthwhile if postcrisis inquiries are going to serve as a tool for establishing ethical conduct and improving public performance in crises.

Some of the chapters (see Chapters 2, 7, 9, & 10) also show us how postcrisis inquiries can create arenas of opportunity in which blame-game politics, political power struggles, and reform efforts play out, often with profound consequences for the future (Chapter 10). Furthermore, commissions can be set up to fail by design, even in their good mission to learn, improve public performance, and gain mastery of the forces that affect our lives and our future. As one of the 9/11 Commission chairmen reflected, "If you want something to fail, you take a controversial topic and appoint five people from each party. You make sure they are appointed by the most partisan people from each party—the leaders of the party. And, just to make sure, let's ask the commission to finish the report during the most partisan period of time—the presidential election season" (Chapter 10, Making it Work). These less-positive aspects of postcrisis inquiries are also things we need to account and plan for in crisis management systems with vital accountability mechanisms.

NOTES

1. They use the term *Aporia* to characterize these unintended outcomes.
2. This was a category the staff created when they needed to prioritize evacuees. This last category consisted of elderly patients judged sick enough by their families that they previously had stated they wanted a Do Not Resuscitate Order for them.
3. Constitutions and extraordinary legal rules designed for contingences in the foreign policy arena give states the right to use great discretionary powers and to create partial information monopolies. These tools make it easier for decision makers to manage foreign policy crises and crises in the international arena. However, the use of these tools and the ambiguity they help to create gel poorly with domestic processes for seeking accountability and allocating blame.
4. There are arguably several other important aims of inquiry commissions and other postcrisis processes, such as creating a psychological effect of closure; identifying areas that need improvement or reform in terms of the crisis management system; or postponing, diverting, masking or politicizing public judgment of a crisis effort (by burying or cooling off a politically sensitive or hot topic in a committee procedure that will take a long time, has few resources and/or has a limited mandate, or heating it up through a formal inquiry process that will put focus on decision makers or increase the pressure and heat on involved crisis managers). For a thorough discussion and perspective on the multiple functions of crisis inquiries, see Chapter 9, The Politics-Administration Dichotomy, Responsibility, and Crisis, The Swedish Tsunami Commission: Crisis and the Limits of Formal Mandates, The Committee on

the Constitution: Principles and Politics; Chapter 10, Three Rationales for Official Postcrisis Investigations; Chapter 11, Introduction, Ethical Functions of Crisis Inquiries.

5. The two committees that examined the Swedish government's response to the 2004 tsunami disaster represent both the authoritative interpretation of the Swedish responsibility doctrine in crises and a qualified discussion on legitimacy from the citizens' point of view, as well as a ruling on the legal aspects of the action/inaction and a debate of ethical considerations made in light of the political environment.

6. Discretion is defined here as the "legitimate right to make choices based on one's authoritative assessment of a situation" (Feldman, quoted in Chapter 5). This is a classic topic in public administration, but scholars have rarely studied the use of administrative discretion in crises (Chapter 5).

7. Another rationale behind organizing in hierarchical layers is "the power superiors have in settling conflicts between units or individuals who have different perceptions of the basic goals of the bureau. A second rationale is that hierarchies can render communication within the bureau more efficient in terms of relaying information appropriately, instead of having all sharing all information with everybody else.... Both rationales push accountability upward. The lower hierarchical levels cannot be expected to determine the agency's goals and values, and their control over information flows is limited" (Chapter 2, Ethical Expectations on Bureaucratic Behavior).

8. Boin and Nieuwenburg suggest in this volume that in response to the need for guidance, rather than merely centralizing the decision making at the top again, we should use a process of deliberation to ensure that street-level expertise is fed into that formation process. If a process of deliberation supplants the practice of dodging ethical bullets (top-level decision makers avoiding tough choices), political-administrative foundations will be upheld while effectively avoiding crisis-induced *Aporia.*

9. Deliberation here refers to a process of interaction that enables policymakers to make informed decisions that prevent *Aporia* (Chapter 5).

10. As Boin and Nieuwenburg point out in Chapter 5, three conditions need to be fulfilled in order for deliberation to be a workable countermeasure to *Aporia.* First, crisis authorities and first responders need to engage in an informed debate of the ends of crisis management in terms of feasibility on the ground. Second, there has to be a suitable measure of involvement or commitment among the participants. It is important that the leaders of a crisis response take the time needed for deliberation and demonstrate this commitment. Third, deliberation has to be transparent. For true deliberation to actually occur, those who participate in it or who need to accept the reasoning actually have to be able to understand and follow the line of reasoning.

REFERENCES

Allison, G. (1971). *Essence of decision: Explaining the Cuban missile crisis.* Boston: Little, Brown.

Dunn, W. N. (2008). *Public policy analysis: An introduction* (4th ed.). Upper Saddle River, NJ: Pearson-Prentice Hall.

Morris, E. (Writer). (2004). *The fog of war: Eleven lessons from the life of Robert S. McNamara*. M. Williams, J. Ahlberg (Producers), & E. Morris (Producer/Director). Culver City, CA: Columbia TriStar Home Entertainment.

't Hart, P., Stern, E., & Sundelius, B. (Eds.). (1997). *Beyond groupthink: Political group dynamics and foreign policymaking*. Ann Arbor: University of Michigan Press.

Vertzberger, Y. (1990). *The world in their minds: Information processing, cognition, and perception in foreign policy decisionmaking*. Stanford, CA: Stanford University Press.

Vertzberger, Y. (1998). *Risk taking and decision making: Foreign military decisions*. Stanford, CA: Stanford University Press.

ABOUT THE EDITOR

Lina Svedin is assistant professor at the University of Utah, Political Science Department, and she teaches in the Master's of Public Administration program. Her research focuses on cooperation, responsibility, perception, and ethics, particularly in crises. Some of her recent publications include *Organizational Cooperation in Crises* (2009) published by Ashgate and *Risk Regulation in the European Union and the United States: Controlling Chaos* (2010), co-authored with Adam Luedtke and Thad Hall and published by Palgrave MacMillan. Dr. Svedin has also published several books on crisis management, and she has led several international research projects. At the University of Utah, she teaches courses in administrative theory, public policy analysis, governance and the economy, ethics, crisis management, and conflict resolution. In 2009, she received the Wendy Rice Award for excellence in service. Dr. Svedin previously served as a senior analyst and Training Director at the Swedish national center for Crisis Management Research and Training (CRISMART). She has also worked as an area specialist in crisis management for the Swedish Government Offices and has extensive experience in training and educating public service professionals from around the world. Her PhD is in political science from the Maxwell School of Citizenship and Public Affairs, Syracuse University.

Ethics and Crisis Management, page 247

CONTRIBUTORS LIST

Lina Svedin
PhD
Assistant professor
Political Science Department
University of Utah
Salt Lake City, Utah

Pär Daléus
M.A.
Training Director and Senior Analyst
CRISMART – Crisis Management Research and Training
Swedish National Defence College
Stockholm, Sweden
and PhD student
Department of Political Science
Stockholm University
Stockholm, Sweden

Dan Hansén
PhD
Research Director
CRISMART – Crisis Management Research and Training
Swedish National Defence College
Stockholm, Sweden

Ethics and Crisis Management, pages 249–252
Copyright © 2011 by Information Age Publishing
249

Fredrik Bynander
PhD
Assistant professor
Department of Government
Uppsala University
Uppsala, Sweden

Lieuwe Zijlstra
B.A.
Research Master student
Graduate School of Philosophy
University of Groningen
Groningen, the Netherlands

Andrej Zwitter
PhD
Assistant professor
Department of International Relations and International Organization
University of Groningen
Groningen, the Netherlands

Liesbet Heyse
PhD
Assistant professor
Department of Sociology
University of Groningen
Groningen, the Netherlands

Arjen Boin
PhD
Associate professor
Utrecht University School of Governance
Utrecht University
Utrecht, the Netherlands

Paul Nieuwenburg
PhD
Associate professor
Institute of Political Science
Leiden University
Leiden, the Netherlands

Sanneke Kuipers
PhD
Senior Researcher
Crisisplan BV
Leiden, the Netherlands

Kasia Kochanska
B.A.
Master of Public Administration student
Public Administration Department
Leiden University
Leiden, the Netherlands

Annika Brändström
M.A.
Crisis Management Coordination Secretariat, Prime Minister's Office,
Swedish Government Offices, Stockholm, Sweden
and
PhD student
Utrecht School of Governance, Utrecht University, Utrecht, the
Netherlands

Eva-Karin Olsson
PhD
Lecturer
The Department of Communication and Media
Lund University
Lund, Sweden

Helena Wockelberg
PhD
Researcher
Department of Government
Uppsala University
Uppsala, Sweden

Charles Parker
PhD
Assistant professor
Department of Government
Uppsala University
Uppsala, Sweden

Daniel Nohrstedt
PhD
Researcher
CRISMART – Crisis Management Research and Training
Swedish National Defence College
Stockholm, Sweden

INDEX

2004 Tsunami disaster, 29, 32, 163, 167, 176, 220, 239, 245
9/11, 16, 46, 51, 53, 137, 161, 179, 181, 183–198, 214, 221, 233, 235, 243

A

Abu Ghraib, 119, 125–132, 135–139, 226, 228
account, 10, 15, 26, 42, 68, 111, 130, 144, 149, 155–156, 185, 189, 194, 244
    accounts, 50, 113, 120, 242
accountability, 8, 9, 11, 15–16, 22, 35, 38, 40, 62, 110, 120–121, 123, 129, 137, 158, 164–165, 173, 179, 181–182, 190, 194, 200, 203, 206, 210, 212–213, 220, 225, 231–232, 240, 244–245
    accountability logics, 203, 206, 210
    accountable, 8, 17, 22, 25, 33, 35, 63, 117, 121, 124, 126, 129, 204, 219, 232
acted, 13, 31, 34–35, 150, 168, 170, 172, 203, 205, 229, 240
    acting, 40, 100–101, 106, 127, 153
action, 3–9, 13, 17, 22–24, 27, 30–31, 34, 46–47, 48, 50–51, 54–55, 59, 62, 73–74, 77–79, 101, 126,

148–149, 152, 166, 173, 184–185, 196, 219–220, 223, 227, 229, 231, 233, 237, 239, 242, 245
actions, 3–9, 13–15, 17, 22, 24, 28–35, 38, 48, 59, 63, 67, 78, 84–85, 100, 106–107, 111, 121, 127, 129, 131, 134, 141, 145, 164, 171, 199–202, 209, 212, 218, 221, 223, 226, 228–238, 241
avoidance, 14, 41, 120, 121, 137, 140, 176

B

bad behavior, 100, 224
Baha Mousa, 127, 129, 130, 132–136, 138–139, 228
bail-out, 102, 110, 111
    bailing out, 111
    bail-out package, 102
    bail-out packages, 110, 111
bank, 105, 115–117
    banks, 99, 101, 102, 104–106, 114–115, 224
bankruptcy, 98, 101, 102–103, 105, 108, 110–111, 116–117
    bankruptcies, 105, 111, 113

Ethics and Crisis Management, pages 253–262

behavior, 7, 9, 14, 22, 24–26, 39–41, 46,
49–50, 58, 77–78, 80, 88, 91–95,
98, 100, 103, 108, 111–112, 120–
121, 124, 128, 135, 138, 187, 200,
201–202, 204, 222–228, 234–235,
238, 242, 245
behaviors, 6, 7, 10, 13, 16, 97, 99,
108, 109, 111–112, 223
belief, 55, 127, 132
beliefs, 46, 65, 69, 187, 218, 244
believing, 45
Blair government, 134
blame, 14, 23, 26, 35, 54, 62, 119, 120–
126, 131–134, 136–138, 140, 144,
158, 163–167, 171–172, 174, 177,
179, 184–185, 190, 194–195, 197,
214, 220, 222, 226, 228, 235, 244
blue ribbon commission, 186
bureaucracy, 12, 14, 21–23, 27, 34, 36,
92, 94, 95, 181, 220, 230, 237–239
bureaucratic elite, 172, 176
Bush administration, 42, 47, 126,
127–128, 131–133, 186, 236

C

centralization, 88–89, 93, 217, 242–243
central command structures, 76
centralized, 8, 91, 210, 212
cheat, 8
CIA, 38, 43–45, 54, 128, 192–194, 233,
68, 76, 78, 80, 94, 97, 207, 307,
310, 370
Clinton, 53, 55, 188, 194
closure, 2, 7, 245
command and control, 75
commission, 6, 184–198, 231, 233–234,
243–244
Commission, 26, 30–31, 33, 72, 103,
113, 115, 118, 167–169, 172,
177, 178, 181, 183–185, 187,
189–197, 220, 233–235, 243,
245
commissions, 25, 33, 184–185, 198,
234, 241, 244–245,

communicate, 7, 32, 78, 149, 189, 211,
217, 236
communicated, 151, 154
communicates, 229
communicating, 16, 149, 153, 160, 206
communication, 23, 28, 32, 36, 45–46,
47, 90, 137, 141–145, 147, 149,
151, 153–155, 157–161, 235–236
communication strategies, 141,
143–144, 154
compliance, 53, 77
confidence, 7–9, 103, 105, 184,
Congress, 128, 186, 188, 193, 196
connecting the dots, 220
consequence, 6, 21, 26, 29, 40, 63, 78,
109, 115, 128, 207, 218, 229,
231–232, 244
consequences, 2, 8, 15, 24, 33, 41,
63, 67, 69, 76, 80–81, 85–87,
90, 92, 104, 109, 134, 184, 194,
212, 218–220, 222, 224, 231,
239–241, 244
consequently, 4, 58, 67, 77, 112, 135,
202, 210, 242
Conservative, 130, 146, 147, 157
Conservatives, 129, 147
controversial, 2, 131, 134, 156, 222–223
controversy, 48, 66, 151, 188
controversies, 185, 187, 235
coordinate, 153, 156, 217
coordinating, 207–210
coordination, 72, 186, 207, 210
costs and benefits, 7, 193
credibility, 43, 49, 134, 142, 153, 156,
185, 189, 222–223, 233, 235
credible, 142, 195
crisis inquiries, 200, 202, 245
crisis management policy, 98
crisis management strategy, 107–108
crisis strategies, 98, 144
cultural, 14, 38, 58, 62, 64–68, 70, 72,
141–143, 145, 146, 148–149, 154,
157, 225, 227
culture, 43, 49, 70, 102, 108, 111,
113, 117, 147, 157, 227
cultures, 64, 65
cynicism, 187

D

debate, 6, 8, 10, 38–39, 45, 53, 56, 65, 70, 73, 90, 95, 119–122, 147–149, 152, 196, 217, 223, 245
   debated, 102, 165, 167, 177
   debates, 46, 51, 63, 123, 151,
decide, 58, 71, 148, 153, 165, 176
   decided, 4, 44, 64, 81, 83, 110, 127–129, 189
   decides, 82
decision, 1–8, 10–18, 23–24, 29–31, 40–42, 46, 49, 51, 76, 78–79, 82–83, 85, 87, 90–91, 94, 109–110, 119, 129, 135, 143, 145, 153, 158, 160, 168, 170, 176–177, 184, 190, 194, 199, 200–201, 203, 204, 210, 212, 217–223, 227–246
decision criteria, 6, 13, 228–229, 241
decision making, 2, 10, 13–14, 17, 23, 40, 46, 76, 78, 87, 91, 94, 158, 160, 170, 176, 210, 217–219, 228–229, 235, 239–240, 245
decision makers, 1–3, 6–8, 12–13, 15, 17–18, 41–42, 90, 109, 143, 145, 177, 199–200, 203–204, 217–218, 220–222, 227–234, 238–241, 244–245
decisions, 2–9, 11, 13–17, 25, 30, 34–35, 42, 55–56, 58, 76–77, 78, 81–82, 85–86, 89, 91–92, 97–98, 105–106, 109, 111–112, 120, 122, 151, 163, 165, 168, 170, 175, 185–186, 193, 199, 202, 207, 219, 221, 226, 228–237, 239–243, 245–246
define, 7, 122, 145, 201
   defined, 76, 110, 200–204, 208, 210–212, 245
   defines, 91, 124, 211
   defining, 24, 39, 47, 122, 199–200, 202, 212, 226, 232
   definition, 38, 65, 90, 212
delegate, 23
   delegated, 90
   delegation, 23, 80
deliberation, 29, 88–91, 93–95

Democratic, 26, 55, 87, 93, 157, 188–189, 233
Democrats, 116, 193, 195
deregulation, 102, 114, 116
detainee, 133, 137, 193
detainees, 126–127, 135, 139, 192–193
   detention, 127, 130, 132, 134–137, 139
dialogue, 73, 142–143, 145–146, 150–151, 155–156
dilemma, 12, 23, 29, 33, 38, 64, 73, 76, 82, 84, 86, 91, 100, 218–221, 229, 242
   dilemmas, 1, 3, 13, 22, 33, 35, 70, 73, 76, 78, 80–81, 83, 85, 88, 90, 94, 97, 99–100, 141, 215, 219, 221, 223–224, 226, 238–240, 242
directing, 123, 210
direction, 41, 80, 125, 210, 212, 230
directives, 77
disagree, 8
disaster, 18–19, 21, 26, 28–29, 32, 34, 58, 66, 71, 75, 77, 86, 90, 102–103, 136, 158, 163, 167, 170–171, 176, 200–202, 205, 210–211, 213–214, 219–220, 223–225, 229–230, 239, 241, 245
   disaster management, 213, 75, 90
discretion, 2, 15, 76–78, 80, 87–93, 176, 228, 238–240, 242–243, 245
distrust, 43, 44, 190
division of labor, 24, 202
division of responsibility, 97, 207, 234
down the chain, 219, 239

E

effectiveness, 5, 8, 14, 87, 134, 136, 166, 174, 176, 210–211, 213, 228
   effective, 9, 40, 87, 98, 108, 110–111, 131, 134, 144–145, 156, 178, 201, 208, 210, 226, 236
efficiency, 5, 17, 228, 237
   efficient, 4, 28, 103, 111, 165, 173, 176, 245

empowered, 87

Enron, 98, 101–103, 108–111, 113–114, 117–118, 160, 230

equal, 39, 61, 69, 111, 148

    equally, 79, 101, 106, 110, 233

equity, 5, 106, 110–111, 213, 228

ethical dilemma, 12, 23, 29, 33, 38, 218–219, 221, 242

    ethical dilemmas, 13, 22, 33, 35, 70, 97, 99–100, 141, 221, 223, 238, 242

evacuate, 4, 5, 81–83, 85

    evacuated, 4, 5, 81, 83, 86, 228, 241

    evacuation, 4, 26, 31, 82–84, 224–225, 228

    evacuees, 244

evaluate, 6–9, 15, 78, 80, 194, 230–231, 241

    evaluates, 4, 5, 98

    evaluated, 24, 25, 196, 234

    evaluating, 6, 9, 16, 160, 165, 214, 230, 233

    evaluation, 3, 6–7, 9, 11, 22, 25, 34, 163, 167–168, 171, 199–200, 212, 214, 226, 229, 231–232, 241

    evaluations, 33, 163–166, 169–170, 172–176, 199–201, 231–232, 234, 241

fair, 1, 2, 13, 22, 49, 110, 120, 143–145, 184–185, 187–188, 201, 210, 235, 238

    fairly, 101, 163, 195, 211

fairness, 166, 175, 232, 239

fall guy, 173

Fannie Mae, 104–105, 116

    Fannie, 104–105, 113, 116

fault, 112, 193–194, 226

    faults, 137

fear, 146, 220, 226, 236

    fears, 173

    feared, 33, 147

feedback, 77, 93, 221, 236, 238

financial crisis, 98, 103–106, 108, 111–112, 115–116, 118, 224

first responders, 75–76, 78, 81, 86, 219, 236, 241, 245

floods, 5, 16, 205–209, 212–214

fog of war, 19, 246

framing, 120–122, 130, 134, 137–138, 144, 151, 155–156, 159, 200

fraud, 103, 112

Freddie Mac, 105, 113, 224

    Freddie, 105, 113, 116, 224

free, 61, 64, 93, 94, 100, 110–112, 146, 148–149, 151–152, 154–155, 170, 177, 187, 240

freedom, 10, 24, 62, 146, 148–150, 152, 156, 159, 177–178, 200

F

fail, 8, 15, 91, 101, 108, 110, 116, 137, 183, 189, 235, 244

    failed, 28, 51, 53, 82, 102, 110, 115, 126, 143, 145, 172, 190, 192, 223, 230

    failure, 19, 38, 41–42, 50–54, 82, 86, 98–99, 102, 105–109, 112–113, 117, 121–124, 127–133, 163, 172, 182, 187, 189, 198, 202–204, 214, 220–221, 224, 231, 233–235, 242

    failures, 2, 16, 26, 33, 40, 98, 123, 136, 158, 164, 167–168, 170, 172–173, 179, 194, 198, 213, 232–234, 243

G

games, 14, 23, 55–56, 120, 122, 124, 134, 165–166, 226

Geneva Convention, 119, 228

governing institutions, 2, 8, 9, 12, 169, 225, 242

Guantanamo Bay, 125, 132, 136

guidance, 3, 23, 82, 87–88, 90–91, 202–203, 209–210, 212, 232, 240, 245

guide, 40, 87, 103, 117, 203, 211, 230, 239, 240

    guides, 23, 91, 212

    guiding, 60, 200, 202, 204, 206, 228

H

human rights, 49, 53, 60–66, 68, 69, 70, 73–74, 125, 129, 136, 138, 146, 156, 229–231, 244

Human Rights, 61–62, 69, 74, 125, 136, 138, 146

humanitarianism, 58, 59, 70, 72–73

humanitarian assistance, 66, 74

Hurricane Katrina, 81, 219

I

illegal, 25, 32–33, 54, 84, 126, 132, 157, 229

illegally, 30

illegitimate, 34, 58–60, 64–65, 67–72, 229, 238–239

ill-structured messes, 78

implementation, 77, 87, 92, 94, 131, 166, 168, 173, 195

implemented, 194, 205

implementing, 11, 74, 87, 92, 108, 122, 173

impossible, 11, 16, 18–19, 53, 72, 75, 78, 80, 87, 89–91, 105–106, 116, 145, 213, 217–220, 228, 241

impossible job, 72, 75

impossibility, 240

incentive, 112

incentives, 14, 52, 87, 98, 100, 107–108, 110, 115

incentivize, 108

incentivized, 100

independent, 67, 106, 127, 129, 130, 134, 139, 167, 169, 176, 178, 186–187

infraction, 79

inquiry, 6, 26, 33, 48–50, 55, 127, 129–130, 132, 136, 138–139, 167, 171, 177, 180, 184, 186, 187–188, 190, 197, 200, 203, 213–214, 233, 243, 245

inquiries, 16, 125, 127, 184–185, 198–202, 205, 212, 231–233, 242–245

insight, 14, 24, 25–26, 33, 85, 204

institutional Aporia, 81, 243

institutionalized lying, 80

intelligence, 37–38, 41–49, 51–56, 95, 136, 138, 186, 191, 193, 195–198, 220, 227, 230, 235, 243

intelligence community, 44, 46–47, 52, 191, 193, 235

intelligence services, 54, 220, 230

interpret, 28, 167, 170, 174

interpretation, 38, 58, 145, 185, 194, 245

intervention, 59, 60, 66, 70–71, 73, 77, 97–99, 106, 114, 218, 227, 229, 230

investigate, 44, 126, 129, 140, 188

investigated, 128, 129, 135, 175

investigating, 133, 138, 168, 184

investigation, 35, 114, 122, 126–127, 132, 134, 137–138, 140, 158, 178, 180–181, 185–188, 191, 197, 233, 235

investigations, 16, 120, 128, 183–185, 189, 198, 243, 245

investment, 104, 110, 112–115, 207

investor, 105, 114

investors, 101, 104, 107, 115

J

judge, 8, 9, 13, 202, 228, 240–241, 242

judged, 6, 25, 114, 200, 229, 244

judging, 202

judgment, 2, 6–7, 9, 13, 23, 46, 201, 205, 211, 218, 225, 229, 231, 240, 245,

just, 1, 4, 9, 38, 46, 56, 64, 85, 89, 104, 107, 109–110, 112, 181, 186, 188–189, 194, 208, 233, 243

justice, 94, 121, 139

justification, 39, 40, 54, 221, 227, 231, 235–236

justifications, 39, 40, 42

justify, 7, 17, 53, 99, 228, 231

justified, 6, 13, 53, 66, 226–227

K

Kissinger, 188–189, 197–198

L

label, 7, 131
  labeled, 156, 164
law, 9, 22–23, 26, 31–32, 34, 39, 43,
    59–61, 65–67, 70, 72–74, 79, 85,
    92, 103, 118, 165–167, 169, 173,
    178, 186, 188–189, 193, 196, 203,
    210, 219, 232, 237, 239
  laws, 4, 24, 60, 79, 91, 118, 135, 167,
    201–203, 219,
learn, 117, 165–166, 175, 187, 244
  learned, 16, 90, 137, 163, 194, 221,
    226
  learning, 15, 35, 117, 136–137, 158,
    163, 176, 180, 182, 184–185,
    187, 195, 200, 212–214, 220,
    232–233, 235, 242
legal, 4, 5, 7, 22, 25, 29–30, 34, 37,
    39–40, 47, 54, 63, 109–110, 126,
    152, 170–171, 178, 201, 209, 221,
    231, 238, 244, 245

M

market, 98–106, 108, 110, 112, 115–117,
  markets, 103–104, 112–114
market failure, 98–99, 117
  market failures, 98
mask, 174
  masked, 226
  masking, 245
meaning making, 185, 188, 195
Memorial Medical Center, 90
metaethical, 3
middle management, 29, 34
mission impossible, 16, 18–19, 219
mistrust, 8
mitigation, 98, 107–108, 155, 205
  mobilize resources, 217

monitoring, 43, 78, 93, 113, 184, 220,
  243
moral, 3, 6, 14, 17, 24, 39, 58, 60–62,
    85–86, 91, 95, 105, 111, 140–142,
    145, 158, 177, 192, 195, 200, 202,
    204–205, 211, 214–215, 223, 238
  moral judgment, 205
  moral obligation, 105
morality, 3, 199
mortgage, 89, 99, 104, 107, 111, 224
  mortgages, 113, 115
  mortgage brokers, 104

N

needs-based approach, 70
negotiate, 79, 88, 102, 242
  negotiated, 44, 142
  negotiations, 10, 186, 237
networks of organizations, 203
New Orleans, 14, 76, 82, 219
norm, 173–174, 176
  norms, 7, 17, 24, 68, 70–71, 87, 91,
    200–205, 228, 232, 239
normative, 3, 58, 163, 199
NPM, 164, 166, 173, 177

O

Obama, 129
objective, 78, 79, 110, 166, 169, 184, 199
  objectives, 6, 128, 176, 202–203, 226
opportunity, 113, 140, 171, 185, 244
  opportunities, 13
outrage, 47, 223
  outraged, 223

P

paradigm, 75
  paradigm shift, 75
Parliament, 157, 169, 177, 180, 182
  parliamentary, 37, 126, 172, 214

partnership, 98
  partnerships, 98
  partnering, 97
Pentagon, 132, 193, 220
perceive, 2, 23, 69
  perceives, 16
  perceived, 2, 8, 14, 21, 39, 41, 51,
      60–61, 66–68, 70–71, 84, 86,
      100, 120, 130–131, 148, 165,
      171–172, 176, 188, 194–195,
      204, 206, 219–221, 225, 227,
      229, 233, 235–236
  perceived legitimacy, 236
perception, 2, 8, 11, 19, 41, 53, 60,
      63–64, 72, 124, 127, 134, 185,
      190, 205, 222, 235, 246
  perceptions, 3, 6, 8, 12, 18, 58–59,
      66–67, 69, 70, 78, 234
  perceptual, 17
policy, 1–2, 4–7, 12, 16, 18, 37, 39, 41,
      43, 45–46, 49, 51–53, 55–56, 74,
      76–77, 79–81, 87–88, 90–94, 98,
      102, 109–111, 116, 120, 123,
      128, 130, 132, 136, 139–140, 142,
      158–159, 173, 181–182, 190, 194–
      195, 197–199, 205, 210, 213–214,
      218–219, 221–222, 226, 228–231,
      233, 235–236, 238–242, 246
  policy change, 130, 132
  policy dilemmas, 80, 90, 219
  policy leaders, 76, 119, 239
  policy options, 2, 4, 242
  policy twilight zone, 219, 239
politicization, 120, 136, 156, 158, 165,
      213
politicize, 7
  politicized, 121, 176, 226
politics-administration dichotomy, 163,
      231, 239
power, 4, 12, 14, 16, 18, 23, 27, 41, 53,
      55, 60, 64, 83, 85, 89, 99, 101,
      116–117, 130, 137, 142, 164, 166,
      173, 185, 191, 198, 200, 203–204,
      213, 231, 240, 243–245
  powers, 22, 37, 135, 168, 237, 244
  power struggles, 244
POWs, 119, 124, 222, 234

practical reasoning, 80, 88–89, 242–243
practitioners, 1, 16, 78
President, 44, 50, 59, 103, 114, 128–
      129, 131–132, 140, 156–157, 186,
      188–189, 191–192, 198, 226
Prime Minister, 26, 33, 48, 55, 66,
      146–147, 148, 150–152, 154, 157,
      234
prioritize, 10, 40, 77, 225, 240, 244
prisons, 80, 92, 126, 222
prisoner, 132
  prisoners, 119, 124, 126, 128,
      134–135, 139, 222, 225–226,
      228, 234
  prisoners of war, 228, 234
private sector, 97–98, 107–109, 112–
      113, 118, 202, 207, 239
problem of many hands, 29, 135, 212
productivity, 80, 89
protect, 4, 14, 15, 51, 60, 62, 76,
      165–166, 169, 175–176, 178
protest, 8, 147, 149, 150
  protests, 152, 155
public diplomacy, 141–142, 153, 159–161
public opinion, 113, 190, 238
public pressure, 186
public sphere, 142, 158
public-private, 97, 98

Q

quit, 8, 83

R

rational, 29, 56, 77–79, 81, 87, 94, 166,
      174–175, 184–185, 237
  rationality, 4, 23, 77, 92, 94, 110, 239
  rationalize, 7
  rationalized, 60
rationale, 4, 5, 17, 23, 98–99, 109–111,
      184–185, 188, 245
  rationales, 4, 97, 109–110, 141, 195,
      228, 230, 233, 237, 239, 245

reason, 8, 13, 48–49, 51, 60, 86, 95, 101, 105–106, 157, 174, 184, 209

reasons, 17, 27, 76–77, 91, 100, 102, 105, 107, 176, 201, 219–220, 235–236, 242

reasoning, 3, 41, 80, 88–90, 112, 117, 173, 201, 215, 242–243, 246

Red River flood, 5

reform, 94, 117, 164, 181–182, 184, 193, 195–196, 198, 233, 235, 243–244

reforms, 103, 130, 173, 197, 212

reforming, 93, 166

regulate, 99, 100, 104, 107, 112

regulation, 20, 99, 103, 106–108, 111, 114, 117, 210

regulatory, 15, 98, 100, 102–103, 107–108, 111, 113, 201, 203, 209–212, 224, 232

regulatory system, 98, 102

regulatory uncertainty, 201, 210, 212

repercussion, 112

repercussions, 83, 85

Republican, 186, 188–189, 193, 233

Republicans, 186, 191, 195

resilience, 207, 208, 211–212, 232

resource, 23, 239

resources, 2, 5, 8, 11, 24, 45, 47, 58, 75, 82, 89, 168, 191, 201, 217, 219, 233–235, 245

response, 11–13, 15–17, 27, 29, 34, 75–76, 80, 90, 109, 112, 117, 128, 137, 150, 159, 165, 167–168, 187, 199, 202, 204–214, 218, 220–222, 229, 231, 236, 245–246

responses, 35, 59, 137, 158, 170, 180, 190, 201, 214–215, 223,

response chain, 76

responsibility, 14–16, 23–24, 26, 30, 33, 35, 77, 81, 97, 102, 110, 113–114, 120–122, 125, 130–131, 134, 138, 144, 153–154, 163–177, 179, 181, 184, 187, 194, 200, 203, 207–211, 214, 223–224, 226–227, 231–232, 234–235, 243, 245

responsibility doctrine, 163164, 166–169, 172, 176, 179, 231–232, 245

responsible, 8, 18, 23, 31–33, 35, 88, 113, 121, 124–125, 127–128, 131, 164, 185, 195, 206, 211, 223, 231, 234, 242

responsive, 23, 35, 110

responsiveness, 5, 23, 35, 228

result, 12, 15, 38, 45, 51, 62, 64, 80–81, 84, 87, 101, 121–122, 128, 155, 166, 187, 189, 194, 201, 205, 220–222, 225, 228, 231, 233

results, 34–35, 88, 110, 124, 144, 209, 229

resulting, 39, 46, 58–59, 67, 69, 128, 131, 201

Rice, 47, 128, 188, 191

right, 3–8, 10, 17, 22, 24–26, 32, 47, 60, 62, 63, 66–67, 71, 73, 82, 91, 128, 132, 138, 145–146, 148–149, 159, 163, 165, 170, 172, 174, 200, 202, 204, 206, 211, 219–220, 225–226, 230, 240, 244

rights, 7, 10, 39, 49, 53, 55, 57, 59–71, 73–74, 119, 125, 129, 136, 138, 156, 163, 218, 229, 230–231, 244

rights-based approach, 62–63, 70

risk, 2, 8, 14, 20, 40, 54, 56, 68–69, 100–101, 106–107, 115, 117–118, 137, 153, 172, 201, 205, 207–208, 211, 214, 218, 225, 238, 246

risks, 15, 18, 45, 108, 113, 201

risky, 32, 100, 104, 108, 112, 115

rule, 24, 77, 79, 110, 113, 115, 118, 122, 166–167, 169–170, 203, 232, 237

rules, 4, 12, 22–23, 26, 29, 31, 33, 40, 78, 87, 100–101, 106, 108, 110, 116, 118, 169, 173, 180, 188, 200–205, 209–210, 219, 224, 227–229, 238, 244

rule-compromise discretion, 77

rules of the game, 100–101, 227

Rumsfeld, 44, 119, 126, 128, 131–133, 136, 138–139, 222

S

sanction, 7, 8, 125, 241

sanctions, 7, 40, 105, 122, 134
sanctioning, 7, 100, 194, 233
scapegoat, 122–123, 132, 134, 173
scapegoats, 130
scholars, 1, 11–12, 61, 65, 76, 116, 144, 166, 178, 194, 212, 245
scrutiny, 2, 25, 27, 35, 39, 54, 169, 173, 178, 221, 226, 232, 235
scrutinized, 7, 26, 35
scrutinizing, 29, 169
Securities and Exchange Commission, 103, 113, 115
SEC, 103, 112, 118
Security Council, 39, 42, 45, 51, 188
self-interest, 185, 187, 195
Senate, 38, 44, 46, 56, 103, 106, 117–118, 126–127, 131, 138–139, 188
sense making, 141, 145, 204
shift, 35, 65, 75–76, 151, 153, 219, 239–240
shifts, 78
shift of authority, 239
shifted, 76, 119
shifting, 222, 243
significant choice, 29
speak truth to power, 173
stake in, 13, 121, 173
stakeholder, 142–145, 155, 158, 217, 221, 230–231
stakeholders, 6, 130, 141, 143–146, 152, 155–156, 221–222, 236
stakeholder groups, 221, 230
standard operating procedures, 34, 210
state agencies, 166–168, 170, 173, 178–179
steal, 8
strategy, 6, 48, 50, 52, 54, 56, 107–108, 151, 153–154, 156, 166, 189–190, 221–222, 230, 233, 238
street-level bureaucrat, 87, 92
street-level bureaucrats, 77, 78, 80, 87–89, 91–92, 236–237, 239–240, 243
structural setting, 98
structure, 16, 54, 60, 65, 202, 239–240
structures, 17, 76, 99, 111, 218, 237, 242

substantive rationale, 5
Swedish Government Offices, 173
symbols, 125, 166, 202
symbolic, 7, 161, 166, 184–186, 188, 190, 195–196
symbolic action, 166
symbolic actions, 7
symbolism, 237

T

The Federal Reserve, 102, 114, 118
threat, 2, 10, 12, 18, 41, 45, 73, 79, 190–191, 199, 220, 241
threats, 3, 147, 156
threatened, 71, 83, 166, 191
threatening, 201
torture, 125, 128–129, 131–133, 135, 137–140, 222, 226, 228, 234, 236
torturing, 119, 128, 226, 234
trade-off, 145
trade-offs, 195
tragic choices, 8, 11, 76, 106, 218–219
transparency, 14–15, 22, 142, 155, 165–166, 170, 175–176, 187, 209
transparent, 90, 103, 169, 190, 233, 245
trust, 1, 2, 8–9, 16, 32, 35, 38, 62, 87–88, 101, 116–117, 170, 187, 218, 225, 240
truthful, 32

U

uncertainty, 2, 8, 10, 12, 18, 40, 52, 80, 101, 199–201, 203–205, 209–212, 220, 232, 236
uncertain, 17, 109, 205, 240
undermine, 68, 103, 129, 229
undermines, 101, 240
unethical, 7, 86, 100, 111–112, 120, 128, 134, 222–223, 225, 227–228, 232, 234, 241
unethically, 121

unfair, 86, 165, 175
United Kingdom, 122, 200
    UK, 35, 55, 92–94, 124, 129, 135,
        140, 158, 180, 182, 197, 214
United Nations, 42, 57, 62, 72, 125
    UN, 38, 39, 42–43, 61, 74, 125, 140,
        147, 150, 156
    UN Security Council, 39
universal rights, 61
urgency, 2, 9, 10, 12, 18, 46, 82
urgent, 185, 199, 207, 226, 235

V

vague, 3, 30, 204
value, 1, 4, 6, 10–11, 23–24, 38–40, 46,
    88, 104, 106, 108–109, 111, 151,
    169–170, 174, 176, 187, 195, 203,
    211, 218, 221, 229, 230, 234–237,
    240, 242
    values, 1, 3, 5–6, 8, 10, 12–13, 17–18,
        23, 38–40, 46, 60–61, 65, 71, 87,
        89, 91, 105–106, 109, 120–121,
        123, 143, 145–146, 153, 155–
        157, 165–167, 169, 172–174,
        176, 200–202, 212, 218–219,
        221, 224–225, 227, 229–232,
        235–237, 239–240, 242
    valued, 79, 109, 166, 174
    valuing, 174
violation, 63, 79, 100, 110, 121, 203
    violations, 63, 101, 120–122
    violating, 63, 100, 125, 156
violence, 39, 58, 63
virtue, 94, 225, 234
    virtues, 164, 175

W

Wall Street, 55, 98, 101, 103–104,
    110–111, 118
waterboarding, 192
White House, 38, 44, 131, 133, 187–188,
    192–193, 198

Z

Zelikow, 188, 190, 193

CPSIA information can be obtained
at www.ICGtesting.com
Printed in the USA
LVOW13s1928251017

553783LV00007B/20/P